D0481530

BELIEF,
EXISTENCE,
and MEANING

BELIEF, EXISTENCE, and MEANING

R. M. Martin
New York University

New York: NEW YORK UNIVERSITY PRESS
London: UNIVERSITY OF LONDON PRESS, LTD.
1969

For
Van Quine,
in gratitude for
the high standards of clarity
in logico-philosophical writing
that he has set for our time.

Truth is to be found, not in a well, but in clinging mud.

Old French Proverb.

While others fish with craft for great opinion,
I with great truth catch mere simplicity;
Whilst some with cunning gild their copper crowns,
With truth and plainness I do wear mine bare.
Fear not my truth: the moral of my wit
Is plain, and true; there's all the reach of it.

Troilus, IV, iv.

Dear Crito, your zeal is invaluable, if a right one; but if wrong, the greater the zeal the greater the danger; and therefore we ought to consider whether I shall or shall not do as you say. For I am and always have been one of those natures who must be guided by reason, whatever the reason may be which upon reflection appears to me to be the best: . . .

Crito, 44.

I feel myself . . . how hard or rather impossible is the attainment of any certainty about questions such as these. . . . For [one] should persevere until he has achieved one of two things: either he should discover, or be taught the truth about them; or, if this be impossible, I would have him take the best and most irrefragable of human theories, and let this be the raft upon which he sails through life—not without risk, as I admit, if he cannot find some divine word which will more surely and safely carry him.

Phaedo, 85.

What reason here discovers, I have power
To show thee, that which lies beyond, expect
From Beatrice, faith not reason's task.

Purgatorio, xviii, 47–48.

Preface

This book is concerned with certain intimately related topics in philosophical analysis at the very forefront of contemporary discussion. The analysis of *belief* is usually thought to involve reference to *meanings* or *intensions* in some form or another. The objects of our beliefs are thought to be "propositions" and propositions are presumed to be intensional entities of some sort. Straightway, then, an analysis of belief is thought to involve the *existence* of, or an *ontology* for, intensions. Conversely, talk of existence and ontology is of especial interest in connection with the problem of analyzing intensions, and the key argument that there are such entities is their supposed need for the analysis of belief. In this book some clarity (hopefully) is achieved on some of the knottily intertwined problems concerning these difficult topics.

The analysis of belief leads directly to the notion of *rational* belief. Now logic provides the conceptual core of rationality. Whatever else it does, it does at least this. In his Carus Lectures, Professor Blanshard has noted that reason "is seen in its most obvious form . . . in the deductions . . . of the logician and mathematician. This may be taken as the narrowest and nuclear meaning of the term."[1] It has also been claimed that "the procedure of induction, . . . far from being irrational, defines the very essence of rationality." The connection between logic, both deductive and inductive, and rationality, in fact, seems so close as to justify the maxim: No logic, no rational belief, no rational behavior.

---

[1] *Reason and Analysis* (La Salle, Ill.: Open Court Publishing Co., 1962), p. 26.

ix

Logic, both deductive and inductive, has undergone an intensive new development in recent years. Many philosophers have come to think of this as of interest primarily to mathematics and hence as largely beyond their concern. The new logic is difficult to master and filled with intricacies and subtleties that often seem "unprofitable." It is easier to dismiss the subject altogether. However, to do so is surely to neglect interconnections of the utmost importance. Because logic provides the very essence of rationality, the task remains of showing explicitly how it is related to the philosophical study of rational belief and behavior. This cannot be done satisfactorily, it would seem, without the sharp conceptual tools of modern logic, including those of *syntax*, *semantics*, and *pragmatics*.

In syntax we are interested only in signs and their interconnections. In semantics, we consider also how signs are interrelated with objects as well as with meanings; and in pragmatics, fundamental account is taken of the human user of signs, his beliefs, his actions, and so on. Semantics conveniently divides into two branches, the *extensional* and the *intensional*. In the former, we consider only the relations of signs with objects and hence such notions as *truth, designation, denotation*, and the like. In intensional semantics, account is also taken of meanings or intensions in some sense, usually regarded as a kind of Platonic idea. They are not so regarded here, where, as it were, a more Aristotelian stand is taken. An intensional semantics usually contains an extensional semantics as a part. When the user of a language is taken into account, a semantics of either kind may be presupposed. Hence, a pragmatics likewise may be either extensional or intensional. Pragmatics may also be developed quite independently of semantics, in which case it need presuppose only a syntax.

One of the main tasks of philosophical analysis is to illuminate what otherwise is puzzling or foggy or confused. This need not be claimed as the only task, but surely it is a major one. An analysis that fails to illuminate, fails of its main intent. However, almost as important is the exhibition of *logical form*. What notion or notions are employed in the analysis? Are they to be regarded as undefined or primitive? If so, how are they to be characterized axiomatically? If not primitive, then how defined? What kind of a logic is being used or presupposed? In short, to be logically interesting, a philosophical analysis should utilize a language system whose syntax, semantics, and pragmatics are given explicit characterization.

One of the main tasks of this book is to formulate the beginnings of a well-knit and urgently needed logic of belief on a clear-cut, extensional foundation. It is often thought that the analysis of belief, knowledge, and related notions must involve in some fashion or other fundamental reference to intensions regarded as Platonic entities *sui generis*. In fact, the key argument in behalf of such intensions is their supposed need in analyzing such notions. Also it is widely thought that intensions *sui generis* are needed for the study of human action. Just how or why, however, has never been very carefully shown, and the status of the underlying semantics needed to characterize them has been in doubt. Intensional semantics has been on the defensive, and many logicians have found its fundamental notions somewhat dubious and obscure; at best they are not above suspicion. Many contend that a foundation for the analysis of belief and action cannot adequately be given in wholly extensional terms. One of the tasks of this book is to try to show that it can. Further, intensions themselves can be fully analyzed, as we hope to show, in terms of their ultimate extensional components.

It is often said that beliefs have no logic, and hence are presumably beyond rational categories. What one believes, it is said, is the result of many factors, some of which may be erratic in the extreme. However, underneath any given set of beliefs some *pattern* that it exhibits is usually discernible. The pattern may be complicated and difficult to unearth, but it is there, and our task is to bring it to light and give it a full characterization. Some patterns no doubt contain desirable features, others do not. Those that do are usually thought to be "rational" in some sense. Those that do not may still be interesting as patterns of actual belief. We tend to use 'rational' rather glibly, as though we knew what it meant and it had one and only one meaning. The fact is, however, that there is a vast number of meanings to be distinguished. The logic of belief, as conceived here, is concerned primarily with patterns of belief, and the study of rationality is seen to be a part of the more general study of such patterns.

Before turning to these patterns, however, we should first try to be clear as to what *linguistic forms* are needed to talk about beliefs and actions. We shall be interested primarily in the locutions 'Person *X believes* such and such' and '*X does* so and so' in the actional sense of doing. We shall wish also to mention, albeit only in passing, *quantitative* forms of belief as expressed in the locution '*X* believes so and so to such and such a degree'.

Belief and action are not approached here in disregard of the experimental procedures of the behavioral sciences. The notion of action is perhaps the fundamental notion in the study of human behavior. A clear vocabulary is needed in which it may be discussed. Because of the importance of the notions of action and of belief for the behavioral sciences, this book may be viewed as a study in the logical and linguistic foundations of these sciences.

The material here is thought to be of fundamental interest also for the philosophy of science in general. In the first place, the so-called *thesis of extensionality* stands or falls with the success of the modes of treatment to be suggested. This thesis maintains that extensional languages should suffice for the purposes of science and philosophical analysis. The notion of belief has heretofore been thought to resist adequate analysis in extensional terms. Also, the philosophy of science is now preeminently concerned with the semantics of scientific language, but the exact character of the semantics used is rarely mentioned or explored. If intensional notions are needed, they are usually brought in rather sheepishly. Also, the status of most theories of intension is ambiguous. Rarely mentioned by the philosopher of science, they seem to serve only as a backdrop. At best, however, many of these theories are suspect, as has been noted, especially those concerned with intensions *sui generis*, and a full argument should be given as to why they are unsuited for the tasks for which they are presumably designed.

In the author's *Intension and Decision*[2] a semantical theory of intensions was suggested, which has turned out to contain an important defect. In place of the theory there, a revised and much improved one is put forward here. Many kinds of intensions are clearly distinguished, and it is shown how they may be constructed or built up in a very natural way. In particular, intensions are *analyzed* here into parts or members in a suitable fashion, and hence are not regarded as entities *sui generis*, as is usual. The analysis will, moreover, throw some light (hopefully) upon what *facts*, *propositions*, and *events* are—another obscure and puzzling philosophical trio—and upon their connection with belief and intensions. The two former appropriately turn out to be intensional entities; the latter do not.

A brief outline of the book is as follows. In Chapter I a very broad and general discussion is given of the significance of modern logic for philosophic analysis. Chapter II is devoted to the so-called *criterion for ontic or ontological commitment*. This topic has been brought to the fore in recent years, especially by Quine. His criterion is subjected to analysis, extended appropriately, and its relevance for philosophic analysis noted. The net result of these deliberations will be to end up with a new notion of ontic *involvement*, of especial significance for the philosophical view that will be put forward. In Chapter III, various reasons for lamenting the approach to philosophical analysis via unanalyzed intensions *sui generis* are given. Several valuable suggestions toward a logic of belief, due to Russell, Church, Ajdukiewicz, Quine, Carnap, and others, are examined in Chapter IV.

---

[2] (Englewood Cliffs, N.J.: Prentice-Hall, Inc., 1963).

Although for the most part they will be rejected later, the suggestions are useful as steps forward.

The logic of belief proper is discussed provisorily in Chapter V along somewhat Platonic lines. Chapter VI is concerned with the theory of so-called *virtual classes* in terms of which an alternative and improved handling of belief may be given. Chapter VII is devoted to an outline of the theory of analyzed, objective intensions, now regarded as constructs. Chapter VIII is concerned with *facts*— for we are often said to believe them—regarded as intensional constructs of a certain kind. *Events* are analyzed in Chapter IX and contrasted sharply with facts. The two are often confused, so that it will not be amiss to explore the logic of both. Also, a treatment of *propositions* is suggested, again as certain kinds of intensional constructs. Propositions are then interrelated with the handling of belief.

In Chapter X the main content of *Frege's* famous paper "Über Sinn und Bedeutung" is examined freshly in the light of the foregoing analyses of objective intensions and belief, with some surprising results. The theory of *action* is discussed in Chapter XI. Finally, in Chapter XII some further *pragmatic* and *epistemic relations* are introduced and commented on briefly.

The material of this book is in part critical and in part constructive. Important suggestions of various authors are profitably examined, even where agreement is not possible. The treatment throughout is discursive rather than formal, so that there is only a minimum of symbolization. The logic presupposed is the most elementary, comprising merely *truth functions*, *quantifiers*, and *identity*, so that no specialized knowledge is presumed on the part of the reader. Much of the material here may appear tentative and inconclusive, and there is concern more with the linguistic foundations than with the theoretical superstructure. At best the beginnings of a program are sketched that may prove worthy of further development. The obvious defects and omissions are challenges to do better. However, on matters wherein there is failure, it would seem that either there has been no previous analysis at all, or only an obviously inadequate one in which logic is for the most part tossed to the winds, or an inadequate one making use of a specious logic itself in need of analysis. Thus any progress made on the difficult matters here and on the basis of what is thought to be a sound logic, will perhaps not be unwelcome.

The material of this book brings together, in its concern with the user of language, some aspects of the naturalist tradition in philosophy with the newer techniques of logical analysis. Perforce the broader metaphysical, epistemological, and value-theoretic issues concerned with belief and action are neglected. However, progress on purely logico-linguistic matters often can be made only at the expense of such neglect. Once a proper logical format has been attained—and this is no easy matter—the wider context may be returned to with renewed and deepened insight.

The author wishes to thank the National Science Foundation for Grant No. GS–273 in support of some of the work reported in this book. Also, Professors Alan Anderson, Ruth Barcan Marcus, Herbert Bohnert, Rudolf Carnap, Alonzo Church, Frederic Fitch, Henry Hiz, Carl Hempel, Ernest Nagel, and W. V. Quine have influenced the material here for the better, although in ways of which they might not approve. Nonetheless, the author wishes to thank each and every one of these for his or her contribution. Some of the material here has already appeared *in nuce* in various philosophical journals, but it has been reworked, improved, or modified to constitute a unified whole. The author wishes to thank the editors of *The Journal of Philosophy*, *Philosophical Studies, Mind, Synthese, American Philosophical Quarterly, Philosophy of Science, Philosophy and Phenomenological Research, The Monist*, The North-Holland Publishing Company, the St. Martin's Press, The University of Massachusetts Press, Blackwell's, The John Day Co., and La Nuova Italia Editrice for kind permission to reproduce or borrow material.

The editors and staff of the New York University Press have been helpful at all stages in the production of this volume. Whatever errors or inadequacies it contains, either as to content or form, are here as elsewhere, it is to be feared, *mea culpa*.

Contents

BELIEF,
EXISTENCE,
and MEANING

CHAPTER I

"In What Sense is Logic Something Sublime?"

There seems "to pertain to logic a peculiar depth—a universal significance."[1] Logic lies, it seems, at the foundations of the sciences and of discourse in general. "For logical investigation explores the nature of all things"—or rather, of the linguistic forms by means of which we talk of things. "It seeks to see to the bottom of things and is not meant to concern itself whether what actually happens is this or that." Logic is not concerned with contingent happenings, as we say, but rather with the abiding truths that hold of all happenings.

> It takes its rise . . . from an urge to understand the basis, or essence of everything empirical. Not, however, as if to this end we had to hunt out new facts; it is, rather, of the essence of our investigation that we do not seek to learn anything *new* by it. We want to *understand* something that is already in plain view. For *this* is what we seem in some sense not to understand.

Logic is not then primarily a tool of discovery, but rather an aid to understanding and clarification. We often think we understand what is in plain view, only to find on reflection that it is vastly more complicated and involved than we thought. Of course we might discover something indirectly in the course of our analysis, but this is not the primary aim.

Saint Augustine's comment, *Quid est ergo tempus? Si nemo ex me quaerat scio; si quaerenti explicare velim, nescio.*

[1] L. Wittgenstein, *Philosophical Investigations* (Oxford: Basil Blackwell, 1953), p. 42.

3

could not be said of a question of natural science. (What is the specific gravity of hydrogen? for example). . . . Something that we know when no one asks us, but no longer know when we are supposed to give an account of it, is something that we need to remind ourselves of. And it is obviously something of which for some reason it is difficult to remind oneself.

The logic we know and use when no one asks us is a *logica utens,* rough and ready, good enough (so we think) for the purpose at hand. When asked to give an account of it, we attempt to formulate a *logica docens,* a more systematic and perhaps even formal characterization of the principles, modes of proof, and so on, being implicitly used or presupposed.[2] The two are related roughly as practice to theory, and a perfect fit is almost never achieved. Nor is the analogous fit between surveying and geometry, between moving particles and the equations thereof, between behavior in the marketplace and economic theory, and so on. Because the fit is not perfect, there is no reason to regard the attempt to gain the exact measure, so to speak, as in some sense superfluous or not needed.

To the contrary, the sciences including mathematics often do well enough, especially in their less advanced stages, without a conscious critique of procedure. A loose *logica utens* suffices for many purposes, and mathematics has done quite well for a long time without a conscious *logica docens.* It may well be contended that modern mathematical logic has done little for working mathematics. To be sure, new areas of theory have been opened up, together with interesting and important applications. However, these are then merely new areas of mathematical theory with interconnections with other known or well-developed areas. The main body of mathematical work goes on largely as before.

In philosophy the situation is remarkably different. Here our task is continually to "remind" ourselves of an underlying *logica docens.* Here the conscious critique of procedure seems essential at every step. The logic, which Wittgenstein refers to as "sublime," is not just *mathematical* logic, but a wider domain of theory. We might call it for the moment '*philosophic logic*', but this would be to suggest erroneously that it is in some sense separate from, and perhaps even opposed to, mathematical logic. Strictly there is only one logic, so we shall contend, but philosophers and mathematicians view it with different eyes. Let us reflect upon this difference, and then try to characterize very roughly the wider terrain.

[2] See C. S. Peirce, *Collected Papers* (Cambridge, Mass.: Harvard University Press, 1931–1958), *passim,* but especially 2.188 ff.

In Section 1 we reflect very briefly upon logic as *divorced* from mathematics, preparatory to a discussion in Section 2 of what an *applied logic* is. In Section 3 we turn to some of *Frege's* comments concerning logic as a philosophic tool. Two or three pertinent criticisms of essentially this view, due to *Findlay*, are parried in Section 4. In Section 5 we reflect upon Frege's intensionalism and related notions, about which a good deal will have to be said in subsequent chapters. Finally, that logic may and should, in Peirce's phrase, "meddle with all subjects" is urged in Section 6.

1. Logic Without Mathematics. The traditional status of logic as a fundamental part of philosophy has been challenged in recent years and today even seems in peril. The subject has all but been taken over by mathematicians, and mathematicians *manqués*; in turn it has been dismissed with indifference or contempt by many philosophers. Even professional logicians (teaching in departments of philosophy) have shown little philosophic concern and have turned to problems of interest primarily to mathematics. In fact 'logic' and 'mathematical logic' have almost become synonyms and are popularly becoming equated with the study of matters connected with computer technology.

Logic in our time has become so intimately associated with mathematics and mathematical methods as perhaps to lose its proper identity. In the mid-nineteenth century, Peirce and Frege had to struggle valiantly to free logic from the algebraic model of Boole and earlier workers. Curiously enough, now in the late twentieth century, after a period of intensive development, there is again a struggle to free logic from the grip of those who have only mathematical interests. The logical positivists among philosophers, it is true, have given eminent lip service to logic for some years, but this has now quieted somewhat with the virtual demise of positivism itself. The "other" tradition, that of using formal logic for the study of more traditional philosophical problems—the tradition of Leibniz, perhaps Peirce, Leśniewski, Russell, and Scholz—has never really taken root and may almost be said to have perished in the bud.

Yet formal logic itself is clearly one of the most perfect intellectual instruments, at once the most fundamental of the sciences and a leading humanity. It is both an *"ars artium et scientia scientiarum, ad omnium aliarum scientiarum methodorum principia viam habens,"* in the great words of Petrus Hispanus.[3] Also it is a most important educative tool, the full value of which we have not even begun to realize.

[3] See the opening sentence of his *Summulae Logicales*.

Logic in the sense of *mathematical* logic is quite well off nowadays as a special branch of mathematics. Actually, the birthday may be reckoned as long ago as 1908, the year that saw the simultaneous publication of Russell's "Mathematical Logic as Based on the Theory of Types" and Zermelo's "Untersuchungen über die Grundlagen der Mengenlehre." The year of inception may perhaps be gauged as 1879 (with the publication of Frege's *Begriffschrift*), the most important year (according to Kneale) in the history of logic in the nineteenth century.[4] For so great and difficult a subject, surely twenty-nine years is not an excessive period of gestation.

These important papers of Russell and Zermelo inaugurated a period of intensive development in mathematical logic, most of which has been carried out by professional mathematicians. It may well be contended that, since 1908, no major contribution to mathematical logic has been made by a professional philosopher. But his task is rather different anyhow. Peirce has put the matter thus:

> In truth no two things could be more directly opposite than the cast of mind of the logician and that of the mathematician. . . . The mathematician's interest in a reasoning is as a means of solving problems. . . . The logician, on the other hand, is interested in picking a method to pieces and in finding out what its essential ingredients are.[5]

Of this more anon.

Contrasted with mathematical logic, the theory of mathematical systems, proof theory, set theory, theory of models, and so on, is the general subject of formal logic as the theory of valid deductive inference. This subject is of course of great concern to the philosopher, as it has been for two millenia. There is considerable disagreement as to its exact nature and extent, however, and it is by no means clear precisely what valid deductive inferences are. Formal logic is a battleground for competing systems, each intended to characterize valid deductive inference in what is hoped is a satisfactory way.

Beyond formal logic is a wider domain of "informal" or applied logic, of the "logical geography" of concepts (to borrow Ryle's felicitous phrase).[6] Here the aim is to help sharpen, clarify, characterize, and explicate notions in current philosophical, scientific, or ordinary use. Although these notions are in plain view, most of them turn out

---

[4] See William Kneale and Martha Kneale, *The Development of Logic* (Oxford: Clarendon Press, 1962).

[5] *Collected Papers.*

[6] G. Ryle, *Dilemmas* (Cambridge: Cambridge University Press, 1954). The characterization here differs from that of Ryle.

upon analysis to be vastly more complicated than imagined. To
analyze is to become technical, to make sharp distinctions, to theorize,
perhaps to take a stand—in short, to become philosophical. Logical
geography is not a pursuit independent of formal logic; rather, it rests
upon it fundamentally. Further, it uses the devices of logical syntax,
semantics, and even pragmatics. These areas of inquiry together constitute what, following Peirce and Charles Morris, is called *'semiotic'*.
Logical geography in the widest sense may be regarded as the syntax,
semantics, and pragmatics of language.

> How then [Ryle asks] is the philosopher a client of the
> Formal Logician?[7] [Formal logic is] rather like what geometry
> is to the cartographer. He [the latter] finds no Euclidian straight
> hedgerows or Euclidian plane meadows. Yet he could not map
> the sinuous hedgerows that he finds or the undulating meadow
> save against the ideally regular boundaries and levels. . . . The
> cartographer is one of the clients of geometry [just as the phi-
> losopher is of formal logic].

The likelihood that his map is "approximately correct or precise" is
the gift both of Euclid and of the formal logician.

2. Applied Logic. No doubt the mathematician is concerned more
with pure theory and the philosopher with its applications. The
mathematician is interested in alternative forms of theory; the philosopher, in using some one form or forms as basic. To suggest that the
logic of this or that specific subject is *sui generis* or in some sense
unique, however, is at best misleading. Logic may be applied to
diverse subject matters, but that which is applied is unique. "One
God, one country, one logic" remains here the underlying maxim.

A fundamental problem in applied logic is that of determining
the nonlogical *predicates* (including symbols for relations) required
for a given subject matter. The choice of predicates goes hand in
hand with determining the objects to which they apply. In logical
analysis the fixing of axioms or primitive sentences governing the
predicates is secondary. Surely no satisfactory axioms—'satisfactory' here in the sense of being true or at least widely accepted
when suitably interpreted—can be framed without clear-cut *semantical
rules* governing the primitives, about which much more later. Mathematicians tend to prefer the converse procedure: Frame axioms no
matter how, and hunt for an interpretation afterward. If none is forth-

[7] *Ibid.,* p. 123.

coming, make one up—hence the artificiality of many mathematical "models" or theories and the forcing of actual data to fit them.

Logical analysis is to be distinguished sharply from the construction of a mathematical model or theory in that the former requires *ab initio* suitable semantical rules of interpretation for the primitives chosen. These rules may be of the form stating that such and such primitives *designate* such and such classes or relations or *denote* such and such objects.[8] The classes and/or relations and objects must be available to start with—otherwise there is nothing to analyze. Strictly, the mathematician has nothing to analyze—he frames axioms and hopes that something will turn up to fit them. Obviously the axioms are the crucial objects of worry for him, and once they are chosen, their parade of consequences is reviewed. The logical analyst, in contrast, will not worry over axioms to begin with, for there is usually sufficient difficulty in choosing suitable primitives. Once he is sufficiently clear about these, he will have ample occasion to explore alternative sets of axioms.

The two approaches or methods just discussed might be called 'the *nomic* or *nomological*' and 'the *ontic* or *ontological*', respectively. The mathematician, being concerned primarily with laws or principles, tends to favor the former. The philosopher tends to be concerned more with what actually is, or at least with what he thinks actually is. He will wish to determine his ontic commitment prior to, or as a basis for, the introduction of laws or principles.

Interesting cases in point are of course *modal* and *deontic* logics.[9] The former are concerned with such notions as 'necessity' and 'possibility', the latter with 'obligation', 'permission', and the like. These logics are usually constructed (as mere calculi) by framing axioms and exploring their consequences, and only secondarily does anyone seek to interpret them. If no suitable interpretation is forthcoming, this does not seem to matter. Some minor mathematical interest may perhaps attach to these logics. We need not attempt to decide whether this is the case or not. It is doubtful, however, that the analyses that deontic logic has provided (to date at least) of obligation, permission, and so on, are of sufficient subtlety and depth to be of much interest for ethics, the social sciences, the law, and allied subjects. Of course, the point is controversial, and more will be said in Chapter XI.

[8] See the author's *Truth and Denotation* (Chicago: University of Chicago Press, 1958), especially Chapter IV, V, and VII.

[9] See, for example and *inter alia*, C. I. Lewis and C. H. Langford, *Symbolic Logic* (New York: The Century Co., 1932) and G. H. von Wright, *An Essay in Modal Logic* (*Studies in Logic and the Foundations of Mathematics*, Amsterdam: North-Holland Publishing Co., 1951). More recent works will be referred to later.

If obligation and the like are to be handled in terms of certain primitive predicates, it is reasonable to ask what the arguments of these predicates are. Straightways some will tell us *propositions*, regarded as the "meanings" of declarative sentences. However, if they are so regarded, they are surely an obscure kind of entity. A better candidate for the arguments of predicates for obligation and the like would be *action kinds*, or *act properties*, as von Wright calls them.[10] However action kinds may in turn be medadic, monadic, dyadic, and so on, depending upon the various factors involved in the action. To light a cigarette is clearly monadic, but to light a cigarette *with* a given match or lighter is dyadic. Also, action types are performed *by* given persons *at* given times. Furthermore, obligation is relative to a given legal code and perhaps also to a given social group. Thus a predicate for obligation should perhaps have at least five arguments: a person, an action kind, an object of the action kind (if it is dyadic), a time, a social group, and a legal code. A full theory of obligation, it would appear, should incorporate each of these factors.

The nomic approach to the theory of obligation via deontic logic is essentially that taken by the mathematician: Get axioms or deontic laws no matter how, and do not worry about such things as codes or social groups. The ontic approach, to the contrary, undertakes painstaking analyses of these various factors and of the whole pragmatic context. It would seem that this latter approach ought to be of greater interest and utility for both the philosopher and legal analyst than is the method of mathematical model building.

Similar remarks pertain to logic as a philosophical tool generally. Laws or axioms without a full analysis and exploration of their context and content are philosophically without interest. Mathematical logic is thus often rightly viewed as philosophically irrelevant. Logic in the broad sense, including semiotic (syntax, semantics, and pragmatics together), in contrast, may be thought to constitute the very core of philosophical analysis. In short, mathematics is a luxury for philosophy, but logic is its daily bread.

3. Logical Perfection. Often regarded as the greatest logician of of the nineteenth century, *Frege* made fundamental contributions to mathematical logic and to the foundations of mathematics. His interests did not stop there, however, and there are many suggestions in his writings reminding us of his broader concern for logic as a philosophic tool. To this day these suggestions contain a most eloquent plea for the use of logical methods in philosophy. Although analytic

[10] *Loc. cit.*

philosophers recently have been giving much lip service to some of Frege, it is doubtful that his real message has been understood. Much of Frege's technical work has been absorbed into the tradition; the same cannot be said of his comments concerning philosophical method. Let us review some of these comments, without attempting an exhaustive exposition or critique. In so doing, we shall be characterizing *Frege's way in*,[11] which is closely allied to that suggested above.

In one of his first ventures into philosophical writing, in 1882, Frege extols the virtues of the use of symbols, that "grand discovery," as he puts it.[12] Sometimes words of ordinary language seem to be included among his "symbols," but for the most part he is concerned with the use of mathematical or other special signs. The "imperfection of [ordinary] language" and "the need for some method of avoiding errors in one's own thought as well as misunderstanding on the part of others" are apparently to be overcome by properly chosen symbols. "Let no one be contemptuous of symbols! A good deal depends upon a practical selection of them." Symbols are aids to memory, Frege reminds us, and without them we "could hardly raise ourselves to the level of conceptual thought." They help to "protect our thinking from error" and help us differentiate flawless from specious argumentation.

It is often said that it takes a great philosopher to make a great mistake. Frege's mistake is often thought—at Oxford anyhow—to be the pursuit of "logical perfection" in the use of a logically perfect language system as in some way a substitute for our ordinary language. However, it is not altogether clear that Frege committed this mistake, if such it be. The shortcomings he finds in ordinary language are caused, he thought, "by a certain softness and instability . . . , which, on the other hand, constitute the reason for its many-sided usefulness and potentiality for development." A logically perfect language system is thus to be contrasted sharply with our ordinary language. For some purposes the one is more appropriate; for others, the other.

Wittgenstein has put this matter well in noting that

> our clear and simple language-games are not preparatory studies for a future regularization of language—as it were, first approximations, ignoring friction and air resistance. The language-games are rather set us as objects of comparison which are meant to throw light on the facts of our language by way not only of similarities, but also of dissimilarities. . . .[13]

---

[11] See W. V. Quine, "On Frege's Way Out," in *Selected Logic Papers* (New York: Random House, 1966), pp. 146–158.

[12] See G. Frege, "On the Scientific Justification of a Concept-Script" (1882), tr. by J. Bartlett in *Mind* LXXIII (1964), 155–160.

[13] Wittgenstein, *loc. cit.*

That this, or something like it, was Frege's view also seems likely. Logical perfection is to be pursued in mathematics and in its foundations. Its pursuit elsewhere does no harm as an object of comparison or as an ideal, and may often be helpful. The "application of my symbols to other fields [than mathematics] is not excluded," Frege writes. "The logical relations recur everywhere. . . . [A] forward-looking representation of the forms of thought has a significance extending beyond mathematics. May the philosophers then give some attention to the matter!"

4. "Pernicious Influence" and "Bedevilment." The "logical relations recur everywhere"; strictly mathematical ones may or may not. Well, wherever the logical relations occur or recur is presumably fit subject for logical study. Logic justifiably "meddles" with all subjects. In contrast, the applicability of mathematics may often be pressed too far with perhaps unfortunate effect.

In his "The Pernicious Influence of Mathematics on Science," Jacob Schwartz has dwelt interestingly with the "single-mindedness, literal-mindedness, simple-mindedness" of mathematics when confronted with the complex data with which the empirical sciences, both physical and social, deal.[14] "Quite typically," he writes, "science leaps ahead and mathematics plods behind." Even more pernicious, it is sometimes claimed, is the influence of formal logic upon philosophy. John Findlay, for example, has recently written that all

> . . . philosophy has been bedeviled by the methods and ideals of formal logic—which may be summed up as the attempt to draw sharp lines round all concepts and to make all inferences rigorously deductive—and increasingly so with the improved formalization of recent times. . . .[15]

The two types of "pernicious influence," if such they be, are to be evaluated very differently. The use of mathematics in the physical and social sciences is a very special matter about which it is difficult to give a definite statement.. Overnight the situation may change, and some new applications of existing mathematics may be brought to light or some altogether new area of theory developed. The applicability of logic to both the sciences and philsosophy is, however, quite another

---

[14] In *Logic, Methodology, and the Philosophy of Science, Proceedings of the 1960 International Congress* (Stanford: Stanford University Press, 1962), pp. 356–360.

[15] In *Values and Intentions* (London: Geo. Allen and Unwin, 1961), p. 15.

matter, as Frege in effect pointed out, the "logical relations recurring everywhere."

The bedevilment of which Findlay speaks seems fictitious. In "drawing sharp lines round all concepts," recent philosophers have perhaps indeed neglected the logical analysis of the "cloudy material" concerned with "family relations" among values and ends with which Findlay is concerned. However, neglect to apply is not inapplicability. The "family relations" are indeed "logical" relations, as Findlay contends. Hence it would seem that logic is needed for their analysis. Further, the bedevilment of "deductivism" is surely exaggerated and is strictly neither a "method" nor an "ideal" of formal logic. Whatever *in*ductive inference is, it is not merely another form of deduction—or if it is, it is of a well-disguised kind within no doubt some suitable semantical or pragmatical metalanguage. Nor should the drawing of sharp lines around concepts be lightly disparaged. Philosophy, to say nothing of mathematics and the sciences, owes much of its advance to such. Although the sciences often muddle along with rather casual distinctions, the drawing of sharp lines and boundaries is often of the utmost importance in professional philosophical discussion.

But let us return to Frege.

5. On Frege's Intensionalism. Another grievous error Frege is supposed to have made is to have searched for the "sense" or meaning, *Sinn,* rather than for the use—or, better, to have supposed in the first place that there are meanings or *Sinne* to be searched for or to be found. Again, however, it is doubtful that this supposition is so grievous an error after all. Frege did not give an analysis of the *internal structure* of meanings, and this is surely unfortunate. Meanings are not merely to be postulated or hypostatized but to be analyzed or dissected into components in some clear way. In other words, we are to start with a well-developed theory of syntax, of designational or denotational semantics for a given system, and then build up concepts, meanings, and the like, as relativized to that language system. Here, we should contend, is Frege's real error in the theory of meaning: that he did not press the purely extensionalist point of view deeply enough. (This is discussed further in Chapters VII and X.)

One of the first to have emphasized the importance of the distinction between the *use* and *mention* of expressions, Frege was perhaps actually the first to have used quotation marks with full correctness. Of course he was not the first to have made the distinction, but probably the first to have realized its significance, at least for the foundations of mathematics. His key statement on this matter, in the

Grundgesetze der Arithmetik, cannot be improved upon and merits being called to attention in full.

> The frequent use of quotation marks may cause surprise. I use them to distinguish the cases where I speak about the sign itself from those where I speak about what it stands for. Pedantic as this may appear, I think it necessary. It is remarkable how an inexact mode of speaking or writing, which was perhaps originally employed only for greater convenience or brevity and with full consciousness of its inaccuracy, may end in a confusion of thought, when once that consciousness has disappeared. People have managed to mistake numerals for numbers, names for the things named, the mere devices of arithmetic for its proper subject-matter. Such experiences teach us how necessary it is to demand the highest exactness in manner of speech and writing. And I have taken pains to do justice to such demands, at any rate wherever it seemed to be of importance.[16]

Out of this basic distinction between use and mention comes that between *object* and *meta*language, between the language being discussed and the language in which the discussion takes place. This likewise is a distinction of fundamental theoretical importance, but one unfortunately more observed nowadays in the breach than in the keeping. So much depends upon the correct use of quotation marks in logico-philosophical writing that, as Donald Davidson has recently remarked, we all should be more puzzled about them than we are.

6. "Logic Meddles with All Subjects." Often it is contended that the Fregean kind of approach leads to no "substantive" analyses in philosophy or methodology, that one merely puts into symbols what one already knows, and that one gains nothing new by its use. Of course philosophers and methodologists are often more interested in the content of what is said than in the way of saying it. Frege made a similar point concerning mathematicians.

> As a rule mathematicians are interested only in the content of a theorem. . . . The novelty of this book does not lie in the content of the theorems [for the most part well known], but in the development of the . . . foundations on which they are based. That

---

[16] G. Frege, *Grundgesetze der Arithmetik,* reprinted by Georg Olms Verlagsbuchhandlung (Hildesheim: 1962), p. 4.

this altogether different point of view needs a quite different treatment ought not to appear strange. . . .[17]

Logical analysis is less concerned with content than with the forms of the expressions used, their syntax and their semantics. To expect substantive solutions to problems concerned with content from logical analysis is to misunderstand its aims. Logic in fact is neutral with respect to variant philosophical aims and is in principle as serviceable to any one as to any other. This is an important point, it seems, yet one that is widely misunderstood.

Logic "meddles" with all subjects, as does no other discipline, and often not just in superficial ways but to the depths. The sooner we learn to welcome this situation, it seems, the better. Nor is it an unpleasant or undesirable situation. Logic meddles, not necessarily to condemn (as in the hands of some), but to help. Logic is primarily a constructive tool, a useful technique, a help-meet in the whole philosophic enterprise. Rather than to try to do without technique, the wiser course is no doubt to master whatever is available, and then go on to use it as best one can.

The charge of "scholasticism" is often urged against Frege's way in to the problems of philosophy via universally applicable "logical relations" and the theory of meaning. Scholastics, in this pejorative sense, make "unprofitable" distinctions beyond those ordinarily needed in critical discussions in analytic phlosophy. Of course it is not always easy to demarcate distinctions that are profitable from those that are not. Profitable for what special purpose? is a question that may well be asked. Sometimes distinctions have intrinsic interest, even if they are not immediately useful. However, making them may lead to something profitable in the future. A high-powered computer is not needed to multiply 2 by 3, but it is useful for certain more complex tasks. However, for the purpose of doing fundamental philosophy, of delving deeply into a matter, or of clarifying *au fond* the logical structure of some area, the help of the most subtle logical tools seems more and more needed.

In the random remarks made concerning Frege, no attempt has been made to survey his many contributions to logic and therewith philosophic method. Instead, attention has been called to a few items against which philosophers (to use Frege's own words) "sin most often." (A good deal more will be said below about the doctrine of *Sinne*.)

[17] *Ibid.*, p. viii. The translations are from *Philosophical Writings of Gottlob Frege*, by P. Geach and M. Black (Oxford: Basil Blackwell, 1952), p. 106.

One final comment. It is sometimes said that the attempt to formalize a given field of knowledge succeeds only in expressing (to use the words of Hao Wang) "in tiresome exactitude more or less commonplace ideas which could be conveyed more easily and more directly in a few sentences of plain language."[18] Wang goes on to say that

> perhaps we can compare many of the attempts to formalize with the use of an airplane to visit a friend living in the same town. Unless you simply love the airplane ride . . . , the procedure would be quite pointless and extremely inconvenient. Or we may compare the matter with constructing or using a huge computer solely to calculate the result of multiplying seven by eleven.

At best these metaphors seem misleading, and it would be interesting to know precisely what formalizations Wang wishes to include among the "many." Surely not the important work on constitution theory stemming from Carnap's *Aufbau,* that on syntax and the semantical truth concept, that on syntactical or semantical categories, on logical or analytic truth, on designation and allied notions, on the theory of intensions, on ontology, on nominalism, on probability, on the logic of explanation, on structural linguistics, and on special branches of various empirical science.[19] In none of these areas of applied logic would a "few sentences of plain language" suffice. In fact it would be difficult to name a single significant instance of formalization in philosophy or the methodology of science that Wang's description would fit. The important point is that we *can* formalize if we wish, that general techniques are available if they are needed, and that to achieve maimum logical candor some explicit formalization is often helpful.

We must also beware lest in philosophical analysis our plain

---

[18] Hao Wang, *A Survey of Mathematical Logic (Studies in Logic and the Foundations of Mathematics,* Amsterdam: North-Holland Publishing Co., 1963), p. 63. The view expressed in the passage quoted is not necessarily that of Wang.

[19] In addition to relevant works already referred to, the following, of outstanding interest, may be mentioned in passing: R. Carnap, *Der Logische Aufbau der Welt* (Berlin-Schlachtensee: Weltkrcis-Verlag, 1928 and [in translation] Berkeley and Los Angeles: University of California Press, 1967) and *Logical Foundations of Probability* (Chicago: University of Chicago Press, 1950); C. G. Hempel and P. Oppenheim, "Studies in the Logic of Explanation," *Philosophy of Science* 15 (1948), 135–175; C. G. Hempel, *Aspects of Scientific Explanation* (New York: The Free Press, and London: Collier-Macmillan Ltd., 1965); Z. Harris, *Methods in Structural Linguistics* (Chicago: University of Chicago Press, 1951); J. H. Woodger, *The Axiomatic Method in Biology* (Cambridge: Cambridge University Press, 1937), and N. Goodman, *The Structure of Appearance* (Cambridge: Harvard University Press, 1951).

language lulls us into thinking that we understand more than we do. Ideas are often "commonplace" merely because we ask no searching questions about them. The point of having airplanes and computers is to be able to use them when we need them. We need not use them every time we wish to cross the street or multiply 2 by 3. However, if we wish to go a good distance or solve a difficult equation, they provide a most serviceable means, and they are becoming increasingly reliable and efficient with the advance of research.

The points made in this chapter are very broad and general, and the reader is asked, in Frege's phrase, to meet them at least half-way. To substantiate them fully would require a more detailed discussion than space permits. Some of them will be elaborated and made more exact below. They are put forward here in a merely introductory way and should be viewed in the light of the by no means orthodox philosophical view underlying what follows.

CHAPTER II

Ontic Commitment and Involvement

Several criteria for "ontic [or ontological] commitment" have recently been formulated, but all are more or less modifications of the one put forward originally by Quine.[1] Roughly, a language or language system *ontically commits* us to the entities over which its variables of quantification range, and the totality of such objects constitutes the *ontology* of that language or language system. Also, we can say that a *sentence* ontically commits us to the entities over which its variables range or (if it contains no variables) to the entities designated by the (nonlogical) individual constants occurring in it.

The phrase 'ontic commitment' is new, but the central idea involved presumably harks back to the first users of variables in antiquity (or at least to the first conscious users of quantifiers in the nineteenth century). Over what do our variables range? Quine has happily focused attention upon this question and has shown its philosophical importance. However, he has left out one most significant factor, so that a new notion of *ontic involvement* will have to be put forward in place of ontic commitment. Ontic involvement, it will be contended, is the more significant notion. The subject is approached gradually by examining first some influential contemporary views on the nature of logic and its relation with ontology.

In Sections 1 and 2 some of *Church's* views on these topics are discussed critically, and in Section 3 some of *Kneale's* are considered.

[1] For a recent formulation, see *Word and Object* (New York and London: The Technology Press of the Massachusetts Institute of Technology and John Wiley and Sons, 1960), p. 242.

That there is *one logic only* is urged in Section 4. In Section 5 the role of *ontology in semantics* is examined, preparatory to a discussion of logic as a *logic-with-ontology* in Section 6. In Section 7 *Quine's criterion* and its connection with the *quantifiers* are discussed in detail. In Section 8 further *critical comments* on Quine's views are put forward. The notion of *ontic involvement* is finally introduced in Section 9. In Section 10, Quine's notion of *semantic ascent* is discussed briefly.

1. Church on the Province of Logic. In his paper read at the 1960 International Congress for Logic, Methodology, and Philosophy of Science, Alonzo Church was concerned with the problem of the province of logic and how it is to be distinguished from that of mathematics.[2] His comments are intimately connected with matters of ontology. Roughly, logic may be said to consist, he says, "in a theory of deductive reasoning, plus whatever is required in object language or metalanguage for the adequacy, generality, and simplicity of the theory." This statement is intended as a "descriptive account rather than a definition, and assuming the notion of deductive reasoning as already known, from experience with particular instances of it." The crucial word 'valid' is left out in this description, and we may assume that Church intends 'deductive reasoning' here only in the sense of 'valid deductive reasoning'. Even so, the clause beginning with 'plus whatever' is not clear. The two paragraphs that follow are presumably intended to make amends. Because these will be commented upon at some length, they should be quoted in full.

> That logic does not . . . consist [Church says] merely in a metatheory of some object language arises in the following way. It is found that ordinary theories, and perhaps any satisfactory theory, of deductive reasoning in the form of a metatheory will lead to analytic sentences in the object language. . . . These analytic sentences lead in turn to certain generalizations; e.g., the infinitely many analytic sentences $A \lor \sim A$, where A ranges over all sentences of the object language, lead to the generalization $p \lor \sim p$, or more explicitly $(p) \cdot p \lor \sim p$; and in similar fashion $(F)(y) \cdot (x)F(x) \supset F(y)$ may arise by generalization from infinitely many analytic sentences of the appropriate form. These generalizations are common to many object languages on the basis of what is seen to be in some sense the same theory of deductive reasoning for the different languages. Hence they are

[2] A. Church, "Mathematics and Logic," in *Logic, Methodology and Philosophy of Science*, pp. 181–186.

considered to belong to logic, as not only is natural but has long been the standard terminology.

Against the suggestion [Church continues] which is sometimes made from a nominalistic motivation, to avoid or omit these generalizations, it must be said that to have, e.g., all of the special cases $A \vee \sim A$ and yet not allow the general law $(p) \cdot p \vee \sim p$ seems to be contrary to the spirit of generality in mathematics, which I would extend to logic as the most fundamental branch of mathematics. Indeed such a situation would be much as if one had in arithmetic $2 + 3 = 3 + 2$, $4 + 5 = 5 + 4$, and all other particular cases of the commutative law of addition, yet refused to accept or formulate a general law, $(x)(y) \cdot x + y = y + x$.

Almost surreptitiously here, an *arrière pensée* as it were, Church has been guided by a conception of mathematical generality as well as by a conception of logic as "the most fundamental branch of mathematics." However, such conceptions are the very points at issue, and we may well ask whether this conception of mathematical generality *should* guide us here, and whether (and if so, why, and in what sense) logic *should* be regarded as the most fundamental branch of mathematics. Why, in fact, should logic be regarded as a branch of mathematics at all? It was not so regarded for many centuries, and surely it does not go without discussion that modern developments have proved this beyond cavil. Indeed, that it should *not* be so regarded has been suggested in the preceding chapter and is urged again below.

Further, the philosopher who is sensitive to matters of existence, that is, to matters of ontology and ontic commitment, will observe an *enormous* difference between admitting infinitely many analytic sentences of the form '$(A \vee \sim A)$', where 'A' is a sentence of the object language, and a generalization of the form '$(p)(p \vee \sim p)$, *where* 'p' ranges over *propositions*. The one formulation carries no ontic commitment other than that carried by 'A'; the other carries ontic commitment to an altogether new kind of entity, abstract propositions. It is clear that the latter are never needed for the purpose of formulating a theory of valid deduction for any given system.

Church himself comments later that "the abstract general laws of logic may satisfactorily be formulated as extensional . . . " and hence presumably without the use of propositional variables, for propositions and *in*tensionality go hand in hand. The formulation of these laws in terms of propositions is in fact more complicated than the formulation of the laws without the propositions, in the obvious sense of requiring a new style of variables together with the entities over which they range. Thus at best the introduction of the form

'$(p)(p \lor \sim p)$' serves neither the "adequacy," "generality," nor "simplicity" of the theory.

Similar remarks apply to the form '$(F)(y) \ldots$', although much depends upon what 'F' is taken to range over. If 'F' is taken to range over properties-in-extension or classes, the ontic commitment of the form '$(F) \ldots$' involves no intensionality whatsoever. The ontic commitment of '$(p)(p \lor \sim p)$', however, presumably involves intensionality no matter what the other kinds of variables of the object language at hand range over. Also, the form '$(F)(y) \ldots$' is a form within a specific object language and is thus linguistically relative. The form '$(p)(p \lor \sim p)$', in contrast, is intended in some sense to hold for *all* languages. In allowing quantifiers over all "propositions," we are no longer speaking of the sentences or statements of just one language but presumably of all propositions expressed in *any language whatsoever*. There is thus an implicit generalization here to all languages or language systems. Such a generalization is not involved in the form '$(F)(y) \ldots$' on the usual interpretation of the quantifiers. There are thus very essential differences between these two forms.

Surely also there is an enormous difference between admitting all laws of the form '$2 + 3 = 3 + 2$', '$4 + 5 = 5 + 4$', and so on, in arithmetic, yet refusing to admit the general law '$(x)(y)x + y = y + x$'. In fact, it is just this difference that has been at the root of some important mathematical work.[3]

Even if it be granted that the difference here is perhaps somewhat special, another point should be observed. We note that the variable 'x' here is presumed to range, say, over the natural numbers or positive integers. Hence the quantifier '(x)' may be read 'for all positive integers x' or 'for all natural numbers x'. The "spirit of generality in mathematics" here carries us from an infinity of statements containing proper names '2', '3', '4', $\ldots$ of specific integers or natural numbers to a statement containing universal quantifiers over integers or numbers in general. Our criterion of ontic commitment may or may not be formulated so that the sentence '$2 + 3 = 3 + 2$' carries ontic commitment to the integers 2 and 3. If it is, and it is not unreasonable to allow this, the ontic commitment of '$2 + 3 = 3 + 2$' consists of a subdomain of the ontic commitment of the sentence '$(x)(y)x + y = x$'. Here the spirit of mathematical generality does *not* lead to a change in the kind of ontic commitment, but only

---

[3] See, for example, D. Hilbert and P. Bernays, *Grundlagen der Mathematik*, 2 vols. (Berlin: Springer, 1934 and 1939) and R. Goodstein, *Recursive Number Theory* (*Studies in Logic and the Foundations of Mathematics*, Amsterdam: North-Holland Pub. Co., 1956).

to an increase within some one kind. This indeed seems as it should be.

For a sentence '$(A \lor \sim A)$', we have the same ontic commitment as for 'A', some objects in a domain D, namely, over which the variables of 'A' (if any) range or which are denoted or designated by the proper names occurring in 'A'. The spirit of generality then carries us to a general formula in which we allow the quantifier over the objects of D, but not to a general formula such as '$(p)(p \lor \sim p)$' where the ontic commitment is not preserved. In short, the spirit of generality in mathematics should be such as to *preserve* ontic commitment *to the same kind of object*, not to change or increase it to another kind. If the ontic commitment is changed, it is no longer the spirit of generality that is guiding us but the desire or need (if such it be) of introducing some altogether new kind of object.

The points raised may seem minute, but out of such minutiae important truths emerge that are essential for the proper understanding of logic, ontology, syntax, semantics, theory of intension, and the like.

2. Logic and Subject Matter. Valid deductive reasoning does not take place in a vacuum; it is always applied to a particular subject matter. There is no specifically "logical" subject matter, it seems, for us to reason about, validly or otherwise. There is no eternal notion *or*, which we introduce the wedge sign '$\lor$' to designate. There are of course *signs* or *expressions*, in particular the signs of logic, but there are no specifically "logical" individuals or things. There are no specifically "logical" classes or relations; there are merely specific classes and relations germane to a given subject matter. The theory of valid deductive reasoning cannot, it would seem, be a theory of a given subject matter. What is it, then, precisely? Church says that it does not consist "merely in a metatheory of some object language." Surely not of any *one* object language. This would be much too narrow a characterization. However, if we consider all object languages formulated as *first-order* systems, say, first-order logic might well be regarded as being merely the theory of valid deducibility within their syntax and semantics.[4]

[4] See *Truth and Denotation*. On first-order systems, see especially D. Hilbert and W. Ackermann, *Grundzüge der Theoretischen Logik*, 4th ed. (Berlin: Springer, 1959) and A. Church, *Introduction to Mathematical Logic*, Vol. I (Princeton: Princeton University Press, 1956). For useful recent expositions see D. Kalish and R. Montague, *Logic, Techniques of Formal Reasoning* (New York: Harcourt, Brace & World, Inc., 1964), B. Mates, *Elementary Logic* (New York: Oxford University Press, 1965), and H. Leblanc, *Techniques of Deductive Inference* (Englewood Cliffs, N.J.: Prentice-Hall, 1966).

If there is no specifically "logical" subject matter, we speak instead of the signs of a languge and of how these signs are connected with each other and with the objects with which the language deals. We consider certain purely *syntactical* relations between certain formulae of the language, on the one hand, and how the formulae are related to the semantical notion of *truth* for that language, on the other. Roughly, in some such way, valid deductive inference for the given language or languages is characterized. Most important here, as Church in effect emphasizes, is the notion of *analytic* or *logical truth*. Given this latter for a language, the set of valid deductive inferences of the language is uniquely determined. First-order logic may then be regarded equally well as the theory of analytic truths for first-order languages.[5]

Church would no doubt regard the foregoing remarks as arising from a "nominalistic motivation." Actually, however, this view of logic is strictly *neutral* with regard to nominalism. Nominalistic, realistic, and conceptualistic systems may all be formulated within the kind of logic discussed. This latter contains no hidden features that require defense. Church's kind of formulation, in contrast, is out-and-out realist, as well as intensionalist. The burden of proof is therefore upon him to provide a suitable philosophical justification for these views. Clearly, the neutral formulation enjoys an important advantage in this respect.

Every language system of the kinds usually considered contains a logic as a part, whether the specific subject matter of the language be from physics, chemistry, biology, musicology, psychology, or other disciplines. Logic might therefore be regarded as the fundamental branch of all of these sciences or areas of inquiry. There is nothing especially privileged about mathematical subject matter and hence no reason why logic should be regarded as a fundamental branch of mathematics any more than of any other science. Of course, mathematical subject matter is especially "clear," and it is especially easy to get at the exact character of mathematical inferences. However this says merely that mathematics affords an especially convenient area to which logic may be applied. Here too, it would seem, a strict neutrality should be maintained. The study of valid deductive inference seems quite neutral as regards specific subject matter. This neutrality permeates the history of logic, from Aristotle and Chrysippus through Leibniz to Bolzano, Boole, Frege and Peirce, and modern

---

[5] See the author's *The Notion of Analytic Truth* (Philadelphia: University of Pennsylvania Press, 1959).

developments do not indicate that it should be abandoned or that it is in any way in error.

3. Kneale on Applied Logic. In *The Development of Logic*,[6] William Kneale has urged a use of 'logic' in accord with which one would not correctly speak of the "logic" of the terms for this or that special subject matter. If this latter were admitted, "arithmetic would undoubtedly be the logic of numerals, just as geometry would be the logic of shape words, mechanics the logic of 'force', analytical economics the logic of 'price', philosophical theology (if such a science exists) the logic of 'God', and so forth." It is clear that this use of 'logic' is roughly the same as what more accurately and customarily is called 'applied logic'.

The use of 'applied logic' does not seem to involve "an enormous extension of a technical term," and it is not clear why, "if we think that the logic of tradition has been concerned primarily with principles of inference valid for all possible subject matters, we must reject as unprofitable such phrases as 'the logic of "God" '." In discourse about 'God' we find, in fact, an extremely interesting and historically important area for the use of logic that might indeed be very profitable to explore on a more modern footing, as Father Bocheński has recently suggested.[7] Logic may be presumed to include the syntax and semantics of such discourse quite as much as it does for any other.

If to the purely logical axioms and rules of a language system nonlogical axioms akin to Carnap's *meaning postulates* are added, the notion of analytic truth for that language need not therewith be altered.[8] Carnap regards meaning postulates as in some sense *primitively* L-true or analytic. However, this is an extension of the word 'analytic' as used here and by Church. Thus meaning postulates concerning 'God' need in no way become logical or analytic truths. Therefore, Kneale's insistence that we cannot properly speak of a logic of 'God' seems gratuitous, if meaning postulates germane to a given subject matter are not regarded as analytic truths.

Of course the general characterization of logic as the study of valid deductive inferences is, as Kneale points out, somewhat vague. Precisely what are valid deductive inferences? Well, each of the vast

---

[6] Pp. 740 ff.

[7] In his Charles F. Deems Lectures. See his *The Logic of Religion* (New York: New York University Press, 1965). See the author's review, in the *International Philosophical Quarterly* VI (1966), 645–664.

[8] R. Carnap, "Meaning Postulates," in *Meaning and Necessity*, 2d ed. (Chicago: University of Chicago Press, 1956), pp. 222–229.

multiplicity of well-formulated logics attempts to answer this question in its own way. We cannot single out one of these logics and say by *fiat* that the inferences it condones are just the valid ones. Nonetheless these various logics are not all on a par, and good arguments can be adduced that the first-order logic mentioned above is the fundamental or basic one.

4. One Logic Only. Philosophers differ remarkably over what they wish to include under 'formal logic', as we noted above. Some wish to include the whole of mathematics, as developed, say, within the *simplified theory of types* or within an *axiomatic set theory*.[9] Others wish to restrict logic to a *second-order logic*, within which (with appropriate nonlogical axioms) mathematical analysis may be developed.[10] Still others consider that even second-order logic involves too much and condone (as here) only the classical *first-order* logic. Intuitionists maintain that even this narrow kind of a logic contains dubious laws, and in its place they have put forward *intuitionistic logics*.[11] Others have attempted to develop *many-valued* logics, with one or more "values" intermediary between truth and falsehood.[12] Also, a syntax presumably should be included in the general province of logic, as well as a denotational or designational semantics. Some even may wish to add a theory of meaning or intension, in the manner of Frege, Carnap, or Church.[13] These latter constitute metalogic, which may then be further supplemented by a pragmatics.

The various alternative kinds of logic clamor for attention, and their respective proponents are eloquent as to the special virtues of

[9] See, in particular, B. Russell, "Mathematical Logic as Based on the Theory of Types," *American Journal of Mathematics* 30 (1908), 222–262; A. N. Whitehead and B. Russell, *Principia Mathematica,* 2d ed. (Cambridge: Cambridge University Press, 1925–27); E. Zermelo, "Untersuchungen über die Grundlagen der Mengenlehre," *Mathematische Annalen* 65 (1908), 261–281; and J. von Neumann, "Die Axiomatisierung der Mengenlehre." *Mathematische Zeitschrift* 27 (1928), 669–752. For more recent developments, see W. V. Quine, *Set Theory and Its Logic* (Cambridge: The Belknap Press of Harvard University Press, 1963), and the works cited therein.

[10] See Hilbert-Ackermann, *op. cit.,* and Church, *op. cit.*

[11] See, for example, A. Heyting, *Intuitionism, An Introduction* (*Studies in Logic and the Foundations of Mathematics,* Amsterdam: North-Holland Publishing Co., 1956) and the works therein cited.

[12] See especially J. B. Rosser and A. R. Turquette, *Many-valued Logics* (*Studies in Logic and the Foundations of Mathematics,* Amsterdam: North-Holland Publishing Co.: 1952).

[13] See especially Frege, "On Sense and Reference," in *Philosophical Writings of Gottlob Frege,* Carnap, *Meaning and Necessity,* and Church, *Introduction to Mathematical Logic,* Chapter I. Concerning this last, see Chapter III, Section 7, below, and concerning *modal* logic, Sections 2 through 6.

each. Unfortunately these virtues usually turn out to be rather special for the most part. The *Entscheidungsproblem* can be solved easily for this logical system; that one has such and such a completeness property; this other contains 256 different numbers all very closely akin to the natural number 2! Important philosophical issues are at stake, however, in the appraisal of the multiplicity of logics. Not all of them are philosophically above suspicion, as has already been suggested, and a strong argument can be made that the classical, first-order logic, with syntax and semantics constructed on its basis, has a privileged status.

In view of the vast multiplicity of logics available, any one, it is often thought, is as good as any other. Just take your pick and, if none of them quite suits, make up a new one or simply disregard the subject altogether. However, this rather cavalier—and widespread—attitude is surely not defensible. Why not reject physics on the grounds that there is no complete unanimity on all details of wave theory, of field theory, or of quantum theory, and how they are interrelated? Why not reject arithmetic on similar grounds?

Very briefly, some of the arguments that first-order logic is more fundamental than the alternatives are as follows.

In the first place, first-order logic is a direct and natural outgrowth of the logic of tradition, stemming from Aristotle and the Stoics and the Scholastics. As Kneale himself notes, ". . . it is desirable that any new rules we adopt deliberately for old words should depart little, if at all, from previously established customs. . . ." What new rules we do adopt should, in Hobbes' phrase, contain "no offensive novelty." This typically British attitude no doubt needs defense in general, but not, it would seem, in the present context.

First-order logic may be regarded as containing the conceptual core of other logics. Most of them may be viewed as arising from first-order logic by a modification of this or that, or by an extension or deletion here or there. Other logics are then viewed and characterized in terms of their similarities to and differences from first-order logic regarded as a kind of paradigm.

No doubt we can argue also for the "simplicity" and "naturalness" of first-order logic as over and against the alternatives. In addition, first-order logic can be formulated wholly extensionally, as already noted, while some of the alternatives cannot; thus first-order logic always enjoys the advantages of extensionality.

Another very important argument is that every logic has a syntax and a semantics—in fact, as we have observed, each *is* a syntax and a semantics in the sense that it is formulated within a syntactical or semantical metalanguage. In turn these metalanguages may be formulated as formal systems and thus contain a logic as a part. This logic is usually the classical logic, irrespective of whether the logic of the object language is or is not. For example, syntax may be regarded as the theory of *concatenation*[14] or logical spelling, even for intuitionistic or many-valued systems. That first-order logic always seems presupposed in the syntactical metalanguage of any logic whatsoever provides a most telling argument; and, *a fortiori*, the semantical metalanguages of such systems usually are built upon the basis of first-order logic.

Of interest as a matter of historical fact is the point that the standard first-order logic has been used more successfully in applications than has any other kind of logic. Most applications in the sciences are of this kind, as are those in the methodology of the sciences. Modal logics, many-valued logics, intuitionistic logics, and the like seem not to have been used very much or very fruitfully in such applications. When philosophers worry about whether such and such an inference in natural language is valid, it is always to first-order logic (whether they consciously realize it or not) that they turn, is it not? Logic in the sense of the "logical geography of concepts" seems to involve only the notions of first-order logic-cum-semantics.

No one of these arguments is by itself conclusive, and each should be developed much more fully. In sum, however, they lend good support to the thesis that first-order logic is the fundamental one. If so, philosophers may well look to this kind of logic as providing the most suitable tools for their work.

We may conclude that not all logics are of equal value for the philosopher. Not all of them are equally sound, nor are all formulations equally acceptable. Mathematicians may continue to explore special features of this or that kind of system, but their results are likely to be of little philosophical interest. The standard, classical, first-order logic provides the most suitable philosophical tools, it would seem, and it is presupposed in one fashion or another even in the discussion of the alternatives.

5. Ontology. It was suggested earlier that syntax and sematics themselves may be viewed as applied first-order systems. That this is the case is most important for philosophy and logical analysis, with significant bearings on ontology.

---

[14] See A. Tarski, *Logic, Semantics, Metamathematics* (Oxford: Clarendon Press, 1956), pp. 165 ff., W. V. Quine, *Mathematical Logic*, rev. ed. (Cambridge: Harvard University Press, 1951), Chapter Seven, and *Truth and Denotation*, Chapter III.

Logical analysis is preeminently concerned with the syntax, semantics, and pragmatics of language, as has already been noted. Only rarely, however, are these three compartments of semiotic clearly distinguished from one another. Some philosophers even make a virtue of blurring them together indiscriminately, especially when natural language is concerned. Blurring may have its merits, but philosophy and logical analysis live and breathe with sharp distinctions, clear groupings, and precise statements. Thus it seems eminently desirable that we always distinguish carefully among logical, factual, syntactical, semantical, and pragmatical rules or assumptions. The question now arises as to how ontology is related to them. What is ontology? Is it a separate subject? A further subdivision of logic? Or is it in some sense reducible to these others? We have been following Quine in using the terminology 'ontology of L' and 'ontic commitment of L' to refer to the domain of objects taken as values for variables in L. This usage seems justified and is a mere sharpening of more or less traditional notions. Ontology in its modern setting is essentially the study of the objects "about" which our language or languages speak. The use of 'ontology' in this modern sense does no violence to traditional meanings. Rather, it is a natural outgrowth of those meanings and of the concerns that prompt them.

Ontology enters into logic via semantics, which is the study of the relations between signs and objects, between words and things. To study such relations we must occasionally make reference to objects as their relata. In semantics we are not interested in objects in any deeper sense, however, so that ontology plays here a rather subsidiary role. It has been urged that the ontology of a semantical metalanguage should involve no objects other than those of the object language under discussion. (See *Truth and Denotation*.) This is clearly essential for economy of ontic commitment. However, it is also essential if the semantician is not to usurp the tasks of the ontologist. In marked contrast are the formulations of semantics, for example, those of Carnap and Tarski, in which all manner of new entities are admitted other than the values for variables of the object language (or translation of such). The narrower kind of formulation of a semantics, presupposing only a first-order logic, involves no such objects and thus is strictly neutral with regard to further ontic commitment. Such neutrality should be part and parcel of the conception of semantics, as it should of the conception of logic.

It is not the logician's task to settle problems of ontology, nor is it his place either to populate or depopulate the universe. He merely accepts what is given him and returns it in an ordered form. This is all—but this is enough. His tools should, then, enable him to do this in the simplest and easiest way. First-order logic and the syntax and semantics built upon it seem explicitly designed for this.

6. Logic with Ontology. In a recent essay, Gottfried Martin has called attention to the traditional distinction between metaphysics as a theory of principles, *scientia universalis,* and as a theory of being, *ontologia generalis.*[15] Martin points out that historically metaphysicians have tended to be interested primarily in one or the other of these theories, rarely in both equally. He concludes by expressing preference for metaphysics as a theory of being and gives several objections to the possibility of metaphysics as a *scientia universalis.* He thinks that

> only regional systems of principles are possible, that is to say, that there are only systems of principles which are relevant to particular realms of being. If this assumption is correct, [he continues] it would be advisable to regard the systems of principles as belonging to the fundamental questions of the respective sciences. If we are dealing with very general systems of principles, and with general questions about systems of principles, then these had best find their place in the theory of science or in logic—logic here understood . . . in the modern extended sense. [Hence it is] appropriate to loosen the old bonds between *scientia universalis* and *ontologia generalis* . . . [and to assign] theory of principles to logic in its wide sense, and to concentrate metaphysics essentially upon the task of theory of being.

By 'the *logical principles* of language system *L*' let us designate the set of logical or analytic truths of *L*. It might be thought that construing 'ontology' in essentially Quine's sense and 'logical principles' in this way does violence to traditional meanings, but this is doubtful. The modern semantical notion of an ontology renders explicit what historically has often been rather obscure. Likewise, the modern notion of analytic truth may be regarded as a kind of paradigm to the precise characterization of which much of traditional logic has been devoted. Both of these comments require, to be sure, a detailed historical justification.

If the foregoing identifications are legitimate, it seems doubtful that we should loosen the bonds between *ontologia generalis* and *scientia universalis*, as Martin recommends. In fact, it is questionable whether this is possible or even meaningful. The two—at least in their

---

[15] See his "Metaphysics as *Scientia Universalis* and as *Ontologia Generalis*" in *The Relevance of Whitehead,* ed. by I. Leclerc (London: Geo. Allen and Unwin, 1961), pp. 219–231.

modern form—seem so indissolubly intertwined as to justify the maxim: No ontology, no logic.

Let us suppose that L is formulated as a first-order system without propositional variables. Such a formulation is designed with special regard to ontology. In each L, formulated this way, the only ontology involved is that of the particular discipline being formalized. In other words, no variables are introduced other than those having as their values the objects with which L deals. This is in contrast to other formulations of logic that involve variables over propositions (as meanings of declarative sentences) and perhaps other kinds of entities not pertaining to the subject matter of L.[16] The formulation of L is such then as to involve the ontology of L, and none other, in a most fundamental way.

It may be noted again that there is no specifically "logical" subject matter. There is subject matter only *of some L.* Thus there is no specifically "logical" ontology. Rather there are specific nonlogical ontologies suitably described in apropriate L's.

It is a thus defensible view that there is no such subject as *pure* logic. There is no subject matter for logic itself. There are only nonlogical subject matters suitably described in given systems. Logic itself may then be regarded as merely the syntactical and semantical theory of valid deducibility of these various systems, as we recall from Section 2.

Because of the generality of first-order logic, there is an important sense in which analytic truths are more than merely "regional." By 'regional truths of L' we could well designate the truths of L that are not analytic. Regional principles are then presumably not common to all disciplines but apply only to "particular realms of being." It is the system of regional principles that "belongs to the fundamental questions of the respective sciences."

The converse maxim—no logic, no ontology—is also attractive. Any ontology and therewith system of regional principles gives rise to a logic, usually to a first-order L. Of course the required L may not actually have been formulated. However, in principle such a formulation can almost always be given. It would seem then that there is a no sharp, clear, or fundamental separation of *ontologia generalis* and *scientia universalis*, of ontology and logic, when each is understood in its proper relation to the other.

Only the logical skeleton of metaphysical language, not its flesh and blood, has been commented on here. However, it is just this skeleton that is so frequently lacking in the metaphysical literature and

---

[16] See especially A. Church, *Introduction to Mathematical Logic* I.

that it is the function of the philosophic logician to provide. Logicians have, for the most part, disclaimed metaphysical interest, and metaphysicians have not mastered the intricacies of the new logic. The result has been an unfortunate severance, as complete as possible. Logic, divorced from its proper role as the *scientia scientiarum*, is merely an arid branch of mathematics. Nevertheless, metaphysics should open its doors to what modern logic has to offer. What is needed now is bridge building between these two areas of philosophy. Each is here to stay. Not peaceful coexistence but intimate collaboration should be aimed at, for which the time seems now ripe.

7. Quine's Criterion and the Quantifiers. Let us turn now to a closer discussion of Quine's criterion of ontic commitment and its connection with the quantifiers. The most recent statement is given in *Word and Object*.

> Insofar as we adhere to . . . [the canonical notation of quantification], the objects we are to be understood to admit are precisely the objects which we reckon to the universe of values over which the bound variables of quantification are considered to range. Such is simply the intended sense of the quantifiers '(x)' and '$(\exists x)$': 'every object x is such that', 'there is an object x such that'.[17]

This formulation is intended primarily for natural languages, but it seems equally applicable to language systems L. An alternative wording is that the language or language system L *carries ontic commitment to* the entities over which its bound variables range. And for the moment we may disregard the presence of individual constants, which almost always are taken to designate objects in the range of the bound variables anyhow.

Let us speak hereafter only of language systems, although much that is said is perhaps applicable also to natural languages.

Howsoever stated, Quine's criterion involves explicit mention of the relevant language system L. After all, it is L that contains the variables and quantifiers by means of which ontic commitment is achieved. Further, L should clearly be an *interpreted* language, that is, a semantical system and not a mere calculus. (An uninterpreted system or calculus presumably carries no ontic commitment with it whatsoever.) One and the same calculus can be given interpretations in different domains of objects. Clearly L is not supposed to carry

[17] P. 242.

ontic commitment with it to all of these domains but only to the one in the intended or principal or relevant interpretation.

In speaking of the ontic commitment of an interpreted *L*, then, it is appropriate to ask *how* the intended or relevant interpretation is to be given. As a matter of fact, it may be given in many different ways, that is, using different technical methods, and expressed in different kinds of semantical metalanguages. These metalanguages must themselves contain variables and quantifiers, perhaps of many different kinds. Thus the ontic commitment carried by the semantical metalanguages of *L* should also be taken into account if a clear description of what is meant by the ontic commitment carried by *L* is to be gained. More will be said about this in a moment.

Central to an understanding of Quine's criterion is the notion of the quantifier. Let us reflect a little more closely upon how best to interpret them.

By 'an *existential quantifier*' we denote an expression of such and such a kind *within some language system L*. Strictly then we should speak only of an existential quantifier *of L*. The clause 'of *L*' is often omitted but only for ellipsis. Actually, it should always be present for explicitness and clarity.

Usually the existential quantifier of *L* is symbolized by '(Ex)', or '$(\exists x)$' (or in some other suitable way) where '*x*' is a variable of *L*. The variables of *L* (supposing for the moment that they are all of one kind) are to be thought of as *ranging* over a certain *domain of individuals,* say *D,* as *values. L* is here a system with a specified interpretation. Part of this interpretation is given by the so-called *semantical rules of range.* For the present we need only one rule of range to specify the domain *D*. In fact the rule of range here may be regarded simply as a definition of the phrase 'values of variables for *L*'. We let

$$\text{'ValVbl}_L\text{'} \quad \text{abbreviate} \quad \text{'}D\text{',}$$

so that the domain of values for variables of *L*, ValVbl$_L$, is by definition simply the domain *D*.

In the usual way of formulating the theory of quantification in *L*, the domain *D* is presumed to contain at least one individual. The universal quantifier of *L* is usually read with the help of the word 'all'. '(x)', for example, is then read 'for all *x*' or 'for every *x*' or 'every *x* is such that' *where in each case x is to be understood as an individual in the domain D*. Better readings are therefore 'for all *x* in *D*' or 'every *x* in *D* is such that'. These readings seem clear and unambiguous. If the phrase 'in *D*' is omitted, this again is mere ellipsis, and it should always be strictly regarded as present. We are not claiming that the various uses of the English words 'all' and 'every' are unambiguous or without need of careful analysis but only that the contexts 'for all x in D' or 'for every x in D' are as "clear" presumably as any concepts of mathematics or exact science ever are, provided D is itself a clear-cut domain of objects.[18]

If the foregoing explanations are acceptable (and indeed they are based on more or less standard semantics), the role of the existential quantifier may be clarified as follows. We let

$$\text{`}(Ex)\text{'}\quad\text{abbreviate}\quad\text{`}\sim(x)\sim\text{'},$$

where '$\sim$' is the sign of negation. Now '$\sim$' is usually read 'it is not the case that' or simply 'not'. Again there seems to be no essential difficulty in this reading. The proper unabbreviated reading of the existential quantifier '(Ex)' is then 'it is not the case that every x in D is not such that' or 'it is not the case that for every x in D it is not the case that'. Clearly these two phrases may be given the abbreviated reading 'there is at least one individual x in D such that' or 'D contains at least one individual x such that' (assuming, as already mentioned, that D is nonnull).

In these readings of '(Ex)' the word 'exists' does not occur. Conceivably '(Ex)' could be read 'there *exists* at least one x in D such that' but all that should then be meant by this phrase is covered by the foregoing explanations. The use of 'exists' here is a mere convenience, a *manière de parler,* a mere abbreviatory reading. There is *some* connection of course with the "ordinary" meaning of 'exists', but not enough perhaps to justify calling the quantifier '(Ex)' 'an *existential* quantifier'. Perhaps it would be better to call it merely 'an *E-quantifier*' or give it some other innocuous label, as Wilfrid Sellars has suggested.[19]

So far as formal logic and semantics are concerned, D may be taken as any nonnull domain of objects whatever, depending upon the subject matter being formalized in L. In practice, however, D is usually a well-defined totality of objects, such as the totality of natural numbers, of real numbers, or of sets in the sense of a mathematical theory of sets, and so on. The philosophical constructionalist is free to choose D *ad libitum,* provided only that it constitute a well-defined totality. In order to have such a totality some clear-cut way of differentiating among the individuals of D must be given, more specifically, a clear-

[18] The requirement that D be nonnull is not strictly needed here. Various methods have been proposed to circumvent it.

[19] See his "Grammar and Existence: A Preface to Ontology," *Mind* LXIX (1960), 499–533.

cut condition under which two distinct objects of D differ from each other. For this in turn we need some clear-cut classes (properties) and relations, so that, for example, we can say of one object that it is a member of the given class and of another that it is not. In any event we have no clear ontology, as Quine has suggested, without a clear condition for identity.

8. "Regimentation." In *Word and Object* (p. 160), Quine states that on the whole "the canonical systems of logical notation [including quantifiers] are best seen not as complete notations for discourse on special subjects, but as partial notations for discourse on all subjects." This passage and its embellishment are central to Quine's philosophy of logic. "Practical temporary departures from ordinary languages," he notes, are to be tolerated on occasion short of using the "canonical notation" of symbolic logic. Certain further departures also may serve the purpose of simplification of theory. The result may no longer be an ordinary language but a "semi-ordinary" one, augmented with the full symbolism of modern logic.

The passage quoted from Quine is not, it would seem, free from ambiguity. Presumably, however, it is intended to say or at least to entail that variables are "best" construed as ranging over *all objects* and hence that the universal quantifier is "best" read 'for all objects x'. No reference to the domain D is needed or called for, nor need any reference be made to a specific language system L.

It was urged earlier that the phrase 'for all x in D' is clear and unambiguous, provided D itself is a clear-cut domain of objects. What meaning now are we to attach to Quine's idiom 'for all x' *without specification of* D as a reading of the universal quantifier? Perhaps the idiom 'for all x' without specification of D is meaningful in ordinary language, but this is doubtful. It is not clear that ordinary language contains any variables and quantifiers. Quine apparently admits this point and therefore speaks of "semi-ordinary" language. However this may be, the modern logic of quantification requires fundamentally the specification of a domain D: no domain D, no quantifiers. In fact it is meaningless, according to modern semantical theory, to use the quantifiers (interpreted in the intended way) without specifying a domain D as the range of the variables.

Very well, then, Quine might answer, take D as consisting of *all objects*. The question then arises as to what precise meaning can be given to this phrase.

Quine and physicalists generally, of course, prefer physical objects to others. One must work hard to defend and justify this preference, however, and it is not easy to give the phrase 'physical object' a wholly clear meaning. Nonetheless, physicalists would not cavil over taking D as the domain of physical objects appropriately construed. Set theorists demand another domain for their variables to range over, a domain of sets or classes. However, the theologian perhaps needs another, and the literary critic perhaps still another, and so on. Whatever literary works of art are, they are presumably not merely one more species of physical object.[20] The thesis of physicalism is a very special one, and it will not do to impose a physicalistic interpretation on the quantifiers as though this were a part of their meaning. Such imposition is not only not justified by logic or semantics, but has been harmful historically. It has led people to suppose that the use of logical procedures in philosophy is inextricably linked with physicalism and, by extension, with other special views in the philosophy of science.

Quine would no doubt allow to the set theorist his domain of sets. However, within a language for set theory the quantified '(x)' should be read 'for all *sets* x' (assuming for the moment that the theory contains no nonsets). Nothing is gained by insisting upon the reading 'for all *objects* x'. In fact, a great deal is lost. What are we to include as objects? Angels, dreams, dispositions, works of art, moral values, and so on? Suitable limitations should be imposed by restricting the variables to range over some fixed domain D.

We see then that Quine's reading of the universal quantifier '(x)' as 'for all objects x' is not the "best" one; it is not a "clear" one; nor in the strict sense is it even a meaningful one. Similar comments apply to his reading of the existential quantifier '(Ex)' as 'there exists at least one object x such that'. All that can significantly be meant by the latter, in some $L,$ is that within the domain D of L there is at least one object x such that.

If D is a domain of physical objects, then and only then is there a connection between the existential quantifiers of L and physical existence (in the sense in which this may be spoken of in L). It is simply an error, in the strict sense, to suppose that this connection rests merely upon the existential quantifier without specification of D and of L.

The relation between the idioms 'for all objects' and 'for some object' or 'there exists at least one object such that' in ordinary language seems much more distant than is ordinarily thought. Strictly speaking, there is no connection at all, for we have no quantifiers (with the intended interpretation) until a language system L with a

---

[20] See, for example, I. A. Richards, *The Principles of Literary Criticism* (London: Kegan Paul, etc., 1924), esp. Chapter XXX and A. Warren and R. Wellek, *Theory of Literature* (London: Jonathan Cape, 1949).

domain D is specified. Once it is specified, we may then study the relations between L and the relevant "parts" of the ordinary language. However, this is a very complex type of interrelationship. Incidentally, similar remarks apply to the interconnections between the truth-functional connectives and the "ordinary" words 'and', 'or', and so on. Logical analysts often speak as though there is a close connection here, but precisely what this connection is is far from clear. (See Chapter XII, Section 10 below.) The enormous variety in the use and usage of words and phrases in ordinary language, even of such simple words as 'and' and 'or', militates against their easy assimilation in any premature or indeed artificial "regimentation."

That Quine's reading of the quantifier '(x)' as 'for all objects x' appears unsound may also be seen by noting the way in which the quantifiers of L are given an interpretation within a systematic semantics. This is accomplished by means of the so-called *Adequacy Condition* for the notion of truth.[21] In particular it should obtain within the metalanguage as a special case that '$(x)(—x—)$', where '$(—x—)$' is a formula of L containing just the one free variable 'x', is *true in L* if and only if $(—x—)$ for all objects x in D. We are assured that the universal quantifier behaves in its proper logical way by this principle of semantics. In fact the *only* method we have of assuring this, that is, of giving the universal quantifier its proper interpretation, is by means of such a principle. Perhaps Quine has some other way in mind to achieve this, but if he does, he does not tell us how. In particular we cannot take L as ordinary language without having an adequate truth concept for ordinary language. (But Tarski has argued forcibly against this very possibility in Section 1 of his *Der Wahrheitsbegriff*.)

Carnap's distinction between questions internal and external to a framework or language system is useful here.[22] Prior to or independent of the selection of a language system L with a domain D of objects as its fundamental domain, the quantifiers are without meaning. They are given meaning only with the formulation of L, that is, by the explicit listing of the syntactical and semantical rules determinative of L. However, Quine apparently wishes to give them meaning *prior* to and indeed independent of such formulation. He seems to mistake an internal matter for an external one. The situation is much as though one would wish to give the integral sign '$\int$' significance independent of the system of real numbers or the 'ϵ' of membership significance independent of some specific domain of sets. The quantifiers

---

[21] Tarski, *op. cit.*, pp. 187 ff. or *Truth and Denotation*, pp. 119 ff.
[22] *Meaning and Necessity*, pp. 205 ff.

are like '∫' and 'ε' in having significance only within well-specified language systems.

The points raised above seem crucial to Quine's view of the way in which logic serves as an instrument of "regimentation" for ordinary language. In fact if the foregoing argument is sound, Quine's view of the interconnection between logic and ordinary language seems inadequate—too simple, perhaps, and premature. A more adequate characterization of this interconnection must await much careful work on the part of linguisticians, logicians, and philosophic analysts. However, this will not be easy, and we must not gloss over difficulties by refusing the help and clarification that modern semantics can give.

9. Involvement. It has been noted that any criterion of ontic commitment for L is itself formulated within a semantical metalanguage of L. To understand any such criterion is presumably therefore to understand the sentences of the metalanguage in which it is given. For this we must inquire into the range of the variables *of the metalanguage* itself. What will be called '*ontic involvement*' takes fundamental account of such a range.

Let us say now that an interpreted language system L *ontically involves* us with, or *carries ontic involvement to*, the *objects over which the variables* (including the *expressional* variables) *of the semantical metalanguage in which it is formulated* (that is, *in which the interpretation is given*) *range*. It is not enough to take account merely of the range of the variables of L. We must look more deeply than this to take note also of the range or ranges of all the kinds of variables used in the semantical metalanguage.

In this characterization of ontic involvement, explicit mention is made of the variables over the expressions of L. This is not altogether essential, but it seems harmless. In a very obvious sense, a language system L carries ontic involvement to its expressions. However, it need not, and in some sense should not, carry ontic involvement to *classes* of its expression, to relations between or among them, and so on.

Let us glance briefly at some of the well-known semantical methods in the light of this criterion.

If L is formulated in a metalanguage of the kind studied by Tarski in his *Der Wahrheitsbegriff*, we note that many types of variables are needed other than those contained in the (translation of the) object language L. Suppose that L is a system for elementary Boolean algebra based on inclusion, as in Section 3 of Tarski's paper. In the semantical metalanguage we need, in addition to the variables (and quantifiers) over the Boolean elements admitted, variables over *expressions*, over *classes* and *relations* of or between expressions, over *various kinds of relations* between expressions and the Boolean elements, over *positive integers*, over *infinite sequences* of Boolean elements, and so on. In fact, with Tarski's method an immense ontology is needed for a very simple L. To give the formulation of L using this method carries ontic involvement a great deal more than seems desirable or intended.

Quine's criterion of commitment seems pointless if Tarski's semantical method is used. We are ontically committed according to it only to entities of the object language, but vastly more is involved in its semantical formulation via Tarski's method. In particular, even *to say what it is that we are committed to* involves more. To say that L commits us to D makes fundamental reference to L, that is, to its definatory syntactical and semantical rules. These presuppose the immense Tarskian ontology. Much of our philosophical talk about a language is of a semantical nature anyway, taking place in a semantical metalanguage. The criterion of commitment fails to take this "semantic ascent" into account. Thus, it is uninteresting if Tarski's semantical method is used, and is to be supplemented with that of involvement.

Carnap also has developed semantical methods, but these are similar to Tarski's in the ways cited, that is, they involve variables and quantifiers over many kinds of entities over and above those used in the object language L.[23]

Until recently the methods described above or variants thereof were the only semantical methods that we had. The semantical metalanguages based on *denotation*, for first-order object languages, have been characterized in some detail in *Truth and Denotation*, and their presumed adequacy for philosophical analysis and the philosophy of science established. The specifically semantical primitive of such metalanguages is 'Den', the relation of *multiple* denotation. Using it (to speak loosely), we say that a class word *a* denotes each individual in the class in question. Thus 'man' denotes severally each and every individual man.

In the semantical metalanguage for L based on denotation we have a situation quite different from that prevailing heretofore. Here in fact we have just *two* sorts of variables, those of the one ranging over the expressions of L and those of the other over the individuals of L. Hence we are ontically involved (by L) with expressions of L

[23] See R. Carnap, *Introduction to Semantics* (Cambridge: Harvard University Press, 1942) and *The Philosophy of Rudolf Carnap,* ed. by P. A. Schilpp in *The Library of Living Philosophers* (La Salle, Ill.: Open Court Publishing Co., 1963), *passim*. Cf. also recent alternatives to Tarski's method emanating from California.

and with the individuals of L and with these only. This, if we mistake not, is what is intended by Quine's criterion of commitment (if we leave aside for the moment commitment to expressions). Here we are able to give the semantical description of L in a metalanguage employing just these two sorts of variables. To have recourse to further kinds of individuals or expressions in the metalanguage would be to commit ourselves to much more than is needed. The metalinguistic description of L must, if Quine's criterion is to have point, be given wholly in terms of the expressions and individuals of L *without recourse to any further expressions or objects*. In other words, the ontic commitment of L should be the same as its ontic involvement.

Within the metalanguage for L, based on denotation, we say that such and such a one-place predicate of L denotes such and such individuals. The reference of one-place predicates is thus wholly described in terms of the individuals to which the predicates apply. We cannot say, as we can with Carnap, for example, that there exists a *property* or *class* that a one-place predicate *designates*. To allow this in the metalanguage would be to involve ourselves with the existence of classes or properties in L.

Bergmann's dictum, "Who admits a single [one-place] primitive predicate admits properties among the building stones of his world," has point if the dictum is taken in connection with semantical metalanguages of the usual kind.[24] If the *only* method of semantic analysis available requires fundamentally variables over properties or classes, and so on, in addition to those admitted in the object language. Bergmann's dictum seems reasonable. The building stones of the world *must* include much more than those admitted in the object language L. Bergmann's dictum loses its point, however, if the semantics of L is formulated within a suitably restricted metalanguage such as that based on denotation. Here the reference of a one-place primitive predicate is determined wholly by stipulating the individuals that it denotes. A full semantics, including a truth concept, is achieved by this method, so that no variables over classes, properties, and so on, are needed.

Thus the point of Quine's criterion of ontic commitment seems better achieved by that of ontic involvement, but only in connection with semantical metalanguages such as that based on denotation. If metalanguages of the usual kind are used, much more is involved than is recognized by his criterion.

The matters raised here are very important and fundamental to

[24] See G. Bergmann, "Two Types of Linguistic Philosophy," *Review of Metaphysics* 5 (1952), 417–438.

the proper understanding of ontic commitment. However, they seem never to have been so much as mentioned by Quine. To be sure he has noted that the idiom 'true of' is useful, and 'true of' is not so very different after all from 'denotes'. However, he has nowhere formulated a semantics on its basis, and he often speaks as though a semantics were not needed. Without explicitly taking into account the accompanying semantics, however, there seems to be no clear way of discussing the ontic commitment of language systems at all.

10. On "Semantic Ascent." Quine's phrase 'semantic ascent' is a felicitous one and what it describes helps to emend the matters just noted.[25] His injunction to "look beyond language to logic" is also admirable. We may applaud the phrases but not agree *au pied de la lettre* with what they are intended to convey.

By 'semantic ascent' Quine designates "the shift from talking *in* certain terms [italics added] to talking *about* them," the shift from talking about miles as certain distances or measures of distances to talking about 'mile'. It is essentially the going from Carnap's old material mode of speech to the formal one.[26] Strictly of course speech in the formal mode takes place wholly in logical syntax. Hence it is only *syntactic* ascent that we have there. One can talk of the word 'mile' *ad nauseam* in syntax without reaching the objective Quine has in mind. Clearly, syntactic should be distinguished from semantic ascent. In semantics, the material and formal modes are, as it were, combined. In semantics, there is concern with the relations between words and objects, not just with words. Quine's use of 'semantic' is misleading. In semantic ascent, we do not transcend any difficulties to be found in the material mode. We merely place them in sharper focus by reflecting explicitly upon the relations, denotation, designation, and the like, between word and thing. However, it is this sharper focusing that is in large part the aim of logical analysis.

Surely, in extolling semantic ascent, Quine is not extolling mere syntax nor, for that matter, semantics. Questions of "usefulness" interest him fundamentally. When, from talk of what miles are, for example, "we ascend to 'mile' and ask which of its contexts are useful and for what purposes, we can get on. . . . The strategy of semantic ascent is that it carries the discussion into a domain where both parties are better agreed on the objects [viz., words] and on the main terms concerning them." The chief merit of ascent is not, then, that we

---

[25] See his *Word and Object*, pp. 270 ff. The recent issue of *Synthese* devoted to this book appeared too late for comment here.

[26] See R. Carnap, *The Logical Syntax of Language* (New York: Harcourt, Brace and Company, 1937).

merely enter the formal mode but that we can better agree on which contexts are "useful and for what purposes," so that among the "main terms" applicable to our words are to be found not merely syntactic and (possibly) semantic predicates but pragmatic ones as well.

Whether Quine is concerned with a pragmatics that presupposes only a syntax, or one that presupposes the fuller resources of a semantics, is not always clear.[27] The fact is that with Quine as our guide we do not know what we are ascending to. Some map, however rough, some *Überblick* as to the lay of the land, some logical geography, seems called for. This is to be found, no doubt, in formal semantics and systematic pragmatics. Nothing short of *pragmatic ascent* accomplishes what Quine wishes.

The injunction 'Look beyond language to logic' aptly suggests that we should look to logic. Of course we should look to language also, with logic as our guide. Of the two, logic seems the more fundamental, meddling with language in ways that language cannot meddle with it. The more proper injunction is therefore 'Look beyond logic to language, with logic as our guide', and if we were to do so wholeheartedly, our language study would no doubt be immeasurably improved. Of course we should look, with logic as our guide, to a great deal else also. Philosophy begins with logic, but in the looking beyond, it knows no bounds.

[27] See the author's *Toward a Systematic Pragmatics* (*Studies in Logic and the Foundations of Mathematics,* Amsterdam: North-Holland Pub. Co., 1959).

CHAPTER III

The Elimination of Intensions Sui Generis

The phrase is Ryle's, but it goes without saying that in our serious philosophical work nothing less than "maximum logical candor" should suffice.[1] Of course no one wishes to be burdened with excessive and wearisome details that obfuscate rather than clarify. No one wishes to be a mere "purveyor of unprofitable subtleties." No one wishes to be "captious about trifles and neglectful of weightier matters, condemning every inference really valuable and admitting only such as are really childish."[2] Nonetheless, philosophers should surely be prepared to furnish any details that might be needed in some specific context to settle a logical point at issue or to bring to a focus obscure relationships. For such purposes a maximum logical analysis with commensurate candor is often indispensable.

It has been suggested above that first-order logic is the basic logic and hence the most suitable as a philosophic tool. Hence also, a first-order semantics may be regarded as the philosophically most appropriate. The very meaning of 'maximum logical candor' is to be found, it would seem, on the basis of this kind of logic and semantics.

One of the tasks of this book is to sketch the framework for a logic of belief, action, and related notions, without reference to intensions *sui generis* and hence upon the basis of the kind of logic and semantics mentioned. Before embarking upon this, we should justify to some extent the exclusion of other kinds of logic, and, if

[1] See G. Ryle, "Philosophical Arguments," Inaugural Lecture (Oxford University Press, 1945), p. 19.
[2] C. S. Peirce, *Collected Papers,* 3.404.

we are to aim for maximum candor, some clarification of the very meaning of 'candor' in this context must be given.

In this chapter it is urged that intensions *sui generis* should play no role in philosophic analysis generally. Thus in particular they are to be avoided when we attempt to formulate a logic of belief. In Section 1 the connection between intensions regarded as entities *sui generis* and so-called *intensional logics* is discussed. In Section 2 we argue that so-called *modal logics* rest upon several rather fundamental confusions and thus that such logics are not suitable as philosophic tools. In Section 3 we reflect critically upon some of *Ruth Marcus'* comments in behalf of intensional logics. In Section 4 we urge that the phrase 'maximum logical candor' be construed, as already suggested, wholly in the light of first-order logic and its applications. Section 5 is devoted to some critical comments on *Anderson's* defense of the intensional point of view. Putnam's *modal picture of mathematics* is discussed in Section 6. Section 7 is devoted to *Church's* reconstruction of a theory of meaning presumably akin to that of Frege, and in Section 8 Church's so-called *translation criterion* is discussed critically. Finally, in Section 9, some merits of wholly *extensional* languages and metalanguages are briefly summarized.

An exhaustive argument against intensionality is not attempted in this chapter. Only a few items of outstanding interest and at the forefront of contemporary discussion can be considered. Many of the points are difficult and controversial, and much will remain to be said after this chapter has done its bit. Although it sets the stage, this chapter is not indispensable, and the reader who is not interested in the niceties of the dispute between intensionalists and extensionalists may well wish to turn directly to the next chapter for the beginning of the constructive development concerning belief.

1. On Intensions and Intensional Logics. First, we should distinguish sharply between the semantical theory of intensions and so-called "intensional logics" such as various forms of modal logic. The former is a branch of semantics and thus should be formulated in a semantical metalanguage. Intensional logics are usually formulated as object languages. The problem then arises of providing a suitable interpretation for them. When we speak of intensions, or of a theory of intensions, it is most important to distinguish clearly these two modes of treatment. Failure to do so has, it would seem, led only to confusion.[3]

---

[3] On the distinction between language and metalanguage it is still good to refer to R. Carnap, *The Logical Syntax of Language.* See also A. Tarski, *Logic, Semantics, Metamathematics.*

In Chapter VII we attempt to formulate a theory of intensions within a semantical metalanguage based upon denotation. This metalanguage in turn, however, is based upon the classical logic and is purely extensional. Yet a strong theory of intensions for given object languages can be built up within it. When intensions or intensional languages are spoken of as being in some sense objectionable, it is not such intensions or metalanguages that are referred to. Within such metalanguages intensions for certain expressions emerge in a very natural way, as we shall see.

In sharp contrast to semantical theories of the extensional kind described above are intensional logics regarded as object languages that take unanalyzed intensions in some sense as values for variables or as designata of names or predicates. Such intensions we regard as *sui generis*. They are merely postulated or assumed, but they are not analyzed. Thus, *properties* or *attributes* are sometimes taken as the designata of one-place predicates rather than classes. A special domain of *propositions* is usually added with special properties applying to them. Thus in modal logic, for example, a proposition *p* may be regarded as *necessary, contingent, possible,* or the like. The problem of *interpreting* satisfactorily such logics, that is, of giving them a clear-cut semantics, is usually left open. Metalanguages are sometimes constructed upon such logics, but their basic features tend to remain obscure. *Individual concepts* are admitted within some of them in addition to individuals as well as *relation concepts* in addition to relations.[4] However, just what these additional entities are is never clearly brought to light. Presumably they have some kinship with Frege's *Sinne*.

What is the individual concept of Socrates, or of 'Socrates'? It is surely something different from Socrates himself as well as from his name. (See Chapter VII, Section 7, below.) Similarly, the relation concept corresponding to the relation of being greater than between integers, for example, is surely to be distinguished from the relation itself as well as from its name. What *precisely* are individual concepts, relation concepts, and their ilk, properties (or attributes or class concepts) and propositions? This we are not told by *sui generis* intensionalists. Instead we are asked to recognize such concepts as indispensable adjuncts to logic or metalogic—it is not always clear which.

Intensions have been spoken of here from an ontic point of view as a kind of entity *sui generis*. An object language is then intensional if such entities are contained among the values for its variables. Metalanguages based upon object languages containing such entities

[4] See especially *Meaning and Necessity*. Some recent works on this subject, also emanating from California, have appeared too late for comment here.

are then intensional in essentially the same sense. These metalanguages should presumably provide a satisfactory semantics for their object languages, but actually they fail to do so, pending a clear-cut analysis of concepts or intensions. Modal logics are typical of the kinds of logic and metalogic we shall decry here and avoid using throughout. However, let us first be clear as to the reasons for the decrial and subsequent avoidance.

2. Does Modal Logic Rest upon a Mistake? The use of an underlying modal logic for the purposes of philosophic analysis is suspect in the eyes of many.[5] Mathematicians have been interested in modal logic because of the mathematical structure or structures involved. However, philosophers who use a modal logic are not concerned primarily with its mathematical structure. They should also be expected to provide a satisfactory interpretation of the calculus or calculi as needed for specific purposes. Just what is meant here by 'satisfactory'? Roughly speaking, an interpretation is satisfactory if and only if it is provided by a metalanguage that itself is sufficiently clear and simple. By this is meant roughly that the metalanguage should contain no "dubious" entities as values for variables and that its nonlogical axioms and underlying logic be suitably economical and restricted. Further, the interpretation should be explicitly formulated in the manner of modern semantics. Some writers insist upon such an interpretation; others do not. The objections here are against only those who do not.[6]

Another closely related point concerns ontic commitment. Formulations of modal logic usually make use of variables ranging over intensional entities such as propositions. What these entities are, however, remains obscure, as has been noted above. Modal logicians, it would seem, have not given a satisfactory account of what propositions are, *precisely.* (See, however, Chapter IX, Section 4 below.) They remain merely obscure and mysterious entities satisfying such and such conditions. Furthermore, because most modal logics primitively utilize variables over such entities that cannot be explained away as mere shorthand or as notational conveniences, the systems usually carry ontic commitment to such entities in a quite fundamental way.

The question arises also as to whether propositions and modal notions are ever really needed, and if so, where. Clearly they are

---

[5] See especially, W. V. Quine, *From a Logical Point of View* (Cambridge: Harvard University Press, 1953) and *Word and Object.* See also his "Three Grades of Modal Involvement," in *The Ways of Paradox* (New York: Random House, 1966), pp. 156–182.

[6] Much recent work has been devoted to this problem, and more will be said on it below.

not needed *in* mathematics, in the sense that they are in any way needed for the definition of specifically mathematical notions. Nor are they needed in discourse *about* mathematics, that is, in meta-mathematics or *Beweistheorie*.[7] Nor do they seem to be needed in natural science or in the logical or methodological analysis thereof. If a specific purpose can be exhibited in which they do seem needed, this purpose can perhaps be better served by regarding propositions as suitable constructs and by identifying the modal operators with their semantical correlates.

Consider, for example, the notion of *logical* or *analytic truth*, as defined within a suitably formulated semantical metalanguage. This notion provides a more or less exact semantical correlate of the modal notion of necessity. And, of course, similarly for other modal notions. Most of the purposes for which the modal notions or operators are used may be more easily and efficiently served by these semantical correlates. Thus most of the purposes of a modal logic itself are better served by an exact semantical metalanguage, which in turn utilizes or presupposes no propositions or modal notions.

It can be explicitly shown in fact, that no form of modal logic is needed for a general semiotic, that is, syntax, semantics, and pragmatics, or at least for these subjects as far as they have been systematically developed to date. There is no reason to suppose that their further development will reveal such need. On the contrary, it seems almost certain that it will not.

It is sometimes claimed, as we have already observed, that modal logics themselves exhibit interesting mathematical structures. This claim is difficult to assess. Indeed, the very notion of being mathematically interesting seems obscure and subject to a good deal of variation. However this may be, a similar claim, it would seem, could be put forward for almost any well-developed logical theory of a sufficient complexity. However, if we are not mistaken, modal logicians have not established that the mathematical interest of their subject is commensurate with that of classical logic or of set theory or of metamathematics or the like. Modal logic seems to have thrown little if any light upon any area of mathematics, pure or applied.

It is often claimed that propositions are needed for the analysis of belief sentences. However, it will be urged in detail below that sentences of this and analogous kinds seem best handled in terms of a systematic pragmatics. Propositions, if needed at all, are handled as constructs of a special kind, and relations such as belief, acceptance,

[7] See especially S. C. Kleene, *Introduction to Metamathematics* (New York: Van Nostrand, 1952) and Section 6 below.

and the like, are characterized in terms of suitable pragmatical primitives without the use of propositions as values for variables.

The classical, two-valued, logic of truth functions and quantifiers seems to provide the only basic logic needed for mathematics and natural science, and for syntax, semantics, and pragmatics (and hence, it would seem, for philosophic analysis generally). For discourse both *in* and *about* these subjects no modal logic with attendant propositions is needed. Perhaps some clear purpose for which a modal logic is needed or for which the use of a modal logic would have clear advantages over other methods can be exhibited. This would seem doubtful and, if we are not mistaken, no such purpose has yet been exhibited by modal logicians.

The answer to the title of this section therefore is: Yes, several. (1) It is doubtful that a sufficiently clear and simple interpretation of modal calculi for philosophical purposes can be given other than in extensional semantics. (2) The analysis of logical or analytic truth seems best handled in terms of the latter. (3) The use of propositional variables ontically commits us to an obscure kind of entity, which, together with the modal notions, (4) is not needed for discourse in or about mathematics or natural science or (5) in or about syntax, semantics, or pragmatics. (6) Modal logics exhibit structures of only dubious mathematical interest. (7) Propositions and modal notions are not needed for the analysis of sentences expressing belief, acceptance, and so on. (8) Classical logic seems to provide the most suitable form of basic logic for the purposes of philosophical and scientific applications.

It might be objected that so many arguments against modal logic are not needed, and that one really good one should suffice. The fact is, however, that in these difficult logico-philosophical matters one can never be too certain of what he contends. Hence the more artillery mustered against a view, the better.

There are still further points that should be noted. Much of modal logic is concerned with the best way to handle *iterated* modalities. Thus there arises concern over how the necessity of a proposition is related to the necessity of the necessity of it. Curiously, philosophers have not worried so much over the corresponding problem concerning *truth*. No alternative theories of truth seem to have arisen that depend upon how the truth of a sentence is related to the truth of its truth. In fact we know from semantics that the truth of a truth is best handled within a meta-metalanguage. Surely necessity, a notion involving truth in some fashion, should be handled similarly. The necessity of the necessity of a sentence should be handled only in a metalanguage of an order higher than that in which we talk merely of necessity *simpliciter*. Of course we can persist in trying to handle the necessity of a necessity otherwise, just as we can persist in regarding the earth as the center of the solar system, as in Ptolemaic astronomy.

3. Further Comments on Intensionality. Ruth Marcus' recent discussions of intensionality[8] and its connection with modal systems are of interest here. We must be extremely careful in all details in discussing intensionality and modal logic, however, and press every point as far as we reasonably can until a suitable logico-semantical bedrock is reached. This is desirable, indeed indispensable, for maximum logical candor. The Marcus discussion hovers amid various historically important logical systems, but it is not clear that it comes to grips successfully with the points raised above.

Marcus seems to agree that intensional logics do nothing for mathematics—they are simply not needed there. However, as she notes, "establishing the foundations of mathematics is not the only purpose of logic, particularly if the assumptions deemed convenient for mathematics do violence to both ordinary and philosophical usage." Presumably among such "assumptions" are: (1) strong principles of extensionality, (2) the distinction between the use and mention of expressions, (3) the usual distinction between object and metalanguage, and (4) clear-cut syntactical and semantical rules.[9] To be sure items (1)–(4) are eminently desirable for the foundation of mathematics and for the methodology of science—nay, they are essential. That they do "violence to ordinary and philosophical usage," however, is doubtful. They do no more violence, it would seem, than modal or intensional logics themselves. If the situation is otherwise, this should no doubt be established by a detailed argument. Indeed, the classical, two-valued logic seems to do less violence to ordinary usage than modal logics with their additional entities (as values for variables) and dangerous assumptions.

Elsewhere, Marcus claims that intensional modal logics are "useful in connection with many interesting and important questions such as

---

[8] Ruth Barcan Marcus, "Extensionality," *Mind* LXIX (1960), 55–62, and "Modalities and Intensional Languages," *Synthese* XIII (1961), 303–322. The rough comments of the text do not of course constitute an exhaustive account of Mrs. Marcus' views. They merely help to indicate reasons for taking a different, semantical approach.

[9] Concerning (1) see especially R. Carnap, *Meaning and Necessity*, pp. 47 ff. and *passim*. A good deal will be said about such principles as we proceed. For a superb statement of the importance of (2) recall G. Frege, *Grundgesetze der Arithmetik*, p. 4, as quoted above. On (3) and (4) see especially Tarski, *op. cit.*, and *Truth and Denotation*.

the analysis of causation, entailment, obligation and belief sentences, to name only a few." The philosophical superstructure, however, is never stronger than its underlying logical foundations. Analyses of causation and other notions that presuppose modal or intensional logics have not to date succeeded where extensional analyses have failed. We remain in the dark on these subjects, even after intensional logics have done their bit. There is evidence, however, that satisfactory extensional foundations are forthcoming for these notions, as we shall see.

Surely it is not the task of the formal logician to do deliberate "violence to ordinary and philosophical usage," nor is it his task merely to serve such usage as if it were in some sense sacrosanct. Before the tribunal of logic all usage is on a par, whether ordinary, extraordinary, philosophical, or whatever. Much ordinary and philosophical usage is no doubt unsound and can be improved by bringing it into conformity with technically established usage. The problem then is *how best to establish logically sound technical usage*. Peirce has said something similar (3.704): "What the usages of [ordinary] language may be does not concern us; language has its meaning modified in technical logical formulae as in other special kinds of discourse."

It is sometimes claimed that "the analytical equipment (of the formal logician) is inadequate for the dissection of most ordinary types of empirical statement."[10] Has this claim ever *really* been put to the test? The analytical equipment of the modern formal logician (including the semiotician) is of course formidable, of such power as to be capable of analyzing many of the most intricate and subtle inferences. To suppose, almost *a priori* and without exploring the matter very deeply, that there are all kinds of exceptions to its applicability, seems premature. Logic itself, including semiotics, is under continual development. However, whether Strawson's claim is true or not is of little interest from the point of view of logic itself, the aim of which anyhow is not to provide a tool of "dissection" for the statements of ordinary language. To suppose that it is is, it would seem, to misunderstand. Peirce disapprovingly has put the matter well, thus (2.67):

> One needs but to turn over the leaves of a few of the first logical treatises that come to hand, especially if they are English, . . . in order to meet with appeals to the ordinary usages of speech as determinative of logical doctrines. Some recent books are quite crowded with this type of argument. It seems usually to be employed unreflectively; but there are works in which it is deliberately laid down as the principal basis of logical science.

[10] P. Strawson, *Introduction to Logical Theory* (London: Methuen, 1952), p. 216.

To attempt to determine precisely how the notions of formal logic are related to notions entering into "most ordinary forms of empirical statement" would of course raise very interesting and difficult questions. However, it is not the task of formal logic or metalogic even to begin to answer them. (See however, Chapter XII, Section 10, below.)

4. The Meaning of 'Candor'. When philosophers or mathematicians speak of classes or of sets, they usually have a reasonably clear conception of what they are talking about. If we plead ignorance at this point, the philosopher can tell us something about the logic of classes, and the mathematician can tell us something about various areas of the mathematical theory of sets. The question as to what classes or sets are, *precisely*, in some perhaps metaphysical sense, may still remain. However, each adequate system of axiomatic set or class theory presumably characterizes a domain of sets and/or classes in a fashion sufficiently clear and rigorous for the purposes at hand. The presence of alternatives presents difficult problems that very quickly lead us to the frontiers of knowledge. The important point is, however, that in choosing any one adequate axiomatization we have a clear basis, explicitly enunciated with maximum logical candor, upon which to build. It is not the notion of set or class as such that is being extolled here, but rather the way in which logicians and set theorists have gone about their task. We may be suspicious of sets, hoping that something simpler can be made to take their place.[11]

Logical syntax and denotational semantics may be constructed along similar lines with a similar candor, as has been noted. The logic of truth functions, quantifiers, and identity is presupposed, as perhaps are fragments of the theory of classes or sets. If new entities are admitted—expressions and sequences (or concatenates) of them—it is at least reasonably clear what is being admitted. Careful attention to the ontology that syntax and denotational semantics utilize seems essential if these areas of theory are to remain clear and unobjectionable.

The extensionalist thus has every right to ask the intensionalist to explain the meaning of the primitives of his theory with maximum logical candor within a mutually agreed upon or accepted vocabulary. If the interrogator wishes to be still more strict, he may question here the very use of 'meaning', and insert 'denotation' or 'designation' in its place. He may ask merely for the denotation or designation (more properly *denotata* or *designata*) of the primitives of the theory. If the extensionalist thinks he knows something about meanings, as distinguished from denotata or designata, he may ask for those as well. In

---

[11] See the theory of *virtual* classes, in Chapter VI below.

addition, he may ask for a clear-cut description of the ontology admitted. He thus ends by asking the intensionalist a fairly elaborate question concerning the semantics and ontology of his theory.

What sort of an answer will suffice? Although progress has been made in attempting to formulate a theory of intensions *sui generis*, it is not clear that this can be done satisfactorily. In particular, any such theory is clearly inadequate for the scientific and philosophical tasks for which it is designed without clear-cut and satisfactory answers to the extensionalist's questions and with candor commensurate to that of denotational semantics.

Occasionally the philosophic logician may say or write 'The man M crossed the street S' where 'The man crossed the street' would serve as well. Where less obvious matters are concerned, the situation is quite different. A philosopher may tell us that the intension of 'man', to cite an instance, differs from the intension of 'animal'. We may then ask: How? Precisely how does the intension α of 'man' differ from the intension β of 'animal'? Here the very introduction of the letters 'α' and 'β' as variables or proper names for intensions is a factor for clarity, and the extensionalist's question is sharpened and deepened.

Intensionalists *sui generis* seem to have failed to tell us what the values for their variables are, what the names or descriptions they use designate, and how the objects so designated differ from one another—how, in other words, intensions can be dissected into parts or components in some fashion. (There is also the closely related problem of the meaning of identity between intensions. Quine has forcefully and repeatedly emphasized the importance of this problem and its bearing on ontology. No clear identity, no clear ontology—according to him.) Until intensionalists do this satisfactorily, writing 'The man M crossed the street S' in place of 'The man crossed the street', is a useful reminder in philosophical analysis that we should try to be explicitly aware of what our vocabulary is, and of the syntax and designational semantics of the language being employed.

5. 'Simpson' and 'Sampson'. Alan Anderson has claimed with some force[12] that there are *two* ways of understanding the notion of extensionality, Ruth Marcus' for one, that of modern semantics for the other. It seems, however, that these two are, or should be, reducible to the same. The semantical approach seems to have the advantages of clarity and explicitness. Anderson thinks it "to be the task of philosophical analysis to try to dissipate the fog with whatever means are

[12] See his "On Professor Martin's Beliefs," *The Journal of Philosophy* LIX (1962), 600–607.

at hand, *even intensional if need be.*" And if need not? The crucial
point is surely that the intensional means are themselves pretty foggy,
as many writers on the subject, including even Anderson and Marcus,
seem to admit. What can be gained in philosophical analysis by using
foggy tools that are themselves in need of analysis? Just as the un-
examined life is not worth the living, foggy tools are not worth the
using.

Let us invoke Anderson's two chaps, *Simpson* and *Sampson*.
Simpson, we recall, is the cube of two, whereas Sampson is the natural
number eight. Clearly, as a matter of arithmetic fact,

$$\text{Simpson} = \text{Sampson}.$$

The names 'Simpson' and 'Sampson' also designate the same object,
Anderson tells us, but *in different ways*. Aye, there's the rub. What are
these different ways? How, precisely, do they differ from each other?
How do we characterize these different ways? By means of semantics,
of course, so let us disperse the fog and talk of semantics again.
'Sampson', we might say, *designates* the cube of two. 'Simpson' also
designates it, but in a different way. Carnap's notion of L-designation
is perhaps useful here.[13] We might say that 'Simpson' *L-designates* the
cube of two. Of course we must then make known what we mean by
'L-designation'. To characterize this notion satisfactorily within a suitable semantical metalanguage would require "fairly subtle and elaborate
techniques," to use Anderson's phrase, involving concatenation, designation, truth, perhaps denotation, logical or analytic truth, and some
derivative notions. None of these notions, however, need involve foggy
methods transcending the extensionalist's requirements. (See again
Chapter VII, Section 2, below.)

6. On the Modal Picture of Mathematics. But modal logic and
the theory of intensions *sui generis* die hard. Recently, several writers
have found new interest in the former. It is not merely that they find
modal logic mathematically interesting in itself, but that they find it of
interest for the foundations of mathematics. Typical of this *new modalism* is the view put forward recently by Hilary Putnam in his "Mathematics without Foundations."[14]

If mathematics doesn't itch you, don't scratch. This is the sub-
stance of Putnam's contention that mathematics neither has nor needs

[13] See R. Carnap, *Introduction to Semantics* and Chapter VIII below.
[14] "Mathematics without Foundations," *The Journal of Philosophy* LXIV (1967),
5–22.

"foundations." The maxim, "Scratch only where it itches,"[15] is a more general principle of which this contention is perhaps merely a special case. It is curious then that Putnam goes on to sketch a philosophy of mathematics that involves both a kind of modal view as well as a set-theoretic one. Both of these views seem intended to provide a kind of "foundation" for mathematics, and, if we take Putnam at his word, it is not clear why he feels that any such view is needed. If, literally, mathematics needs no foundation, why put forward a foundational view at all?

A "model" for a language system is, roughly speaking, some one interpretation of it. (A more technical definition is unnecessary for present purposes.) Throughout our discussion we have for the most part spoken of just *one* model, the normal or standard or preferred one. Of course there are also other models of perhaps more mathematical than philosophic interest. Philosophers are interested primarily in *this* world and in the logical theory that seems to fit it best. Mathematicians are interested in all worlds, hence in all models. The phrase 'all models' is not too clear, however. Think of the vast metaphysical totality of objects to which the theory concerning all models ontically commits us, and then reflect upon its staggering ontic *involvement*. The mere thought makes us gasp. At any event, a more constructive, *seriatim* approach to model theory is advocated here. In the theory of the single, preferred model, we seem to have all that is needed to construct a viable semantical theory of sufficient power for philosophical analysis. The theory of the single model might then well be called '*philosophic* semantics' to distinguish it from mathematical semantics or model theory.

It has already been mentioned that some writers have sought to interpret various systems of modal logic within suitable semantical metalanguages. These latter are usually of the customary model-theoretic kind, and much is made of the requirement that they be extensional metalanguages. We do not claim that all recent writers on the problem of interpreting modal logic have sought an interpretation within an extensional metalanguage. (If modal logic does not itch you, you will think scratching unnecessary.) Nonetheless, wholly extensional interpretations have been clearly demanded by many writers, and modal logics are then regarded as satisfactory insofar as such interpretations are forthcoming.

Thus Carnap notes that "the translation of a modal language into an extensional one provides an extensional interpretation of the concepts of logical modalities. . . . It is thereby shown that these controversial concepts are unobjectionable and acceptable even to those phi-

[15] Paraphrased from *Word and Object*, p. 160.

losophers who profess to understand only an extensional language, provided they are willing to admit class variables of higher types."[16] The variables of higher type are of course needed in the usual model-theoretic metalanguages. Richard Montague has likewise proposed an interpretation of such phrases as 'it is logically necessary that', 'it is physically necessary that', and 'it is obligatory that' within an extensional model-theoretic metalanguage.[17] Others have more or less followed suit. The demand for an extensional interpretation now seems so universal that its achievement has become a *sine qua non* for our "understanding" of modal logic.

The important item to note here is the clearly felt need for the extensional, model-theoretic interpretation. Modal logic becomes of interest only insofar as this interpretation is achieved. Until it is achieved, modal logic is thought to be vague and unsatisfactory, controversial, objectionable, and unacceptable. Once the interpretation is achieved, we can in effect throw modal logic away, for its interest now lies in the semantical interpretation. Semantics is here to stay, being needed for many other purposes. Modal logic, however, can be sacrificed without loss. There is no inner mystique in the modalities that cannot be spelled out with maximum logical candor in the clear, cool terms of semantical model theory. Modal logic need no longer bother us, and we need scratch no more.

Curiously, Putnam goes on to scratch even where there is no itch. He reads into the modal picture a philosophy of mathematics that, to put it bluntly, is simply not there. Consider his schema

(S)   '$\Box[\mathrm{Ax}(S,T) \supset {\sim}\mathrm{Fermat}(S,T)]$',

one of pure first-order modal logic, with the dummy predicate letters 'S' and 'T', '$\Box$' the sign for necessity, and 'Ax' and 'Fermat' as suitable predicates. We are invited to note that the "mathematical content" of the "assertion" (S) is "certainly the same as that of the assertion that *there exist numbers x, y, z, n* $(2 < n, x, y, z \neq 0)$ *such that* $x^n + y^n = z^n$." Let us not quibble about what "content" and "assertion" are, pragmatical notions perhaps, both surely in need of analysis. What is more important is that, even with the dummy letters 'S' and 'T', Putnam

[16] *The Philosophy of Rudolf Carnap*, p. 895.
[17] See, for example, R. Montague, "Logical Necessity, Physical Necessity, Ethics, and Quantifiers," *Inquiry* 4 (1960), 259–269. See also, for example, J. Hintikka "Modality and Quantification," *Theoria* 27 (1961), 119–128 and "The Modes of Modality," *Acta Philosophica Fennica* 16 (1963); S. Kanger, "The Morning Star Paradox," *Theoria* 23 (1957), 1–11; and S. Kripke, "A Completeness Theorem in Modal Logic," *The Journal of Symbolic Logic* 24 (1959), 1–14.

regards (S) as in effect saying something about "the existence of numbers," or at any event about "objects" in an ω-sequence or progression.

> Yet the pictures in the mind called up by these two ways of
> formulating what one might as well consider to be the same mathe-
> matical assertion can be quite different [Putnam continues]. When
> one speaks of the "existence of numbers" one gets the picture of
> mathematics as describing eternal objects while (S) simply says
> that $Ax(S,T)$ entails $\sim$Fermat(S,T), no matter how one may
> interpret the predicate letters '*S*' and '*T*' and this scarcely seems
> to be about "objects" at all. Of course, one can strain after objects
> if one wants. [This latter, however, he thinks] hardly necessary.

If the extensional interpreters of modal logic are right, we *must*
strain after objects here for (S) to make any sense at all. We must,
namely, have some objects in our models. In fact for (S) to make the
modal sense that Putnam wishes, the formula

$$\text{'}[Ax(S,T) \supset \sim\text{Fermat}(S,T)]\text{'}$$

must hold in *all models*. Indeed we must "strain after" a staggering
multitude of objects for this formula to make either model or modal
sense. It is thus very strange indeed that Putnam thinks that it "scarcely
seems to be about 'objects' at all."

So much for the "object" picture. Let us now turn to the intrinsically "modal" one.

> One can interpret '$\square$' as a predicate of statements, rather
> than as a statement connective [Putnam continues], in which case
> what (S) asserts is that a certain object, namely the statement
> [statement-form (?)] '$Ax(S,T) \supset \sim$Fermat(S,T)' has a certain
> property ("being necessary"). But still, the only "object" this
> commits us to is the statement '$Ax(S,T) \supset \sim$Fermat(S,T)', and
> one has to be pretty compulsive about one's nominalistic cleanli-
> ness to scruple about *this*. In short, if one fastens on the first
> picture (the "object" picture), then mathematics is wholly ex-
> tensional, but presupposes a vast totality of eternal objects; while
> if one fastens on the second picture (the "modal" picture), then
> mathematics has no special objects of its own, but simply tells us
> what follows from what. . . .

This key passage seems confused. If we interpret '$\square$' as a predicate of
statements, we still need to give an *analysis* of it, an interpretation of it,
and this presumably within model theory.

It is quite beside the point to speak suddenly of 'Ax$(S,T) \supset$ ~Fermat(S,T)' as an "object"—a linguistic one of course—as though it had not been so all along. It is thus doubtful that Putnam is making any real contrast here between the two pictures. In the "object" picture we have a vast totality of eternal mathematical objects, especially those within the normal or preferred model. In the modal view, "mathematics has no special objects of its own, but simply tells us what follows from what." Of course mathematics has no special objects of its own if none is so regarded. On the other hand, the various "objects" of model theory are fit subjects for mathematical study. Even in Putnam's picture it is not mathematics but modal *logic* that tells us "what follows from what." There is also the question as to whether Putnam is taking 'follows from' here in the syntactical or semantical sense. If the former, then no "interpretation" for (S) is provided, and we are left with mathematics as a purely syntactical concern with linguistic expressions. No "picture" can be involved, so that Putnam presumably takes 'follows from' here in the semantical sense. If so, an interpretation for (S) must be provided, and this in model-theoretic terms. It seems doubtful then that Putnam has drawn any real contrast.

Putnam wants to use "these two ways of looking at mathematics . . . to clarify each other." If the modal notions are obscure unless looked at from model theory, not much would be gained by using them to view the latter. If we look through a glass darkly not much that otherwise might be clear will be seen.

Putnam expressly disclaims that his purpose is "to start a *new* school in the foundations of mathematics." We want rather *both* views, he tells us in effect.

> Even if in some contexts the modal-logic picture is more helpful than the mathematical-objects picture, in other contexts the reverse is the case. Sometimes we have a clearer notion of what 'possible' means than of what 'set' means; in other cases the reverse is true; and in many, many cases both notions seem as clear as notions ever get in science. Looking at things from the standpoint of many different "equivalent descriptions," considering what is suggested by *all* the pictures, is both a healthy antidote to foundationalism and of real heuristic value to the study of first-order scientific questions.

The rub here is that science is never satisfied with the *Herumspringerei* —to use Schrödinger's word—of "equivalent descriptions." Their presence is always a challenge to go on to a "unified view" where possible. Nor is a Monday-Wednesday-Friday Tuesday-Thursday-Saturday dichotomy tolerable in the foundations of mathematics. At best we could allow Putnam to be urging here a kind of unified set-theoretic and modal picture. However, this is then presumably nothing other than our old friend modal logic interpreted within a wider model-theoretic meta-language. What is "clear" to you or me here or there now or then, is beside the point. What we want is a *technically sound* theory accommodating our "picture."

Putnam goes on to suggest that statements of the Zermelo set theory in the "modal-logical language" can be "translated" into certain statements about graphs and about standard concrete models of that theory. (The details need not detain us.) In the resulting translation, a phrase of the form 'it is possible that there is a graph G' occurs fundamentally. This can be construed, Putnam says in effect, as 'there exists a possible graph G satisfying such and such a condition'. To "understand" this latter we must presumably know something about graphs. How do "possible" graphs differ from actual ones? How many are there? What are their properties? It seems doubtful that anything intrinsically modal is involved here that would not come to light clearly in a fully spelled-out theory of graphs. Aside from such a theory, Putnam's suggested translation is surely unenlightening.

Curiously, the vast ontic commitment required for semantical model theory does not seem to have worried philosophers and semanticists. The phrase 'all models', however, is surely as dangerous as 'all sets'. In some contexts Putnam thinks 'all sets' is "clear," for example, in the statement of the existence of the union of any two sets. However, a philosopher should itch all over—this is his business—and if a phrase is not clear in one context it is presumably not clear *überhaupt*. It is a strange view that the phrase 'all sets' gains in clarity from the environing context. It is rather, we should contend, the other way around: a context containing a quantifier is no clearer than the quantifier itself. We can only conclude that Putnam has failed to make his point. He has not shown that mathematics needs no foundations nor has he even sketched an intelligible unified picture incorporating an intrinsically modal view.

Defenders of the new modalism might contend that the various objections put forward against modal logic in Section 2 have in effect been overcome. However, we should distinguish, as already noted, between a modal logic construed within an object language and its semantical interpretation within a suitable extensional metalanguage. We may call proponents of the former without the latter '*intrinsic modalists*'; and their view, 'the *intrinsic view*'. The objections of Section 2 have been raised primarily against the intrinsic view. The new modalists themselves have in effect argued against the intrinsic view by insisting upon the extensional interpretation. As has been mentioned, a shift of interest is involved here. It is now the extensional interpretation that is interesting, no longer intrinsic modalities, as we may call them. These latter may now be disregarded with impunity. Modal logic has been a historical *cul de sac*, and it has not helped in getting ahead with the important tasks of philosophy. Nothing can be accomplished with a modal logic that cannot now be done more clearly, directly, and efficiently by using semantics instead. The new modalists have in effect done away with their own subject.

One further point already hinted at concerns ontic involvement. The interpretations of the new modalists are usually given only within higher-order or set-theoretic metalanguages. We are thus ontically involved by a modal system with a great deal more than seems necessary. The ontic involvement is far in excess of the ontic commitment. The interesting technical problem remains as to whether suitable interpretations of modal systems can be given within only first-order metalanguages and without the excessive ontic involvement.

Just as modal logic dies hard, so does the theory of intensions *sui generis*.

7. On Church's Theory of Meaning. Let us turn again to the writings of Church, one of the foremost contemporary proponents of intensions or meanings *sui generis*. The most recent and readily available exposition of his views on meaning is to be found in the Introduction to his *Introduction to Mathematical Logic*.[18] The theory there, however, turns out to be extremely involved and artificial, contrary to the spirit and practice of science and analytic philosophy, and not only lacking in clarity but also possessing little if any evidence in favor of the entities that it postulates. Yet curiously, this theory, like modal logic itself, has attracted a good deal of interest in recent years on the part of logicians and philosophers of language.

The Church theory of meaning gains much of its motivation from its supposed need for the analysis of belief. In the most fundamental sense, it is contended that beliefs are not "about" objects such as individuals, classes, or relations, but "about" concepts or meanings. Before reflecting upon the merits of such a contention, let us explore briefly this theory of meaning in its own right. No exhaustive critical analysis will be attempted. Instead, we shall concern ourselves primarily with the vast ontic commitment of the theory, but only to the extent of a few critical remarks.

Under *proper names* Church includes not only such names as 'Rembrandt', 'the Mississippi', and 'eight', but also phrases involving

---

[18] See especially pp. 3–9.

a functional sign, such as 'five hundred times nine', and descriptive phrases, such as 'the author of *Waverley*', 'the cube of 2', and so on. A proper name is said to *denote* or *name* the object of which it is a name, this being "the most conspicuous aspect of its meaning." However, "the meaning of a proper name does not consist solely in its denotation." Hence meaning has a second "aspect" that must be sharply distinguished from the first. This second aspect is the *sense* of an expression.

Note that Church uses 'denotation' not in the sense of 'multiple denotation' but rather in the sense of 'designation'. A word or term designates one and only one object, but it may denote (in the sense of 'multiple denotation') many different objects. However, Church's usage will be followed throughout this section.

That the sense of an expression must be distinguished from that which it denotes, that is, its denotatum, may be seen by citing examples of "names which have the same denotation [denotatum] though their meanings [that is, senses] are in some sense different." Thus, following Russell, Church notes that 'Sir Walter Scott' and 'the author of *Waverley*' have the same denotatum but different senses. Therefore "we must ascribe to every proper name another kind of meaning, the sense. . . . Roughly, the sense is what is grasped when one understands a name. . . ." In a footnote Church adds that it "is not meant by this to imply any psychological element in the notion of sense. Rather, a sense (or a concept) is a postulated abstract object, with certain postulated properties."

Note the ambiguous use of 'meaning'. Denotation is spoken of as one *aspect* of meaning and sense as another *kind* of meaning. Here we have either two kinds of meaning or only one kind with two aspects—it is not clear which is intended. Kinds and aspects are presumably not the same. Perhaps the meaning of a term should be regarded as involving in some fashion both its denotatum and its sense, in which case meaning is unique but analyzed into two aspects or components. No doubt some factor or factors concerned with the usage of the term must also be added, so that meanings involve at least three factors. Church, however, has no concern here with the analysis of usage and seems not to admit it in any guise as a factor in meaning.

"The possibility must be allowed," Church continues, "of concepts which are not concepts of any possible thing, and of names which express a sense but have no denotation." Further, in "a well constructed language of course every name should have just one sense. . . . " The force of 'must' in the first sentence is by no means clear. We are not *compelled* to allow this possibility, just as we are not compelled to admit a realm of "possible" and hence presumably "impossible" things. Likewise, the force of 'of course' in the second sentence needs comment. Why should any name in a well-constructed language have just one sense? Perhaps there are different kinds of sense. Why not two, or perhaps none at all? Perhaps only *some* names should be allowed a sense, but not all.

Church does not go on to develop this theory in meticulous logistic detail.[19] No doubt he would welcome such a development, and no one in recent years has been more eloquent than he as to the importance of the logistic method in philosophy. We need not to be concerned here with details of formulation, but only with the underlying ontic commitment, which, as we shall see, appears excessive.

Church tells us nothing concerning the *inner structure* of senses. Do senses have *parts* of some sort? Can one sense enter into, in some fashion, or be determinative of, the sense of another, or are senses indivisible wholes not further to be analyzed? One will search in Church's writings in vain for an analysis of senses that will reveal their internal structure. Yet without at least a hint of what this internal structure is, we cannot be said to have a very clear idea of what senses are supposed, according to this theory, to be.

One passage does suggest that parts of meanings are to be explicitly recognized. Thus, Church tells us that "it is contained in the meaning of . . . ['Sir Walter Scott'] . . . that the person named is a knight or baronet and has the given name 'Walter' and surname 'Scott.'" It would be helpful to have an analysis of 'contained' as used in this passage. This notion of being a part of (or of being contained in) is central to any clear theory of meaning, yet curiously seems not to have been given much attention by logicians. Church in particular makes no further mention of it.

Without an analysis of the inner structure of senses, we are free to reconstrue them more or less *ad libitum* as any ethereal objects satisfying the meager conditions laid down. Thus, by way of an example, we seem to be able to construe senses as *guardian angels* and thereby gain a legitimate interpretation of Church's theory. We are motivated to introduce guardian angels because clearly the guardian angel of an expression must be distinguished from its denotatum. If we are not very clear as to what a guardian angel is here, we are no clearer as to what a sense is when one says that the *sense* of an expression must be

---

[19] See, however, Church's "A Formulation of the Logic of Sense and Denotation," in *Structure, Method, and Meaning, Essays in Honor of Henry M. Sheffer* (New York: Liberal Arts Press, 1951), pp. 3–24 and "The Need for Abstract Entities in Semantic Analysis," *Proceedings of the American Academy of Arts and Sciences* 80 (1951), 100–112.

distinguished from its denotatum. Likewise, names may well have the same denotata but different guardian angels. The guardian angel is of course of the *expression,* not of the thing named. Thus, 'Sir Walter Scott' and 'the author of *Waverley*' have very different guardian angels, although their denotatum is the same. We may also admit guardian angels of expressions that are not the names of actual things as well as names that have guardian angels but no denotata.

In addition to senses of proper names, the theory in effect admits names for these senses. For the moment, let 'w' abbreviate 'Sir Walter Scott', and '$s(w)$' be a name for the concept of Sir Walter Scott, that it, for the sense of 'w'. Expressions such as '$s(w)$' may then also be admitted, 's' being in effect a kind of functional sign absorbing quotation marks. '$s(w)$' likewise then is a proper name, that is, the proper name of a sense, and hence itself has in turn a sense $s(s(w))$. However, '$s(s(w))$' in turn is a proper name and hence has a sense $s(s(s(w)))$, and so on. The staggering array of abstract senses that results is presented without qualms.[20] We are simply told that we "must" admit them and that a simpler theory is not known to be possible.

It is significant that, after the introductory pages of his book, Church makes no essential reference to senses. His exposition of mathematical logic is, in fact, quite independent of his theory of meaning. This is a most interesting fact. The theory of senses is not needed in mathematical logic nor in metamathematics. In fact it is not the kind of theory in which mathematicians have shown much interest to date, nor has it played any role in the logical analysis of science, let alone within science itself. Similarly, syntax and denotational semantics have no need of the theory of sense, nor does systematic pragmatics, as far as it has been developed at the moment. Neither Goodman's theory of qualia, nor Woodger's biological analyses, nor Carnap's theory of probability nor anyone else's—none of these important areas of applied logic—needs the notion of sense. This seems strange indeed. If the notion is as fundamental as Church seems to regard it, should it not play a rather central role in logic itself as well as in its applications?

In his *Toward Reunion in Philosophy*[21] Morton White has argued forcibly against philosophical theories that contain or presuppose notions of meaning akin to those of Church. Without agreeing with all details of White's argument, we can applaud his attempt to show that such theories are not only not needed but have been harmful for epistemology, ethics, and philosophic analysis generally.

[20] Carnap has also made essentially this point in *Meaning and Necessity*.
[21] (Cambridge: Harvard University Press, 1956).

There is of course motivation for seeking a theory of meaning. However, these purposes are as well if not better served by using the devices of a systematic pragmatics. The need not be argued here, where we are concerned primarily with ontic commitment. There are also meanings in the sense of objective intensions, as will be urged in Chapter VII. Intensions, however, are to be analyzed in terms of more fundamental entities already available. Without such an analysis we cannot claim to have put forward a sound conception as to what they are. By getting at its clear-cut parts or components, we give an intension or sense some modicum of concrete specificity.

We see then that the Church theory involves a host of artificially postulated entities of dubious character, for whose existence there seems to be no evidence. These *sui generis* entities, unlike the "theoretical constructs" of mathematical physics, are not of the kind that can significantly enter into scientific discourse. Theoretical constructs are presumably connected in some manner with observation terms or predicates by "coordinating definitions" or postulates. The relation between a sense and the term of which it is a sense, however, remains as mysterious and unanalyzed in the Church theory as the sense itself. Thus we cannot defend that theory by showing similarity in some regard as between senses and the theoretical constructs of science. At any event, it seems that this has not been done to date by proponents of that theory.

To base logic and philosophical analysis—to say nothing of mathematics and the sciences—upon such artificially postulated, mysterious, and unanalyzed entities *sui generis*, with no attempt to explicate their use in science and actual discourse, is to return to a sterile scholasticism, barren as a tool of philosophical clarification and devoid of interest for the methodology of the sciences—indeed, devoid of interest for the methodology of the humanities as well, where a clear theory of meaning is urgently needed. Indeed, the tools of modern logic are as useful for the humanistic scholar as for the scientific one. Unfortunately, the exact study of the logic of the humanities has as yet not even begun. One can be sure in advance, however, that it will be hindered rather than helped by theories of meaning akin to that of Church.

8. On Church's Translation Argument. Suppose it be granted for the moment that the ontic commitment of Church's theory is excessive. Proponents would urge that his theory is still needed, because the objects of belief, that is, what is believed, are in some sense intensions—"propositions" no doubt—and one cannot do without them. So the argument runs.

Some few years ago Church made some comments purporting to show that alternative analyses of belief, in terms of sentences rather than propositions, are defective.[22] This argument has been much discussed in the literature and has become rather widely accepted. It will be urged now that Church's argument fails to establish its point.

For statements such as

(1)   *Seneca said that man is a rational animal*

and

(A)   *Columbus believed the world to be round,*

[Church writes], the most obvious analysis makes them statements about certain abstract entities which we call 'propositions' . . . , namely the proposition that man is a rational animal and the proposition that the world is round; and these propositions are taken as having been respectively the object of an assertion by Seneca and the object of a belief by Columbus. We do not discuss this obvious analysis here [Church continues], except to admit that it threatens difficulties and complications of its own, which appear as soon as the attempt is made to formulate systematically the syntax [and semantics (?)] of a language in which statements like (1) and (A) are possible. But our purpose is to point out what we believe may be an insuperable objection against alternative analyses that undertake to do away with propositions in favor of such more concrete things as sentences.

Of the various attempts to analyze (1), say, in terms of sentences, the most significant seems to be to construe (1), where we take 'said' in the sense of 'wrote', as

(2)   *There is a language S' such that Seneca wrote as sentence*
             of S' words whose translation from S' into English is 'Man
             is a rational animal'.

The objection to this kind of analysis, Church thinks, is that (2) does not "convey the same information" as (1) and is therefore inadequate as an analysis. That this is the case may be brought out more sharply, Church suggests, following Langford, by translating both (1) and (2) into another language and noting that the two translated statements

---

[22] A. Church, "On Carnap's Analysis of Statements of Assertion and Belief," *Analysis* 10 (1950), 97–99. See also the lengthy footnote 5 in "A Formation of the Logic of Sense and Denotation."

"would obviously convey different meanings" to a person who knew the second language but not the first. Clearly, one who knows German but not English will understand a German translation of (1). The material in single quotes in (2) will have to remain untranslated of course, so that a German translation of (2) would not convey to a German who knows no English the essential information within single quotes.

Note first that Church's argument here is very complicated indeed. To make precise, a comparative semantical metalanguage, in which at least two object languages L and L' may be systematically compared and contrasted, would have to be employed. It is not clear that such a metalanguage has ever been satisfactorily formulated. This point may be waived. More important is the fact that the argument makes explicit use of a relation of *conveying the same information as*. It is apparently presupposed as a requirement for an adequate analysis that *analysans* and *analysandum* stand in this relation.

Let us reflect upon this last point. Whatever information the sentence constituting the *analysandum* conveys to the user (presumably even before analysis) must also be conveyed by the *analysans*. But suppose '$1 + 1 = 2$' is analyzed, say, in the manner of *Principia Mathematica*. The *analysandum* here is this very sentence itself, as occurring say in ordinary informal arithmetic. We now carry out its analysis, ending with a complicated statement as *analysans* concerning classes of classes, cardinal addition, the identity of classes of classes, and so on, in primitive notation. (The complications brought in by the "typical ambiguity" of the formula '$1 +_c 1 = 2$' (*110.643) of *PM* may be disregarded.) Whether these two statements convey the same information is far from clear. Surely they do not to someone who does not know *PM*. Yet they should, according to Church's apparent requirement, else the analysis of *PM* is inadequate. That this is the case on such grounds seems doubtful; perhaps on other grounds, but surely not these.

Consider Tarski's celebrated analysis of 'true', already referred to, to the effect that a sentence a of language L is true in L if and only if a is satisfied in L by every infinite sequence of objects. Here again we would not wish to claim that the analysis is inadequate merely on the grounds that *analysans* and *analysandum* do not convey the same information to one who does not understand 'infinite sequence of objects' or 'is satisfied by'.

Note that the German translation of (2) will contain ' 'Man is a rational animal' ' untranslated. This term—it is a noun, not a sentence—is a perfectly good term of German. However, it is a term of German not understood by one knowing German but not English. A new term of a natural language can always be formed, apparently, by putting foreign words and phrases in single quotes. Thus any word of English enclosed in single quotes is a noun of German. Hence it is difficult to determine just how much information a German translation of (2) would convey to one who knows German but no English. How much information does a sentence convey to someone who does not understand all the words occurring in it? Church does discuss this, yet his argument here depends upon a suitable measure of information. The German translation of (1) would presumably convey more information than that of (2), but at any event not the same as that of (2). That this is the case seems to have nothing whatsoever to do, however, with the adequacy or inadequacy of (2) as an analysis of (1). It merely follows from the presumed fact that a sentence containing only German words does not convey the same information to one who knows German but no English as does a German sentence containing a name of an English sentence.

Church's translation criterion, it seems, does not establish what it is intended to. The requirement for sameness of information for *analysans* and *analysandum* seems too strong. Furthermore, it is beside the point, not being germane to the analysis of belief. This is evident from the example concerning '1 + 1 = 2', which does not involve a belief context or even a context containing quoted material. It is extraordinary that an irrelevant, overstrong requirement should have become so widely accepted as having established an "insuperable objection" against analyses of belief in terms of sentences.

Church does not discuss here the experimental basis for establishing belief sentences. It is difficult to see how a sentence such as 'Columbus believed the world to be round' could be established directly other than by finding out something about Columbus's reactions to certain sentences in a suitable language or by studying his actions as related to such sentences. (We leave aside here the establishing of this indirectly by an inspection of historical documents.) At any event, the invocation of a realm of propositions is of no help here. Further, Church does not distinguish between *acceptance* and *belief,* nor between the *objects* and *conditions* of belief, as we shall urge be done in Chapter V. If the experimental basis of the theory of belief is to be brought out clearly and contrasted with the part depending more on semantic analysis, such distinctions seem essential.

We are not concerned here with defending (2) as an analysis of (1). We have tried to show only that Church's objections to the kind of analysis involving sentences rather than propositions are without force. In place of an analysis such as (2), various alternatives will be put forward as we go on.

9. On Extensional Metalanguages. In subsequent chapters an attempt will be made to formulate a logic of belief within a wholly extensional metalanguage in which all reference to objects such as Church's senses or intensions *sui generis* is avoided. Several important advantages to purely extensional, as against nonextensional or intensional languages, may be summarized as follows. (Some of them are related to some of the points urged above against modal logic.) The net result of these advantages seems to be that analyses given within nonextensional languages or metalanguages should be regarded as defective and unsatisfactory in some sense.

First there is the point due to Ajdukiewicz (to be discussed in Chapter IV, Section 8, below), that an intensional formula containing a free variable does not uniquely determine a class of objects satisfying it. Such formulae are therefore meaningless in the strict sense that they do not behave in a semantically proper way. This is an extremely important and fundamental point, one not lightly to be disregarded.

Secondly, extensional metalanguages are usually simpler in structure than corresponding intensional ones. In particular, no intensional entities *sui generis* can appear as values for variables. Hence, no additional primitives applying to such entities and no additional axioms characterizing them are required. Most intensional languages contain an extensional one as a proper part anyhow, and if the proper part can be shown to suffice for the whole, this is surely all to the good. This, likewise, is a very fundamental point. Simplicity is most devoutly to be striven for in all theoretical work, but not easily attained.

Another important point is the following: Certain types of laws permeate logic and mathematics and science generally; these are the so-called *substitution, replacement,* or *extensionality* laws. Mathematics, for example, is unthinkable without them. Replacing equals by equals, equivalents by equivalents, and so on, is a most "natural" logico-mathematical procedure. To restrict the contexts within which such replacement is to be allowed seems most artificial and *ad hoc*. It is as if we were to restrict the principle of the conservation of energy in physics or to limit in some manner the principle that $2 + 2 = 4$ in ordinary mathematics. Well-entrenched laws and kinds of laws are to be preserved, not at all costs, to be sure, but at least in the absence of compelling reasons for "giving them up." So it is also with laws of extensionality. These are not casual laws thought up yesterday by some Oxford don, which we can give up or restrict with impunity. Rather, they are part and parcel of the very fabric of logic and mathematics, and therewith of science and rational thought generally.

Suppose for a moment that "propositions" in some sense are available and that 'p' and 'q' are variables ranging over them. In contrast to the extensionality or replacement laws just mentioned, let us consider the following:

(1)   If p if and only if q and X believes p at time t, then
             X believes q at t.

Clearly this does not hold generally, as Russell, Carnap, and others have repeatedly pointed out; there can be no doubt of this. However, is it not a rather extraordinary circumstance that it does not? Surely it is the *kind* of law we should like to have hold, if possible, and the fact that it (or appropriate laws like it) does not is an occasion for surprise.

The preservation of laws of certain types is often a driving motive in scientific research. It is curious that philosophers have so casually rejected extensionality and replacement laws concerning belief and knowing. Clearly (1) is to be rejected, and hence it has been concluded that extensionality in general is to be abandoned, at least in connection with meaning and belief. This seems premature, for other matters may be amiss instead. Perhaps the very use of unanalyzed propositions, and hence of propositional variables and the entities to which they commit us, provides part of the trouble.

Incidentally, it may be observed that many of these points are in accord with Church's suggestions concerning the formulation of a logic of belief.[23] Church recommends that we first gain a logic of belief, but that it would seem

> unwise to impose restrictions in advance on such a logic, as that it should not be intentional [sic] or that it should not involve commitment to objective meanings. It is difficult enough [he says], to find any sound logic of belief at all, and the search should be unhampered by extraneous demands. . . . But once such a logic were found, it might then be profitable to discuss the question of modifications to meet this or that special demand (if it did not already do so). The discovery of some sound logic of belief may well be a necessary first step toward a formulation that meets other demands in addition. . . . Meanwhile we should not prescribe in advance, but should be prepared to accept objectively the results of research.

In the light of the foregoing arguments, however, it seems doubtful that the demand of extensionality is "extraneous." Rather it is part and

---

[23] A. Church, "Logic and Analysis," *Atti del XII Congresso Internazionale di Filosofia,* Venezia, 1958, Vol. 4 (Firenze: Sansoni, 1960), pp. 77–81.

parcel of the very notion of being sound. A logic of belief that does not meet this requirement, or carries with it a dubious ontology, or employs formulae that do not behave in a semantically proper way or notions and concepts of immense complexity not even remotely akin to those of mathematics and the sciences, can scarcely be regarded as above suspicion.

The reader might be tempted to think that a straw man has been built up in this chapter merely to be knocked down. This is surely not the case. The differences between the extensionalist and intensionalist points of view are very real and fundamental and with broad ramifications for the various areas of philosophy. The differences amount to that between a sound logic and a spurious one, and hence between a reliable philosophic method and one that is not. Curiously, these differences are rarely understood fully, nor have all of the philosophical issues involved been explored to their depths.

In this chapter we have merely cleaned the Augean stables. We should not rest content merely with this, however. We must also attempt to leave something better in place of the material removed.

CHAPTER IV

Some Steps Forward

One of the most pressing problems in contemporary philosophy is that of giving a *materially correct* and *theoretically sound* analysis of sentences expressing belief. To say that person *X believes such and such* seems simple enough, but difficulties emerge as soon as we try to state precisely what it is we are saying. By 'materially correct' is meant, roughly, that the analysis should reflect more or less accurately common use and usage of the term 'belief'. It is difficult, to be sure, to determine precisely what this common use is. Nonetheless, an analysis that violated it in any fundamental respect would surely not be acceptable. And an analysis is presumably theoretically sound if it is incorporated within a well-knit system of notions, each of which is acceptable in turn, the whole system satisfying certain general requirements of adequacy. The problem of giving such an analysis of belief sentences is by no means easy.

This problem impinges upon many others, and the kind of "solution" we give to it will determine to a large extent the kind of solution we should give to the others. In particular, *knowing* (in the sense of *knowing that*) and *believing* are cognate notions, and an analysis of one presumably carries with it *mutatis mutandis* an analysis of the other. An analysis of belief involves determining an ontology. If the fundamental locution allowed is of the form '*X* believes *p*', our ontology involves persons *X* and presumably "propositions" *p*. The difficult task then remains of determining precisely what propositions are and of characterizing them in a satisfactory way. An analysis of belief involves determining the kind of relation (if such it be) expressed by 'believes' in sentences of this form. The analysis of belief is fundamental to the philosophy of *mind*, and hence of crucial importance in discussions of the mind-body problem. It is also central to the analysis of purpose or intentionality. Intentionality (with a 't') is presumably closely related with intensionality (with an 's'), although precisely how is not too clear. Also, problems concerned with intensional, as against extensional, language systems are key problems of philosophic, as against purely mathematical, logic, as has been noted.

In crucial ways, beliefs enter into analyses in ethics and value theory, to say nothing of theology and the philosophy of religion. A satisfactory handling of belief is therefore essential for these disciplines also. Much of psychology and social science is concerned with beliefs in one form or another, and a philosophic analysis of belief sentences seems needed for the foundations of these sciences. Moreover, such an analysis is needed equally in the *methodology* of these sciences, and indeed in the methodology of science in general. Scientists believe in some sense that such and such laws hold or that such and such is the case, or that such and such will obtain in the future or did obtain in the past. The intellectual activity of the scientist can be described largely in terms of his beliefs, and this activity should be accounted for, analyzed, and explained in any adequately developed methodology of science.

The very fundamental character of the problem of belief has been well described by Russell in *The Analysis of Mind*.

> Belief [he says] . . . is the central problem in the analysis of mind. Believing seems the most "mental" thing we do, the thing most remote from what is done by mere matter. The whole intellectual life consists of beliefs, and of the passage from one belief to another by what is called 'reasoning'. Beliefs give knowledge and error; they are the vehicles of truth and falsehood. Psychology, theory of knowledge and metaphysics revolve around belief, and on the view we take of belief our philosophical outlook largely depends.[1]

In Sections 1 to 3, some of Russell's comments on the analysis of belief are reviewed, in order to obtain, if we can, the essential ingredients. Some suggestive points due to *Ramsey* are commented upon in Section 4. In Section 5 we reflect upon some further comments by *Church* on the need for a well-knit logic of belief. In Section 6 *Quine's* suggestions concerning the idiom 'believes-true' are discussed. Some of *Carnap's* work on belief is examined very briefly in Section 7. An important paper by *Ajdukiewicz* is discussed in Section 8. Finally, in

---

[1] B. Russell, *The Analysis of Mind* (London: Geo. Allen and Unwin, 1921), p. 231.

Section 9, *certain linguistic forms* are chosen or settled upon tentatively for further discussion and analysis.

We are concerned here only with those views that in some direct way contribute to the constructive development in subsequent chapters. See, however, Chapter XI, Sections 8 and 9.

1. On Russell's Analysis of Belief. Let us reflect a little upon Russell's discussion of belief, especially as contained in *The Analysis of Mind.* Although written over forty years ago, this book, and in particular the chapter on "Belief," contains much that is still valuable. Although in his later works, particularly *An Inquiry into Meaning and Truth* and *Human Knowledge,* Russell is preoccupied with belief in various ways, there is little if any improvement over the earlier treatment. In fact clear-cut and defensible items there become obscured in his later works. For the purposes of the presystematic limning of a sound logic of belief, we find in his earlier treatment some of Russell's best pages on this subject.

Let us reflect upon the linguistic form or forms required to say that a person believes so and so, or that a person believes (at a given time perhaps) so and so *of* such and such objects. These presumably are, or should be, the fundamental forms for a well-knit logic of belief. Epistemological matters underlying these forms will be touched upon only derivatively. Russell is concerned with both the logic and epistemology of belief and frequently confuses the two. By separating them sharply, we may well gain linguistic forms that will help to clarify matters and pave the way for a more fruitful epistemology.

First Russell notes that beliefs

> are characterized by truth or falsehood [just as] words are characterized by meaning. . . . You may believe [he writes] that such and such a horse will win the Derby. The time comes, and your horse wins or does not win; according to the outcome, your belief was true or false. You may believe that six times nine is fifty-six; in this case also there is a fact which makes your belief false. . . . What makes a belief true or false I call a 'fact'. The particular fact that makes a given belief true or false I call its 'objective', and the relation of a belief to its objective I call the 'reference' or the 'objective reference' of the belief. Thus, if I believe that Columbus crossed the Atlantic in 1492, the 'objective' of my belief is Columbus's actual voyage, and the 'reference' of my belief is the relation between my belief and the voyage. . . .[2]

This passage merits rather close examination.

[2] The quotations are from the chapter "Belief" in *The Analysis of Mind,* pp. 231–252.

Some beliefs may surely be regarded as true, and some as false. Strictly, however, as we know from semantics, only declarative *sentences* or *statements* can properly be said to be true or false in the most fundamental sense. Other uses of these notions should be definable. If a person believes what is expressed by a declarative sentence that is true, we might then *by definition* say that his belief in that sentence is true (or correct). Similarly, his belief may be false (or incorrect) if the sentence expressing what is believed is false. 'True' and 'false' (or 'correct' and 'incorrect') as applied to beliefs may presumably be defined in this way. Minute as it may seem, the distinction between applying 'true' and the like to sentences and beliefs is important if we are to achieve maximum clarity in our discussion and remain free from obvious ambiguities and blunders.

Columbus's actual voyage is a certain historical occurrence in space-time, whereas the "fact" that Columbus crossed the Atlantic in 1492 is expressed by a declarative sentence (or statement or proposition, if you like). Now clearly, spatio-temporal occurrences such as Columbus's actual voyage are very different *entities* from whatever it is that propositions (in the sense of declarative sentences) express. Thus, the example Russell cites cannot be an instance of an "objective" as defined. Russell is here merely confusing different types of entities. (See Chapters VIII and IX below.)

The "fact" that Columbus crossed the Atlantic in 1492 may be broken up or decomposed into suitable components, namely, by distinguishing *Columbus*, the *Atlantic*, the year *1492*, and the *triadic relation of crossing such and such at such and such a time*. In place then of speaking of Russell's "objective" we have these various components. Where Russell's "objective" is a fuzzy "fact," there are now clear-cut individuals, times, and relations to consider. In place of the one "objective," there are now the various *objects* constituting it in some sense, where relations (and perhaps classes) and times are included as objects.

Now as to the relation between the belief and its objective in Russell's sense, the "objective reference." If the notion of an "objective" is fuzzy, surely the relation of "objective reference" is also. If, properly, there are no "facts" (in the explicit sense of having them as values for variables), there can be no relation of "objective reference" of beliefs to them. Having decomposed the "objective" into constituent individuals, classes, and/or relations, we may well ask: What relation emerges here in place of that of "objective reference?" It would be a many-placed relation between, or rather among, the belief (that is, the statement believed) and the many objects (taken in some suitable order) into which the "objective" is decomposed.

def: Belief
+ its objects.

Are beliefs, according to Russell, a part of the "furniture of the world?" Are there beliefs in the sense that we must have variables ranging over them? Must these variables be of a special sort or may they also include entities other than beliefs in their range? Surely there are persons who believe such and such of such and such objects. The totality of declarative sentences believed, or believed at a certain time, constitutes a well-defined class of declarative sentences. If by 'beliefs' we designate such a class, surely we have a clear notion. However, we often speak of beliefs not simply in this sense, but also in the sense of a special kind of act or activity on the part of the believer. That such activities should be recognized as constituting a separate domain of entities, however, is not clear. People believe such and such, surely, but we should not infer from this that there are such things as believings or acts of belief (again, in the explicit sense of being values for variables). (See, however, Chapters IX and XI.)

By 'belief', hereafter let us denote a declarative statement be- *statement* lieved by someone at some time. Taking 'belief' in this way, we may then construe Russell's relation of "objective reference" as a semantical relation between a declarative sentence and the individuals, classes, and/or relations that are the "objects" of the belief.

Russell goes on to distinguish between believing and what is believed.

> I may believe that Columbus crossed the Atlantic [he notes], that all Cretans are liars, that two and two are four . . .; in all these cases the believing is just the same and only the contents believed are different. . . . I may remember my breakfast this morning, my lecture last week, or my first sight of New York. In all these cases the feeling of memory-belief is just the same, and only what is remembered differs. Exactly similar remarks apply to expectations. Bare assent, memory and expectation are forms of belief; all these are different from what is believed, and each has a constant character which is independent of what is believed.

To handle bare assent, memory, and expectation, some theory of time flow presumably must be presupposed. But bare assent is no doubt mere acceptance *now*; memory, acceptance now of statements concerning the past; expectation, present acceptance of statements concerning the future. Perhaps these suggestions do not do full justice to Russell's triad, but he tells us nothing more in the present context or elsewhere concerning time and how it relates to the analysis of belief.

The *believing* is the same in all cases of belief and "is an actual experienced feeling." Believing is presumably to be handled relationally, as no doubt feeling in general should be. The relation is then constant, so to speak, in all cases. Of course the relation may take different *arguments*, and much of the problem in the analysis of belief is to try to be as clear as possible concerning the arguments admitted. *What precisely are the arguments of the relation of believing?* Although Russell is not too explicit, his remarks are illuminating in helping to gain a reasonable answer.

2. "Content." Let us consider Russell's somewhat obscure notion of *content*.

> What is believed, and the believing [he says] must both consist of present occurrences in the believer, no matter what may be the objective of the belief. Suppose I believe, for example, 'that Caesar crossed the Rubicon.' The objective of my belief is an event [fact!] which happened long ago, which I never saw and do not remember. This event itself is not in my mind when I believe that it happened. It is not correct to say that I am believing the actual event; what I am believing is *something now in my mind* [italics added], something related to the event . . . , but obviously not to be confounded with the event, since the event is not occurring now but the believing is. . . . What is believed, however true it may be, is not the actual fact that makes the belief true, but a present event related to the fact. This present event, which is what is believed, I shall call the 'content' of the belief. . . .

In addition to the other factors, the something-now-present-in-the-mind or "content" is discriminated as presumably an essential ingredient in belief. The precise relationship between this something-now-present-in-the-mind and the "objective" is unfortunately not characterized. It may well be doubted that the something-now-present-in-the-mind should be admitted as an additional factor. It seems a mere obfuscating encumbrance and the logic of belief gets underway more readily without it.

Russell comments that the

> first thing to notice about what is believed, i.e., about the content of a belief, is that it is always complex. We believe that a certain thing has a certain property, or that it occurred or will occur . . . ; or we may believe that all the members of a certain class have a certain property, or that a certain property sometimes occurs among the members of a class; or we may believe that if one thing happens, another will happen . . . ; or we may believe that something does not happen, or did not or will not happen . . . ; or that one of two things must happen. . . . The catalogue

of the sorts of things we may believe is infinite, but all of them
are complex.

Of course what is believed is complex when analyzed into its constituents. It is instructive to note Russell's catalogue of objects about
which we have beliefs: things, properties, relations, classes and their
members, happenings—clearly the logician's catalogue. What then is
believed of them? That a thing has a property, that a thing has a
relation to another thing, that such and such happens or fails to happen,
that all members of a given class have such and such a property, and
so on—again, the logician's catalogue. And fine catalogues they are,
not lightly to be added to, subtracted from, or altered. Note, however,
that the comments quoted are supposed to be about the "content" of
a belief, that is, about the something-now-present-in-the-mind. Hence
Russell cannot be talking about things, properties, relations, classes,
and happenings, but only presumably about these as now-present-in-
the-mind. The universe thus becomes populated apparently with real
things as well as with things-now-present-in-the-mind; with real properties as well as with properties-now-present-in-the-mind, and so on.
Surely this duplication is gratuitous, particularly for a logic of belief,
and we had best construe this paragraph as having to do with the *objects* of belief rather than with "content."
  Further, the

> content of a belief involves not merely a plurality of constituents,
> but definite relations between them; it is not determinate when
> its constituents alone are given. For example, 'Plato preceded
> Aristotle' and 'Aristotle preceded Plato' are both contents [sic]
> which may be believed, but, although they consist of exactly the
> same constituents, they are different, and even incompatible.

Again, this passage is literally absurd on Russell's meaning of 'content'.
Clearly, we must distinguish between '*X* believes that Plato preceded
Aristotle' and '*X* believes that Aristotle preceded Plato', but the distinction is only obscured if drawn in terms of "content." The two linguistic
forms suggested may be analyzed in terms of a certain quadratic relation, with differing arguments. Thus the first might become '*X* believes
of *Plato* and of *Aristotle* that *Plato preceded Aristotle*' and the second
'*X* believes of *Aristotle* and of *Plato* that *Aristotle preceded Plato*'.[3]
  Let us turn now to the three kinds of beliefs, those involving bare
assent, memory, or expectation. The difference among them lies not
in the "content" but in "the nature of the belief-feeling." In addition to

[3] Of this more anon.

the something-now-present-in-the-mind constituting content are belief feelings, presumably of various kinds, consisting of "sensations." "I, personally," Russell says, "do not profess to be able to analyze the sensations constituting respectively memory, expectation, and assent; but I am not prepared to say that they cannot be analysed. There may be other belief-feelings, for example, in disjunction and implications; also a disbelief-feeling." Such an analysis would surely be difficult, and Russell does not offer one. Precisely what are disjunctive or implicative "sensations," and how are they related to the presumably simple sensations that comprise them? It is doubtful that satisfactory answers to these questions can be given and that a realm of sensations need be recognized for the logic of belief.

It was suggested above that bare assent may be handled relationally, in terms perhaps of an experimentally characterized notion of *acceptance*, or acceptance to such and such a degree.[4] If so, relations of remembering or of expecting may then perhaps be defined in terms of acceptance together with an underlying theory of time flow. To remember now, for example, that such and such occurred in the past is to accept now the statement that such and such occurred in the past. To expect, in the bland sense and without any particular anticipation of joy or pleasure, that such and such will happen at time t in the future is to accept now the statement that such and such will happen at t in the future. Russell notes that there "is no way of distinguishing, in words, between a memory and an assent to a proposition about the past," and that "exactly similar remarks apply to the difference between expectation . . . and assent to a proposition about the future. . . . " The need for an underlying theory of time flow is obvious here but rarely explicitly recognized.

When acceptance or assent are available, there is presumably no need for an ontology of "belief feelings." If one assents to a given "proposition," one then and only then has the "belief feeling" or "feeling of assent" appropriate to that proposition. Does each proposition have a unique feeling of assent appropriate to it, relative, that is, to the same person and time? (Of course, there may well be *degrees* of assent, in which case we must add: and of the same degree?) Russell does not consider this. In any event, belief feelings as values for variables, it would seem, are not needed for the logic of belief.

3. The Essential Ingredients. Russell's summing up may be paraphrased as follows. (a) We have a "proposition" consisting of inter-

---

[4] See the author's *Toward a Systematic Pragmatics* and *Intension and Decision*.

related words. (b) We "have the feeling of assent, which is presumably a complex sensation demanding analysis." (c) We "have a relation, actually subsisting, between the assent and the proposition, such as is expressed by saying that the proposition in question is what is assented to." This relation may presumably be construed experimentally as that of acceptance. Clearly (a) and (c) enunciate essential ingredients for the basic forms needed in the logic of belief. This is also true of (b), but it need not be listed as a separate factor. The "feeling of assent" is no doubt present when the relation of (c) "actually subsists." If person X stands in the relation of assent or acceptance to a given declarative sentence, he then presumably has the "feeling of acceptance" appropriate to that sentence.

For explicitness, the following factors should also be listed. (d) There is always an agent, usually a human person, who does the believing. (e) There is a time at which the believing takes place. (f) There are the objects (entering constitutively into the "objective") that the sentence is "about." Finally, (g) there is a semantical relation of designation or denotation between the (nonlogical) words of (a) and the objects of (f). An adequate logic of belief must surely take fundamental account of item (a) and of items (c) through (f). Clearly it must presuppose both logical syntax and semantics in some form or other.

Russell has been dwelt on at length because, in spite of its defects, his discussion contains the historically first hints of the kind of analysis that seems correct and that will be found especially useful in the sequel.

It is interesting to note that the kind of analysis that emerges from these remarks, characterized roughly by item (a) and items (c) through (f) just given, makes no use of intensions or meanings in the sense of Frege's *Sinne*. It is usually thought that such entities are indispensable for a logic of belief (as noted in the preceding chapter), and this indispensability is often taken as an argument for the existence of such entities. If we can now succeed in formulating an adequate logic of belief without them, we shall have a most telling argument against such entities. One of the main tasks of this book in fact is to attempt to provide such an argument, as has already been remarked.

We shall attempt to formulate, then, albeit tentatively and as a basis for further reflection and research, foundations for a well-knit logic of belief in what it is hoped is a theoretically sound way. A logic of belief is not a total philosophy of belief, and we should not expect from a logic answers to all the pertinent questions we may ask. On the contrary, to formulate a logic of such and such a term is a rather limited enterprise, and we must not expect of it more than it is designed to supply. This is a very important point, it seems, and one frequently misunderstood.

Clearly it is not the business of a logic of belief to supply *criteria* in accord with which we can decide who believes what, and when. If such criteria are given, the logical consequences of sentences stating that so and so believes such and such may be explored. The logic supplies no means of deciding whether or not such sentences should be affirmed. This is to be done presumably on the basis of suitable observations and experiments or in accord with critical common sense.

An adequate analysis of belief cannot be given merely within a syntax or a semantics. Reference to the person seems essential, and this reference involves us at once in pragmatics. However, syntactical and semantical features of language play a fundamental role in the analysis of belief. Hence we should not wish to attempt such an analysis independent of them. Within a suitably developed pragmatics, however, we hope to be able to show that a logic of belief is forthcoming *without the introduction of any new primitive notions.* Of course, suitable primitives must be available for the underlying pragmatics, but no additional ones are required for the analysis of belief. The analysis is thus to be wholly definitional rather than postulational, the definitions being given within the underlying pragmatics. This, however, is anticipating.

4. On Ramsey's Analysis. Ramsey agrees with Russell that "a judgment has no single object, but is a multiple relation of the mind or mental factors [or person] to many objects, those, namely, which we should ordinarily call constituents of the proposition judged."[5] Ramsey supposes "for simplicity that the thinker with whom we are concerned uses a systematic language without irregularities and with an exact logical notation like that of *Principia Mathematica.*" He is perhaps the first to make such a supposition explicit and to recognize its need in limning a logic of belief.

However, Ramsey errs, it would seem, in saying that "just as in the study of chess nothing is gained by discussing the atoms of which the chessmen are composed, so in the study of logic nothing is gained by entering into the ultimate analysis of names and the objects they signify." The analogy is inexact. Surely a study of chess must make fundamental use of the relations between chessmen, moves, and the structure of the chessboard. So, logic in the broad sense must make use of relations of designation, denotation, and the like, as between

[5] F. P. Ramsey, "Facts and Propositions," in *The Foundations of Mathematics* (New York: Harcourt, Brace and Co., 1931), pp. 138 ff.

certain signs and objects. However, the physico-chemical constitution of the objects is irrelevant to the study of these relations, just as it is to that of the chessmen. Unfortunately, the main development of modern semantics came only after Ramsey's death.

Having agreed with Russell that belief should be handled as a polyadic relation of some kind and not merely as a dyadic one, Ramsey notes that "to leave it at that, as he [Russell] did, cannot be regarded as satisfactory. There is no reason to suppose the relation simple; it may, for instance, result from the combination of dual relations . . . ; and it is desirable that we should try to find out more about it, and how it varies when the form of the proposition believed is varied." This is precisely what we shall try to do below. Curiously, in all these intervening years, no one seems even to have attempted to carry on where Ramsey left off.

We shall make much of *patterns* of belief later. It is interesting that Ramsey plunges into them directly. He thinks somehow that disbelieving '*p*' (we follow for the moment his inconsistent use of '*p*' and quotation marks) is somehow equivalent to believing 'not-*p*'. Also, he thinks that to determine precisely what we mean here by 'equivalent' is "the central difficulty of the subject." "There would be many occasions," he writes, "on which we should expect one or the other [disbelieving '*p*' or believing 'not-*p*'] to occur, but not know which, and whichever occurred we should expect the same kind of behavior in consequence." It seems preferable to speak here of a certain *pattern* of belief concerning 'not'. To determine just which patterns are in some sense the proper or best ones is by no means easy. Ramsey thinks that "the significance of 'not' consists . . . in this equivalence between disbelieving '*p*' and believing 'not-*p*'." We should say rather that when this equivalence obtains, a pattern of belief concerning 'not' is exhibited, that is, a pattern of rationality of a restricted kind. (See Chapter V, Sections 8 and 9, below.)

Ramsey is less clear concerning a rational belief pattern for 'or'. "Thus, to believe *p* or *q* [that is, '(*p* or *q*)'] is to express agreement with the possibilities *p* true and *q* true, *p* false and *q* true, *p* true and *q* false, and disagreement with the remaining possibility *p* false and *q* false." Perhaps we can say here that a rational belief pattern for 'or' is established for person *X*, if whenever *X* believes '(*p* or *q*)' then and only then he believes both '*p*' and '*q*' or believes '*p*' but disbelieves '*q*', or disbelieves '*p*' but believes '*q*'. (If to disbelieve '*p*' is simply *not* to believe '*p*', we need not add the paraphrase of Ramsey's last clause, for it would be logically equivalent to the whole of the preceding disjunction.) We shall reflect upon such a pattern, which is perhaps too strong, later.

Ramsey's comments show extraordinary acumen. A major scandal of recent British philosophy is that no one seems even to have tried to carry on where he left off.

The next explicit comments to be discussed, concerning the need of seeking a well-knit logic of belief, are those of Church of 1958.

5. Church on the Logic of Belief. Church notes that

> problems of philosophical analysis are often in effect problems of logic—not, that is, of logical *inference*, but of formulating some system of ideas in coherent logical form. In such a case the situation usually is that the ideas in question are already known to common sense, as expressed in ordinary language. But the common-sense formulation requires amendment and supplementation, in order to remove uncertainties and perplexities, or even perhaps to resolve paradox. And this process of reformulation is then a matter of logic.[6]

In particular, the problem of giving an adequate analysis of belief, he continues,

> is not to be solved by any single statement of analysis, saying in one sentence of ordinary informal language that to believe is so and so and so and so, or that A believes that p if and only if so and so. But rather *the solution requires stating a logic of belief in a full and systematic way, removing the uncertainties and variabilities of ordinary language* as to what is admissible—first as meaningful, and then as logically compatible—*by a complete statement of formation and transformation rules* [italics added].

According to Church, a full analysis of belief

> must consist of three things, a logic of belief, a theory based on special postulates, and an account of the observational criteria for recognizing or testing belief. But especially the formulation of a satisfactory logic of belief is very much an open problem, and presents peculiar difficulties.

Concerning the observational criteria, Church notes that

> a logic of belief must be distinguished from the question of operational and observational criteria by which belief is to be recog-

---

[6] Alonzo Church, "Logic and Analysis." All the quotations from Church cited here are from this paper.

nized. . . . We may test a man's belief by putting him in a test situation in which he must reveal his belief by acting on it in his own interest. And in order to isolate the belief of the subject in regard to one particular matter, and eliminate the influence of his belief in other matters, we may use a series of test situations in which the circumstances of the test are appropriately varied. Or we may simply ask him. If we doubt the truthfulness of his answer, we may attempt to trip him on cross-examination, or we may ask others about his reputation for veracity. And if we doubt his understanding, we may ask questions to test understanding, or we may resort to various procedures of explanation, verbal and other, in order to remove misunderstanding. To be sure, this common-sense procedure leaves a considerable fringe of vagueness within which doubt arises as to whether *A* believes *p* or not; and though this fringe may be reduced by devising more efficient testing procedures, it can in principle never be wholly removed. In this respect the nature of belief is not different from other observational notions, and no problem seems to arise that is special to the notion of belief as against others. But the question of a logic of belief is another matter.

These admirable statements are in almost complete agreement with what is said above and in *Toward a Systematic Pragmatics* and with what will be said below. It is difficult, however, to see how *Church* can make these statements if propositions are taken as the objects or termini of belief. Propositions at best are entities beyond the direct reach of "operational and observational criteria." The relation of belief—regarded as relating persons with propositions—can never be put to the test unless, of course, propositions are suitably "represented" or "expressed" by sentences. Just how propositions are so expressed, however, is by no means clear. Similarly, one can never *ask* a proposition. There are no interrogative propositions, only interrogative sentences. If operational and observational criteria are regarded as appropriate for testing belief, we must have a clear theory *precisely* as to how abstract entities, such as propositions, are related to operationally testable phenomena, such as sentences (sentence designs) or tokens of sentences (sentence events) "expressing" propositions. This, unfortunately, has not been supplied. Suppose, however, that it were. The question would then arise as to whether the testable phenomena alone may be made to suffice, without the excess weight of unanalyzed propositions.

When a person's belief in a "proposition" is put to the test, the way in which the proposition is expressed must be taken into account. One plausible way of construing a "proposition" is as a class of logically equivalent sentences. The proposition remains the same, no matter how it is expressed. However, a person might well accept or take as true one sentence of that class without accepting or taking as true every other. Hence, propositions construed as classes of logically equivalent sentences do not seem suitable termini for beliefs.

Church is not too clear as to the difference between a "logic of belief" and a "theory based on special postulates." Surely any theory based on special postulates presupposes a logic for its adequate formulation. Concerning belief, we should presumably have special postulates characterizing the suitable primitive or primitives required. For this, a logic is presupposed, that is, specifically logical axioms and rules. However, this logic should not be called 'a logic of belief', even though the word 'believes' might well occur vacuously in the various logical theorems. We should not speak of logical principles, as applied to arithmetic, as providing a specific "logic of arithmetic," or as applied to physics, a "logic of physics," as though they were fundamentally different. It is thus not clear why Church speaks here of a "logic of belief." More properly, the logic of belief would consist of the whole theory based on special postulates including, of course, logical axioms and rules.

Because of the reference to special postulates, it is clear that Church conceives the theory of belief to be postulational rather than definitional in character. Curiously enough, this is in marked contrast to the usual preference of mathematicians for definitional rather than postulational procedures in semantics.[7]

Much of the motive in seeking a logic of belief arises, according to Church, from his conviction that the "very special difficulty of the logical problem [of explicating belief] is indicated by the fact that plausible verbal analyses of believing have repeatedly failed over some point of logic. And the new analysis of believing which Professor Ayer has offered . . . [in his report to the Venice Congress in the *Relazione Introduttive*] provides one more illustration of this." Whether Church's criticism of Ayer on specific points is wholly justified may be doubted, but this is beyond our present concern. Nonetheless, we are indebted to Church for pointing out so forcefully that recent analytic philosophy has failed to provide an adequate analysis of believing, and that such an analysis cannot be given satisfactorily independent of the detailed formulation of a full-fledged logic of belief. Logic has been with us now for a long time and is not to be tossed lightly to the winds, as some would have it, when we turn to analytic philosophy and natural language. Although the latter is unruly, to be sure, logical tools are as

---

[7] See especially A. Tarski, *Logic, Semantics, Metamathematics* and Alonzo Church, *Introduction to Mathematical Logic*, Vol. I.

useful for the study of it as are the exact notions of mathematical physics for the variable and evanescent phenomena of nature.

6. On Quine's 'Believes-True'. Belief and knowledge are among what Russell has called 'propositional attitudes'. Doubt concerning the use of propositions, whatever they are, has been expressed above. Foremost among those who distrust an analysis of knowing and believing that in any way involves intensions, including propositions, is Quine.

In his "Quantifiers and Propositional Attitudes"[8] Quine notes that "instead of:

$$X \text{ believes that } . . .$$

we may say:

(1) X believes-true '. . .'."

Likewise "instead of:

$$X \text{ believes the attribute } y(. . . y . . .) \text{ of } x,$$

we may say:

(2) X believes '. . . y . . .' satisfied by x."

Here '. . . y . . .' is a sentential function of the one variable 'y', and 'y(. . . y . . .)' designates the attribute (a dubious intensional entity, according to Quine, to be condoned only in passing) determined by '. . . y . . .'.

The phrase 'believes satisfied by' used here, Quine notes, "would be viewed as an irreducibly triadic predicate." Quine does not offer a *definition* of this predicate, which presumably could be given under suitable circumstances. The occurrence of 'satisfied' in 'believes satisfied by' suggests that a suitable definition can be given in terms of the semantical relation of *satisfaction*.[9] Likewise, 'believes-true' is perhaps definable in terms of the semantical truth concept; not, however, without suitable additional notions of pragmatics.

---

[8] In *The Ways of Paradox*, p. 183.

[9] An object x is said to *satisfy* a formula a containing just one free variable if the result of replacing throughout (uniformly) occurrences of that free variable by a grammatically admissible name of x is true. For a more general definition, see Tarski, *loc. cit.*

It is interesting to ask what is involved in 'may say . . . instead of'. The 'may be said' does not necessitate being in accord with good Oxford usage, for 'believes-true' or 'believes satisfied by' are already departures. Quine here seems rather to be searching for suitable logical forms, as it were, for suitable atomic sentential forms, in terms of which belief sentences may be expressed.

The forms (1) and (2) are to be extolled as of unusual interest. Quine is perhaps the first writer to have suggested such forms of locution, especially (2), which are free from the defects of most of the alternatives that have been proposed.

Quine states that the semantical reformulations (1) and (2) are "not, of course, intended to suggest that the subject of the propositional attitude speaks the language of the quotation, or any language. We may treat a mouse's fear of a cat as his fearing true a certain English sentence. This is unnatural without being therefore wrong." Similarly, *we* may treat Caesar's belief that Rome is situated on the Tiber as Caesar's believing-true a certain English sentence. If the subject of the propositional attitude speaks no language, however, it is not clear how his reactions to language can be tested. His behavior may be observed, to be sure, but presumably his reactions to language must also be taken into account. Fear may no doubt be handled as fearing true an English sentence by an experimenter or logician who speaks English, but not presumably by one who does not. In the case of belief we have both the language of the quotation (the object language) as well as that of the experimenter (presumably the metalanguage). These should no doubt be sharply distinguished if we are to formulate a satisfactory logic of belief.

If one objects to this dichotomy of language and metalanguage, we may recall the need for such a dichotomy in semantics. A logic of belief presupposes a semantics. Since this dichotomy is essential in semantics, why should we think it could be dispensed with in a logic of belief? This latter patently cannot be simpler than the underlying semantics. Rather, it must involve factors, that is, kinds of variables and modes of locution, other than those needed for semantics or syntax. Indeed, the complexity is there and not to be avoided.

Quine notes that (1) and (2) involve reference to language, which, however, he says, "must be made explicit. When we say that . . . [person X] believes-true S, we need to be able to say what language S is thought of as belonging to; not because . . . [X] needs to understand S, but because S might by coincidence exist (as a linguistic form) with very different meanings in two languages." In the significant case, S will be a sentence within the language that X speaks, if his reactions to language are under test. If not, S will be a sentence within the language (metalanguage) of the experimenter. In either case, S might by coincidence be a sentence in some other language, where perhaps it has a quite different "meaning." A formula in a chemistry book may "mean" one thing; when embedded in a poem, quite another. There is no problem here peculiar to the logic of belief.

The reference to a language should surely be taken into account, but we need not therewith have *variables* over languages and give significance to 'believes-true in *L*'. Quine objects rightly to the "need of dragging in the language concept at all. What is a language? What degree of fixity is supposed? When do we have one language and not two? The propositional attitudes," he goes on, "are dim affairs to begin with, and it is a pity to have to add obscurity to obscurity by bringing in language variables too. Only let it not be supposed that any clarity is gained by restituting the intensions."

To bring in language variables is surely an unnecessary complication. There have been attempts to characterize the values for such variables.[10] Even if some of them are partially successful, the complications remain. There is hope here, however, and the notion of a language as a value for a variable is perhaps less obscure than that of an unanalyzed intension. Even so, it seems more profitable to aim for a logic of belief referring to just *one language*, the logic of belief itself being couched in a suitable metalanguage. There are difficulties enough here. There will then be time to bring in a second language, a third, and so on. This stepwise procedure has been used in logic generally, and in syntax and semantics. Why now all of a sudden should it be abandoned in the search for a logic of belief?

In his *Word and Object*, Quine gives up the notion 'believes '. . .' satisfied by' in favor of 'believes '. . .' true of', an immaterial change. As an alternative, which Quine says he finds "as appealing as any[,] is simply to dispense with the objects of the propositional attitudes" altogether. In other words, Quine proposes in effect to treat

'Tom believes that Cicero denounced Cataline'

not as a relational sentence but as one of subject-predicate form, 'Tom' being the subject, the remainder of the sentence the predicate. This alternative is similar to a method suggested by Ajdukiewicz. (See Sections 7 and 8 below.) Actually, Quine's formulation involves a complication entailed by the "intensional operators" of a certain kind. "The verb 'believes' here," Quine says (p. 216), "ceases to be a term and

[10] See, for example, K. Schröter, "Was ist eine Mathematische Theorie?" *Jahresbericht der Deutschen Mathematiker-Vereinigung* 53 (1943), 69–82; A. Tarski, *loc. cit.*; and *Truth and Denomination*.

becomes part of an operator 'believes that', or 'believes [ ]', which, applied to a sentence, produces a composite absolute general term whereof the sentence is counted an immediate constituent." This involves, as Quine himself says, "a very wayward set of idioms. To have cleared away the ontology of the propositional attitudes is not to have made scientific sense of them." Surely not. There are objections against Quine's procedure similar to those that will be urged later against Ajdukiewicz. Here Quine seems to have taken a backward step.

We have found much to agree with in Quine's comments. There are some important items to take into account, however, to which he perhaps does not do full justice. (1) Evidently more emphasis is to be placed upon the experimental means of testing beliefs than Quine indicates. The experimental foundation must be clearly brought to light. (2) The underlying theory of time should be made explicit.[11] There are no insuperable problems here, but they should be faced nonetheless. (3) A logic of belief is not a mere matter of "regimenting" our everyday modes of speech. It requires explicit determination of the relevant language and metalanguage alike and of the atomic and other sentential forms allowed in each. (4) Quine is concerned only with belief sentences of, as it were, atomic form. Of course the proper determination of these is the first important step. Once these are determined, however, there is still much to do in developing the theory of belief, more particularly in framing various definitions, in fixing axioms, in sketching types or patterns of belief, and in drawing out their consequences. (5) Quine is concerned almost entirely with ordinary language. His discussion reflects a more or less common-sense approach supplemented occasionally with logical symbols to make ordinary language behave properly. Against this approach the more Wittgensteinian view of Chapter I, Section 3, is urged.

It is of interest, finally, to compare Quine's discussion with the items (a)–(g) of Section 3. Quine takes adequate account of (a), (d), and (f), but nowhere seems to attempt a definition in terms of (c), nor does he explicitly take account of (e) or (g).

7. On Carnap's Analyses. No one has worried more deeply than Carnap about the logic of belief sentences, and we are indebted to him for fundamental contributions on this topic as on so many others. Carnap's work is well known, however, and much of it is absorbed in

----

[11] See J. H. Woodger, *The Axiomatic Method in Biology,* pp. 56 ff., and *The Technique of Theory Construction* (*International Encyclopedia of Unified Science,* Vol. II, No. 5, Chicago: University of Chicago Press, 1939), pp. 32–33.

the point of view underlying this book. Therefore, his analysis of belief need be touched upon only very briefly here.

In *The Logical Syntax of Language* (pp. 247 ff.) the sentence(s)

(1)   Charles thinks (asserts, believes, wonders about) A,

where 'A' abbreviates a sentence, is regarded as an "intensional sentence of the autonymous mode of speech," the subsentence 'A' occurring autonymously, that is, as a name of itself. The sentence (1) can be construed, Carnap thinks, as an "extensional sentence of syntax," more particularly as

(2)   Charles thinks (asserts, believes, wonders about) 'A'.

Intensional sentences such as (1) are thus syntactical in disguise and can be translated, so Carnap maintains, into correlated extensional sentences.

In spite of its brevity and seeming simplicity, this early analysis is extremely important in bringing to light a crucial feature of the theory of belief, namely, its relativity to syntax. In their desire in part to avoid the technical complexities of logical syntax, most subsequent writers have neglected to consider sufficiently the merits of (2).

In *Meaning and Necessity,* especially in the second edition, Carnap again reflects upon the linguistic forms needed for a logic of belief. There also Carnap tends to favor forms such as (2) to the alternative in terms of propositions. He notes, however, that "both forms must be further investigated before we can decide which is preferable." Also, he thinks that beliefs should be handled as theoretical constructs and thus presumably cannot be defined wholly in terms of observables. Some additional semantical factors are no doubt required. Much of what will be said subsequently will tend to corroborate this view.

8. Ajdukiewicz on What Caesar Knew. A suggestion that will be of use later is due to Ajdukiewicz. In his "A Method of Eliminating Intensional Sentences and Sentential Formulas" (also presented at the Venice congress in 1958),[12] Ajdukiewicz points out that intensional formulae concerning knowing and believing and containing a free variable are semantically defective in a most important respect. As a result they are in the strict sense *meaningless.*

---

[12] *Atti del XII Congresso Internazionale di Filosofia,* Vol. 5 (Firenze: Sansoni, 1960), pp. 17–24.

Consider the formula

(1)   'Newton knew that $x = 8$'.

The sentences that result from this formula, by substituting for the free variable 'x' different expressions designating one and the same number, should surely have the same truth value. (In other words, the formula (1) should be such as to establish a many-one or functional relation between the values of the variable and truth or falsity.) With some substitutions for 'x', we should expect (1) to come out as a truth, and with others, as a falsity. If for 'x' different expressions for one and the same number are substituted, we should expect (1) to come out with the same truth value in all cases. However, this is precisely what need *not* happen, as Ajdukiewicz shows.

If for 'x' we substitute '$6 + 2$', (1) comes out as a truth, for Newton surely knew the truths of elementary arithmetic. If, on the other hand, we substitute 'the atomic number of oxygen' for 'x', the result is false, for although the atomic number for oxygen is in fact 8, Newton could not have known it, for this did not become known until later. Hence an intensional formula containing a free variable "does not determine unequivocally . . . [a] . . . class of objects which would satisfy that formula."

If we turn now to intensional *sentences,* containing, of course, *no* free variables, the situation is likewise unfortunate. Sentences such as

(2)   'Newton knew that $6 + 2 = 8$',

if analyzed in terms of propositions, would state that Newton stood in the relation of knowing to the proposition that $6 + 2 = 8$. Ajdukiewicz does not even consider this possibility. Presumably, and in accord with "clean" Polish logic, he does not recognize that there are such things as propositions at all.

Another suggestion is that (2) be analyzed in terms of a relation between Newton and some sentence expressing that $6 + 2 = 8$. Or, following Ajdukiewicz with another example,

(3)   'Caesar knew that the capital of the Republic is situated
        on the Tiber'

should perhaps be regarded as an 'inexact formulation" of

(4)   'Caesar recognized as true the sentence 'The capital of the
        Republic is situated on the Tiber' '.

The difficulty with this analysis, as Ajdukiewicz points out, is that (3) is true but (4) false. Caesar could not have recognized as true any sentence in English. However, he would no doubt have recognized an appropriate Latin translation as true. Thus, if the material in single quotes following 'the sentence' in (4) is written in a language known to Caesar, this difficulty is overcome. Even so, it is doubtful that we would accept this analysis as a legitimate rendition of (3). The objects of knowing are to be presumed *extra-linguistic* in some sense, although, of course, what is known must be statable in language. Nontheless, some relation such as *recognizing as true* is no doubt needed in an acceptable analysis of knowing.

Incidentally, 'to recognize as true' is surely not to be equated with 'to know', as is done in Ajdukiewicz's example. To recognize or take some sentence as true is no doubt the same as to *accept* that sentence in some sense. To accept a sentence, which in turn is *true*, is perhaps to know that sentence—in one sense, at least, of 'to know'. However, to recognize or take a sentence as true is clearly not the same as to recognize a sentence that is true.

Ajdukiewicz goes on to suggest a way of overcoming the difficulties noted. To avoid for the moment concern over the descriptive phrase 'the capital of the Republic', let us consider

(3')   'Caesar knew that Rome is situated on the Tiber'

in place of (3). This sentence (3') may be analyzed or "developed," as Ajdukiewicz puts it, as a sentence about *Caesar*, about *Rome*, about the relation of *being situated on*, and about the *Tiber*. Thus

(5)   'Caesar knew about Rome, about the relation of being
        situated on, and about the Tiber, that Rome is situated
        on the Tiber'

is true "if only Caesar recognized as true a sentence in which the main operator denoted [denotes] the relation of being situated on, and the arguments of that operator denoted [denote] Rome and the Tiber respectively." In other words (5) may be regarded as a sentence involving a certain quadratic relation and four arguments. The relation may be written as 'knew-that-Rome-is-situated-on-the-Tiber', the four arguments then being Caesar, Rome, the relation of being situated on, and the Tiber. Hence we may write (5) more accurately as

(6)   'Caesar knew-that-Rome-is-situated-on-the-Tiber of Rome,
        of the relation of being situated on, and of the Tiber'.

Clearly (6) is extensional in the sense that any sentence that results from it by replacing any of the argument expressions by expressions denoting or designating the same objects or relations, has the same truth value as (6). Of course, 'knew-that-Rome-is-situated-on-the-Tiber' is an indivisible expression in which no replacement is grammatically possible.

9. The Admissible Atomic Sentential Forms. Ajdukiewicz's suggestions are of interest, but his method has the disadvantage of involving a vast infinity of unanalyzed relations where only one analyzed one should suffice. Also, his method fails to bring out important syntactical similarities between sentences with essentially the same structure. For example, the sentence

(1)   'Caesar knew that Ostia is situated on the Mediterranean'

clearly has the same grammatical form as (3') of Section 8, differing only in the second and fourth arguments. Hence it is reasonable to think that the "developed" form of (1) likewise should differ from the "developed" form of (3') of Section 8 only in having different arguments. However, the developed form of (1) is

(2)   'Caesar knew-that-Ostia-is-situated-on-the-Mediterranean
         of Ostia, of the relation of being situated on, and of the
         Mediterranean'.

The quadratic relation of knowing-that-Ostia-is-situated-on-the-Mediterranean is a very different relation from that of knowing-that-Rome-is-situated-on-the-Tiber. Taking these two relations as indivisible and as both unanalyzed and even unanalyzable, Ajdukiewicz cannot bring out the obvious similarity between (3') of Section 8 and (1) above in terms of a common relation.

In short, Ajdukiewicz's method does not provide an analysis of knowing in terms of a relation common to all sentences of the form

'*X* knows that - - - - -'.

Rather, he invokes an infinity of relations of the form

'knows-that-so-and-so',

but these relations are not analyzed into their constituents, as they clearly should be. The so and so is surely ingredient in some sense of knowing-so-and-so. How and in what way? To this, no answer is forthcoming. It is to be feared, therefore, that an analysis of knowing in terms of an infinity of unanalyzed relations is not very illuminating.

The question also arises as to whether these relations are all to be regarded as primitives or whether some are to be defined in terms of others. If each is an unanalyzable unit, it is not clear how one could ever be defined in terms of another. Presumably, therefore, they are all unanalyzed primitives, each requiring *ad hoc* some axioms characterizing it.

Let us reflect upon how these difficulties might be avoided. Consider again the sentence (3') of Section 8 and its developed form (5) of Section 8. Ajdukiewicz regards (5) as having the grammatical form exhibited in (6) of Section 8. (6), we recall, involves a quadratic relation of knowing-such-and-such with four arguments. In lieu of this quadratic relation let us use a certain pentadic relation, with the fifth argument being a clause beginning with 'that'. Thus, (5) of Section 8 may be regarded as involving a pentadic relation of knowing (or rather of having known) with the arguments Caesar, Rome, the relation of being situated on, the Tiber, and the "fact" or "circumstance," so to speak, that Rome is situated on the Tiber. Treating (5) of Section 8 in this way, we in effect analyze out, as it were, one of the constituents of the quadratic relation of (6) of Section 8. The question now arises as to how we are to handle the clauses beginning with 'that'. Surely not as propositions nor as facts or circumstances in any literal sense, for it is not clear what such entities are in the sense that we have variables (of any usual kind) ranging over them. (See Chapters VIII and IX below.) We propose, then, to regard the clauses beginning with 'that' as *sentences* of some language system *known at least to us, perhaps to Caesar also.*

Let 'c' designate Caesar, 'r' Rome, 'S' the relation of being situated on, and 't' the Tiber. We may then write the developed form of (5) of Section 8 as

$$(3) \qquad\qquad \text{'c K r,S,t,'rSt''},$$

where 'rSt' expresses that Rome is situated on the Tiber and 'K' reads 'knew'. Similarly, where 'o' designates Ostia and 'm' the Mediterranean, (1) may be developed as

$$(4) \qquad\qquad \text{'c K o,S,m,'oSm''}.$$

The proposal here is to attempt an analysis of knowing and its cognate believing in terms of grammatical forms akin to (3) and (4).

We do not take 'K' as a primitive, however, as has already in effect been suggested above. Rather, it will be defined within a framework provided by pragmatics.

One more preliminary observation should be made. Given a sentence of ordinary language expressing belief, we wish its developed form to be both unique and unambiguous as to truth or falsity. It is to assure this latter that beliefs should be analyzed *maximally*, by bringing out all the structural or grammatical components of the sentence expressing what is believed. To show the need for this, let us consider another example due to Ajdukiewicz, namely,

(5)   'Caesar knew that the capital of the Popes is situated on the Tiber'.

This sentence might be developed as

(6)   'Caesar knew *of the capital of the Popes*, of the relation of being situated on, and of the Tiber, that the capital of the Popes is situated on the Tiber',

or as

why break up the description?

(7)   'Caesar knew *of the relation of being the capital of*, *of the Popes*, of the relation of being situated on, and of the Tiber, that the capital of the Popes is situated on the Tiber'.

Now (6) is presumably true, whereas (7) is false, for Caesar knew nothing whatever about the Popes. We see then that the sentence (5) itself is ambiguous, and we must choose between (6) and (7) as its developed form. (7) clearly affords the deeper analysis of (5) by taking every grammatical component of (5) into account. (7) in fact gives the maximum analysis, if the various constituents, 'capital of', 'the Popes', and so on, are regarded as primitives of the language.

In the general definitions to be given, we shall require always the maximum analysis. When we are dealing with language systems, the primitives may always be given, and hence it will be clear whether or not the maximum analysis is achieved. In the case of a natural language, the situation is more difficult. What are the primitives of a natural language? Well, strictly, it would seem, there are none. However, in a given context or for given purposes, some terms may presumably be picked out and regarded as if they were primitives. Their meaning or behavior is presumably known; they are "good enough" for the purposes at hand. Our analysis would then be relative to those selected terms. A maximum analysis in one context need not then be a maximum analysis in another. Such a relativity is to be expected in connection with natural language, and indeed welcomed in true pragmatic spirit.

It might be objected that the developed form of a sentence expressing belief is often awkward and already represents a departure from natural language. Indeed, it might be claimed that the developed form is no longer one of natural language at all. Form (5) seems natural enough, but (6) and (7) are already *outré*, with a queer ring to them. Part of this is no doubt due to the pleonasm, the repetition of 'capital of', 'the Popes', and so on. Later, some alternative forms will be considered that avoid this repetition. Even so, it is not claimed that the developed form is in any way "natural." The process of developing a sentence rather should be viewed as an attempt to exhibit a suitable *logical form* for it. That such a form departs from ordinary use or usage, then, goes without saying. Indeed, the use of any logical notation whatsoever represents a similar departure. For example, quantifiers, idioms of the form 'for all x' or 'there exists at least one x such that', only rarely if ever occur in ordinary speech in an undisguised way. Nonetheless they are useful in helping to exhibit the logical forms of certain locutions of ordinary speech. So, likewise, with the developed form of a sentence expressing belief. We are to think of it no longer as a sentence of ordinary language but as an out and out departure. It serves as a heuristic, leading us to suitable atomic sentential forms for a logic of belief.

Observe that in forms such as (3) and (4), K is a *hexadic* or six-place relation. Believing and knowing are *not* then to be handled as merely *dyadic* relations, as is so commonly thought. It is interesting that Ajdukiewicz recognized this explicitly. We have already noted that both Russell and Ramsey had done so. The historically first suggestion that belief and related notions are not adequately to be handled in terms of dyadic relations is perhaps to be found as early as 1914 in Russell's *Our Knowledge of the External World*.[13] The suggestion is admirable and has all but been forgotten in the resurgence of interest in Frege, and merits quotation in full.

> The problem of the nature of judgment or belief [Russell writes] may be taken as an example of a problem whose solution depends upon an adequate inventory of logical forms. . . . [T]he supposed universality of the subject-predicate form made it im-

[13] Second edition (New York: W. W. Norton and Co., 1929), pp. 61–62.

possible to give a right analysis of serial order, and therefore made space and time unintelligible. But in this case it was only to admit relations of two terms. The case of judgment [or belief] demands the admission of more complicated forms. If all judgment were true, we might suppose that judgment consisted in apprehension of a fact, and that the apprehension was a relation of a mind to the fact. [See Section 4 above.] From poverty in the logical inventory, this view has often been maintained. But it leads to absolutely insoluble difficulties in the case of error. Suppose I believe that Charles I died in his bed. [Actually he was beheaded in 1649.] There is no objective fact "Charles I's death in his bed" to which I can have a relation of apprehension. Charles I and death and his bed are objective, but they are not, except in my thought, put together as my false belief supposes. It is therefore necessary in analysing a belief, to look for some other logical form than a two-term relation. Failure to realize this necessity has, in my opinion, vitiated almost everything that has been written on the theory of knowledge, making the problem of error insoluble and the difference between belief and perception inexplicable.

If belief is analyzed in terms of a dyadic relation between a person and a fact or proposition, either negative facts or propositions must presumably be admitted to handle error. Such admission seems at best highly artificial and unwarranted. The situation is very different if we separate out one argument of belief as a certain *sentence*. Of course there are negative sentences—given any sentence, its negative is also a sentence. I can well accept 'Charles I died in his bed', or, better, 'Charles I was not beheaded', and hence believe such and such of Charles I, his bed, and so on even though what I believe happens to be false. The problem of error can thus very easily and naturally be handled in terms of such forms as (3) and (4).

Some of what is said in this chapter may seem inconclusive. That we have really taken some steps forward, however, should be clear from the next chapter.

CHAPTER V

On Knowing and Believing

In the preceding chapters some requisites for a logic of belief have been informally explored. Important suggestions made by a number of authors have been examined with a view to adapting those that seem especially appropriate. We have reflected upon the elimination of intensionality as a *sine qua non* for adequate philosophic analysis, and in particular for the logic of belief. It has been remarked that a logic of belief presupposes a pragmatics, which in turn presupposes either a syntax or a semantics (perhaps both). In the present chapter let us first reflect upon the kind of pragmatical underpinnings needed, and then go on to sketch some basic features of the logic of belief as here conceived.

The first task will be the selection of an atomic sentential form or forms for expressing simple sentences of belief, that is, with a form for 'X believes so and so'. Several historically important attempts to characterize the logical form that such sentences exhibit have been examined. Of course, the determination of the atomic sentential forms to be admitted is one of the first steps in the attempt to limn a logic of belief. One form will be settled on here as of special interest, involving explicitly both the objects and condition of belief. Further forms will be introduced as we go on.

Once the atomic sentential forms are selected, however, an enormous task still lies ahead. All manner of sentences must be examined, those involving truth functions, quantifiers, identity, and Russellian descriptions—not only as occurring in the sentences believed (in the conditions of belief) but also in the full sentences reporting beliefs.

This examination leads at once to the study of *patterns* of belief. An exhaustive analysis and classification of all possible patterns cannot be undertaken, for the subject quickly becomes highly technical. Hence we need discuss here only a few rather basic ones.

Beliefs do not occur in isolation but in clusters. And clusters of beliefs are not ordinarily haphazard but exhibit some degree of order or coherence. Indeed, some clusters of beliefs may be said to be *rational* (in the accepted senses of the term), some not. The central task is to try to unearth the characteristics of rational patterns of belief. In getting at these characteristics, we shall find that many kinds of such patterns emerge. It will not be assumed that there is only *one* pattern of rationality. Rather there are many equal claimants to the title, all deserving respect.

In Section 1, some syntactical and semantical technical *preliminaries* are presented. Some notions of *pragmatics* are introduced in Section 2. In Section 3 the distinction between the *objects* and *conditions* of belief is sharply drawn. Some *crucial definitions* are given in Section 4, with some *examples* thereof in Section 5. In Section 6 we reflect upon such "objects" as *unicorns, purple cows,* and *mermaids.* In Section 7 some comments concerning *knowing that one knows* are given. In Section 8 we glance at some *normal acceptance patterns* prior to characterizing some *patterns of rational belief* in Section 9. In Section 10 there is mention in passing of the notion of *degree of rational belief.* In Section 11, finally, we allow the relation of *denotation* to supplant designation as the underlying semantical primitive, with some attendant gain.

1. Syntactical and Semantical Preliminaries. Philosophical theories are expressed in language. To characterize a theory is therefore to unearth the linguistic forms employed. Among such forms are those of logic. Hence, every theory contains a logic as a part. The notions of logic, more particularly of first-order logic, are thus fundamental ingredients in language systems.

Perhaps 'is a member of', in the sense of class or set membership, should be added to the list of logical ingredients. However, whether class or set theory belongs to logic or to mathematics is not too clear.[1] Given a class or set theory of sufficient power, the usual arithmetic of real numbers may be formulated within it, so that mathematics and set theory are, in a rough sense at least, coextensive. Further, they in-

---

[1] See especially Quine's *Set Theory and Its Logic*; also M. Davis, "First-order, Second-order, and Higher-order Systems," an address before the Association for Symbolic Logic, Dec. 27, 1963.

volve notions that seem to belong to higher-order logic. However, many theories may be formulated without presupposing a class theory or higher-order logic. Thus, class or set theory appears less fundamental than first-order logic, since the latter does not involve the notion of class membership.

Some ways of construing formulae of the form '*X* believes so and so' require commitment to sets of classes, others do not. It is of interest to avoid such commitment if possible, not only in connection with nominalism but also with a view to using only such tools as are actually needed. Logical tools and linguistic forms should not be multiplied beyond necessity. Nominalists condone only very restricted, perhaps too restricted, tools. However, keeping tabs as well as not multiplying beyond necessity are fundamental desiderata. One can keep tabs without being a nominalist. If, however, to philosophize is to know what one is doing, one must surely at least keep tabs.

Let us consider as object language some first-order language system *L* of the usual kind. We may suppose this to contain a finite number of nonlogical *predicate constants* as primitives, each of specific degree. Further, we may suppose it to contain a finite number of nonlogical primitive *individual constants* if desired, each designating a distinct individual. It may also contain a symbol for identity as a logical primitive. As variables we have only individual variables ranging over some well-demarcated collection of objects. The variables are to be '*x*', '*y*', '*z*', and so on, with or without numerical subscripts.[2] We have been using the '$\sim$' as the sign for negation throughout and 'V' for disjunction (or alteration), as is customary. The universal quantifiers likewise have been expressed with parentheses and variables in the usual way. The '$\sim$', 'V' and quantifiers, together with '$=$' for identity, are the only special logical symbols we need introduce *primitively*, for all others are forthcoming by definition.

A theory based on *concatenation* may be assumed by way of syntax for *L*. Concatenation, it will be recalled, is the operation of logical *spelling*, as it were. The concatenate of two expressions *a* and *b* is (loosely) the result of writing first *a* and then *b*. This may be symbolized by '$(a \frown b)$' as is customary. We let '*a*', '*b*', and so on, with or without numerical subscripts, be syntactical variables ranging over the expressions of *L*.[3]

To provide the (extensional) semantics of *L*, we may take as primitive for the moment a relation of *designation*, symbolized by

[2] For further details, see *Truth and Denotation*, Chapters II and X.
[3] See again Tarski, *op. cit.*; W. V. Quine, *Mathematical Logic*, pp. 291–305; and *Truth and Denotation*, Chapter III.

'Des'. The object language *L* contains only variables for individuals. It will be convenient for the moment to allow in the semantical metalanguage of *L* not only variables over these same individuals but also variables over properties (in extension) or classes of these individuals and over relations between or among them, as well.[4] The semantical metalanguage for *L* may thus be assumed for the moment to be of *second order*. Let '*F*', '*G*', '*F_1*', '*F_2*', and so on, be the second-order variables. Their degree, that is, the number of arguments they significantly take, need not be specified, for this will always be clear from the context. This rough sketch of the underlying syntax and semantics is all that is required for present purposes.

Several alternative analyses of belief will be suggested as we go on. In particular we cannot rest content with using a second-order semantical metalanguage. (See Chapters VI through X below.) Nonetheless, for two reasons, it will be of interest *pro tem* to use such a metalanguage. Higher-order metalanguages seem commonly presupposed and used by most philosophic analysts. Secondly, we wish to present a kind of "rational reconstruction" of the views of Ajdukiewicz, Ramsey, Russell, and others already discussed. The most direct way seems to be via a second-order metalanguage. Later we shall see that such a metalanguage can be avoided altogether, with many resulting advantages.

2. Acceptance. The analysis of belief cannot be given only within a syntax or semantics, as has been noted. Fundamental reference must be made to the human user of the language, and such reference takes us at once into pragmatics.

A pragmatics for *L* of the following kind is to be employed. Let *a* be some sentence of *L* that we, as an experimenter *E* (or experimenters), wish to *test* in certain ways. In particular, we wish to test whether a person *X reacts* to this sentence in such a way as to lead us to think that he *accepts* this sentence at the time. We assume for the present that *X* knows the language *L*, at least well enough for present purposes. Let

$$\text{'}a\ \text{Tst}_E\ X,t\text{'}$$

express that the sentence *a* of *L* is *put to the test* at time *t* by the experimenter *E*. *E* might *ask X* whether he, *X*, (1) accepts *a* or (2) regards *a* as true, or (3) is disposed to regard *a* as true, or (4) gives *a* a high degree of probability or confirmation on the basis

[4] For details, here likewise see *Truth and Denotation*.

of evidence known to X, or (5) is disposed to give such, or (6) is willing to base his actions on a, or the like. Or (7) E may merely observe X's behavior over a long time perhaps and under varying circumstances in order to decide whether X acts as though he, X, regards a as true. In various such ways, perhaps all or some of them together, would E test a relative to X at time t. If E notes that in fact X answers 'Yes' to the questions (1)–(6), or the like, or concludes under (7) that X in fact does act as though he accepts a at t, he, E, may state his result by writing

$$\text{'}X \text{ Acpt}_E \, a,t\text{'}.$$

The pragmatical metalanguage to be employed for the analysis of belief is to be built around the two notions 'Tst' and 'Acpt' taken as primitives. Each of these is assumed to be characterized experimentally somewhat in the fashion suggested. Two new types of variables are introduced, 'X', 'Y', and so on, for human beings, and 't', 't_1', and so on, for time stretches. We then need also a simple theory of time flow, akin somewhat to that of Woodger.[5]

The notions 'Tst' and 'Acpt' are akin to notions required in behavioral science. Acceptance is surely of interest to the behavioral scientist, and it is to him that we would wish to turn for its more exact characterization. No doubt there is a multitude of cognate characterizations, many of which would be suitable for present purposes. Acceptance and allied notions, such as cognitive preference and even quantitative cognitive preference, howsoever characterized, do seem to be suitable notions to be taken primitively—as is done, for example, with related notions in the von Neumann-Morgenstern theory of utility.[6] If we take a term as primitive, we do not cease to be interested in its further analysis. However, rather than seek an explicit definition, we try to characterize it implicitly by formulating a theory on its basis. The analysis then proceeds by using the theory and determining the extent to which it is adequate for this or that intended purpose.

Clearly only *sentences* of L are under test or accepted. Also, if a is under test at some temporal part of t relative to X, and at every temporal part of t at which a is under such test X reacts affirmatively to a, E is then surely justified in concluding that X accepts a during the whole time interval t.

Suppose, however, a is not under test relative to X during some

[5] See Woodger, *op. cit.*

[6] J. von Neumann and O. Morgenstern, *Theory of Games and Economic Behavior*, Second Edition (Princeton: Princeton University Press, 1947).

temporal part of t. E might still wish to say that X accepts a at t, there being no grounds to the contrary. a might have been under test relative to X at some earlier time. Thus it might be required also that X Acpt$_E$ a,t if there is some time t_1 prior to t such that a Tst$_E$ X,t_1 and for every time t_2, which is a part of t_1 or t or is between t_1 and t, if a Tst$_E$ X,t_2 then X Acpt$_E$ a,t_2.

Should we require that X does *not* accept a sentence at t if it has not been under test at a part of t or prior to t? Presumably E might have other grounds for concluding that X accepts a at t. Perhaps a is sufficiently similar to other sentences b such that X Acpt$_E$ b,t. Or a might be accepted by most members of X's social group, where there are no grounds for thinking that X differs from the group in this respect. Thus, to require that every accepted sentence be, or has been, under test seems too strong.

The full logic of testing and acceptance is of course a big topic, and one that we have scarcely begun to explore. Yet, it is surely fundamental to the logic of belief as well as to the philosophy and methodology of science. Science after all determines the acceptability of a proposed hypothesis or principle in part by means of appropriate tests. Sometimes these tests are simple and direct; sometimes they are highly involved and indirect. Let us think of aceptance throughout in the sense in which a scientist, in his official work, may be said to accept a given observation sentence or theoretical hypothesis. In the former case the scientist may accept the sentence directly as a result of immediate observation or indirectly by means of some experiment or by the use of instruments or the like. In the case of a theoretical hypothesis, the sentence is accepted more on trust or faith, as it were. It is posited as a premiss for explanations and predictions, but the trust may be withdrawn at any time should its explanatory or predictive power be found wanting.

Occasionally we may wish later to refer to an *inscription* of an expression. Expressions throughout are to be regarded as *sign designs* or *shapes* rather than *sign events* or inscriptions.[7] Clearly, however, the primitives 'Tst' and 'Acpt' seem more appropriate when applied to inscriptions than to shapes. It is an actual inscription that is under test at a given time and an actual inscription that is assented to or recognized-as-true. Hence, 'X Acpt$_E$ a,t' may be taken to express that, according to E, X accepts at t an inscription of the shape a. And similarly for 'Tst'. We have chosen shapes rather than inscriptions as the values for the syntactical variables here because they are easier to deal with. The syntax of shapes is much simpler in relevant

---

[7] See especially *Truth and Denotation*, Chapters XI and XII.

respects than the syntax of inscriptions. Nevertheless, 'Tst' and 'Acpt' can be reinterpreted in the manner suggested. In this way full justice is done to inscriptions in terms of the simpler syntax of shapes.

3. "Objects" and "Conditions." The individuals, classes, and relations about which there is belief are called '*the objects of belief*'. These have already been mentioned as item (f) in Chapter IV, Section 3. That which is believed about them is called 'the *condition of the belief*'. The condition must always, it would seem, be a linguistic expression or at least something very intimately asociated with a linguistic expression. This is item (a) of the list in Chapter IV, Section 3. The objects of belief, on the other hand, may be of many kinds and from many kinds of subject matter. For a given *L,* the objects in their totality comprise all objects of *L* about which anyone has ever believed anything—insofar as this anything is expressible in *L*. In similar vein there are *objects* and *conditions* of knowledge.

There are indeed objects of belief and conditions of belief, but strictly speaking there are no beliefs. There are no special entities recognized as beliefs that are supposed to populate some mental, conceptual, or logical space. There are no beliefs in the sense that they constitute the range of some separate set of variables. Belief here is to be analyzed in terms of *believing,* and believing is handled as a certain kind of complex *relation.* Similar comments may be made about knowledge and knowing.

In analyzing belief and knowledge in terms of objects, conditions, designation, testing, and acceptance, we are in effect separating the ontological, logical, semantical, pragmatical, and experimental factors involved. All of these ingredients appear essential, and it is by no means clear that any one could be left out. Indeed it would not be desirable to do so. As with most notions of any philosophic interest, there is a specific logic to be explored, the "logical geography" of that notion, as it were, as well as the experimental basis for it. The task of philosophic analysis is in large part to separate clearly the various ingredients and to attempt to formulate the kind of "logic" needed.

The following two abbreviations will be useful. Let

(1)   '$b_1,...,b_n$ DistPrimPredConsLRa'

be defined within the syntax of *L* to express the following: $b_1, \ldots, b_n$ are all primitive predicate constants distinct among themselves; each occurs at least once in the expression a; every primitive predicate constant occurring in a is b_1 or $b_2, \ldots,$ or b_n, and $b_1, \ldots, b_n$

are taken in the order of their first occurrence in a. (1) may thus be read '$b_1, \ldots, b_n$ are just the distinct primitive predicate constants of a taken in the order of left to right occurrence in a (omitting repetitions)'. Similarly, let

(2)   '$c_1,\ldots,c_k$ DistPrimInConsLR a'

express that $c_1, \ldots, c_k$ are just the distinct primitive individual constants of a taken in the order of left to right occurrence in a (omitting repetitions), in analogous fashion. It is clear that these two notations will be helpful in spelling out the primitive predicate and individual constants occurring in sentences known or believed, and thus in helping to achieve the maximum analysis mentioned in Chapter IV, Section 9.

    4. Some General Definitions. A general definition for belief may now be introduced, with the time reference and the objects and condition of the belief made explicit.

    Let a be a sentence of L, consisting of just one occurrence of a primitive one-place predicate constant followed by an occurrence of an individual constant. We can then let

(1)   '$X \, \mathrm{B}_E \, F,x,a,t$'

express that $X \, \mathrm{Acpt}_E \, a,t$ where the sentence a consists of some predicate constant b designating F followed by some individual constant c designating x. Expression (1) may conveniently be read 'Person X believes of F and of x at t that so and so'. The individual x and the class F here are the objects and a is the condition of the belief.

    More generally,

(2)   '$X \, \mathrm{B}_E \, F_1,\ldots,F_n,x_1,\ldots,x_k,a,t$'

may be regarded as an abbrevation for

    'a is a sentence of L (in primitive notation) such that $X \, \mathrm{Acpt}_E \, a,t$, and there are expressions $b_1, \ldots, b_n, c_1, \ldots, c_k$ such that $b_1 \, \mathrm{Des} \, F_1$, $b_2 \, \mathrm{Des} \, F_2$, $\ldots$, $b_n \, \mathrm{Des} \, F_n$, $c_1 \, \mathrm{Des} \, x_1$, $c_2 \, \mathrm{Des} \, x_2$, $\ldots$, $c_k \, \mathrm{Des} \, x_k$, $b_1,\ldots,b_n \, \mathrm{DistPrimPredConsLR} \, a$, and $c_1,\ldots,c_k \, \mathrm{DistPrimInConsLR} \, a$', for $n \geq 0$ and $k \geq 0$.

    Expression (2) may be read as 'Person X (at time t) believes (according to E) of the classes or relations $F_1, \ldots, F_n$ and of the individuals $x_1, \ldots, x_k$ that a holds'.

might not This mean $E \, B_E \ulcorner X \, B_E \, F_{1,\ldots,}F_n, x_1, \ldots x_k, a, t \urcorner$

For the definition of the cognate locution 'X (at time t) *knows* (according to E) of the properties of relations $F_1, \ldots, F_n$, and of the individuals $x_1, \ldots, x_k$ that a holds', the semantical truth concept must be employed. Let 'Tr a' express that a is *true* in L. The exact definition of this may be given within the underlying semantics. We may then define

'$X \ K_E \ F_1,\ldots,F_n,x_1,\ldots,x_k,a,t$' as '$X \ B_E \ F_1,\ldots,F_n,x_1,\ldots,x_k,a,t$
and Tr a', for $n \geq 0$ and $k \geq 0$.

Note that no restrictions have been placed upon the sentence a, which may be of any complexity. Further, a may contain quantifiers but no abbreviations.

It is not claimed that these definitions are materially adequate in the sense of being in accord with *all* uses of 'knows' and 'believes' in ordinary language. However, they are surely in accord with at least some of the normal or principal uses. This cannot be proved or verified in the absence of clear-cut experimental conditions under which we could determine what the normal or principal uses are. The presumption, however, is certainly in the positive. At the very least it would seem that our ordinary uses can be harmonized or brought into accord with these more technically developed forms. (We need not consider further here the difficult matter of the exact relationship between a sentence of ordinary language expressing belief and its developed form. See Chapter XII, Section 10.)

The reader may object that these definitions do after all presuppose notions of testing and acceptance as primitives and that they are as obscure as that of belief itself. However, both 'Acpt' and 'Tst' are presumed to have clear experimental meanings attached to them, and of course *some* primitives, for which usually alternative interpretations are possible, are needed for any system of applied logic. If those selected, in one or more of the suggested interpretations, should not turn out to be wholly satisfactory in the light of subsequent research, let better ones be forthcoming, in terms of which 'Tst' and 'Acpt' will perhaps be definable. Meanwhile it should be recognized parenthetically that these or allied notions play a crucial role in the logical analysis of experimental method and thus are needed in methodology anyhow. If we can use them in the logic of belief also, this is surely to the good.

It seems commonly agreed that knowing differs from believing by involving truth. The condition of the belief is presumed to be true. Now 'true' is surely to be handled in terms of the semantical truth concept, for no other satisfactory meaning seems to have been put forward.

Still another factor is often thought to be needed for the analysis of belief and knowing, namely, that for X to believe such and such he must have *adequate grounds* for it also; more specifically, that X must accept some sentence or sentences constituting adequate grounds for the condition of the belief. What, however, are adequate grounds? Adequate subjectively according to X? Or according to E? Or in some intersubjective or objective sense? To give adequate grounds for the condition of a belief is, at any event, to answer a question as to *why* one believes so and so. The answer is then presumably that one believes so and so *because of* such and such, in one sense of 'because'. For example, I may believe that it is now raining because you told me, or because I looked out the window to see, and so on. My reason may or may not be adequate, but merely to state *simpliciter* that I believe it is raining is not always surely to involve a reason, let alone an adequate one. Ordinary language is no doubt ambiguous on the point. The above definition is intended to capture, to some extent at least, the ordinary meaning *simpliciter*. For the notion *believes because of* and on adequate objective grounds, some notions of inductive logic would presumably be needed.

Of course there is the possibility that X might accept a sentence a, casually or as a sheer guess, and the sentence might happen to be true. We would perhaps then not wish to say that he has genuine knowledge, but has simply made a lucky guess. Whether E would say in this case that X has knowledge depends of course upon how 'Acpt' is interpreted. If X merely guesses, E might not regard X as genuinely accepting a. E himself tests X under controlled conditions, and might well rule out lucky guesses and the like. To rule these cases out, E would no doubt use the *because of* idiom, and then X's inadequate grounds for accepting a would come to light.

5. Some Examples. As examples of the general definition given of 'B', let us consider a few cases involving simple sentences of the object language containing only one-place predicates. Let these predicates be, for the present, 'P', 'Q', and 'R'.

For E to say that person X believes (at t) of P that every object has P or does not have P (that is, that X believes one form of the law of excluded middle), is for E to say that

(1) $X \, B_E \, P, '(x)(Px \lor {\sim}Px)', t.$

E here of course uses '${\sim}$', '$\lor$', and the quantifier in their normal senses to express one form of the law of excluded middle. E is presumed to be conversant with (that is, knows or speaks or at least is familiar with the syntactical and semantical rules of) both the object language L and its syntactical and semantical metalanguages. Hence E can formulate the form of the law of excluded middle under discussion in the notation of L, and it is this form that he tests relative to X.

If X knows the language L, it follows from (1) that X accepts '$(x)(Px \lor \sim Px)$' at t. However, we need not presuppose always that X knows L. Of course X might not recognize this sentence to be a form of the law of excluded middle, nor need he even take '$\sim$', '$\lor$', or '(x)' in their proper senses. If he, X, knows L, E may well be interested in determining whether X's acceptances and beliefs satisfy certain conditions or patterns of *normalcy* for '$\sim$' or '$\lor$' and the like.

If X *does* not know L, the experimenter E can instruct him sufficiently at least for him, E, to decide whether X accepts '$(x)(Px \lor \sim Px)$' or not. It is reasonable to assume here that E can communicate with X in some language that both can use and understand, enough at least for this purpose. It is reasonable also to allow E to be able to say that X accepts a sentence a of L, even where X himself does not know L and hence could not recognize a as true.

That X believes (at t) that every object that has P has Q may be expressed (by E) by

(2) $\qquad\qquad$ '$X \ B_E \ P,Q,'(x)(\sim Px \lor Qx)',t$'.

Recall that for significance E must always spell out the nonlogical primitive predicates in the sentence under consideration in their left to right order of first occurrence, the sentence itself being wholly in primitive notation. Hence E must express that all P's are Q's by '$(x)(\sim Px \lor Qx)$', not (as is more usual) by '$(x)(Px \supset Qx)$', which would contain a defined, albeit a logical, symbol. X may or may not be familiar with the usual definition of '$\supset$' in terms of '$\sim$' and '$\lor$'.

Note that (2) might obtain whereas X might not B_E at t of Q and of P that '$(x)(Qx \lor \sim Px)$' holds. X might not be familiar with the commutative law for disjunction. If he is and accepts it, E may establish therewith a certain pattern concerning X's beliefs.

Consider now a sentence containing *no* primitive nonlogical predicate or individual constants, that is, where both n and k of the general definition are 0. '$(x)x = x$' would be such a sentence, '$=$' being regarded as a primitive logical constant of L. Hence,

(3) $\qquad\qquad$ '$X \ B_E \ '(x)x = x',t$'

merely reduces to

$\qquad\qquad$ '$X \ \text{Acpt}_E \ '(x)x = x',t$'.

Belief in statements of L that do not contain any nonlogical primitives reduces to mere acceptance. That this is a "natural" state of affairs may be seen as follows, at least to some extent.

We have distinguished above the objects and the conditions of belief. Some beliefs may well be such as to have no objects. The objects of course are designated by the primitive individual constants or denoted by the one-place predicate constants. If no such constants now occur in the condition of belief, there are strictly no "objects" of the belief. Of course *quantifiers* may occur in the condition of belief and these quantifiers range over the objects of L. This, however, is quite another matter. We see then that the conditions of belief are in this sense more fundamental than the objects: no beliefs without a condition, but we may well have beliefs without objects.

Let 'a' be a primitive individual constant of L. That X believes of P and of the individual a at t that a has P is expressed by

$$\text{'}X \text{ B}_E \text{ P,a,'Pa'},t\text{'}.$$

Other beliefs concerning P and a are expressed by appropriately varying the condition. Thus,

$$\text{'}X \text{ B}_E \text{ P,a,'}(\sim (x)Px \lor Pa)\text{'},t\text{'}$$

expresses that X believes at t of P and a a certain instance of a logical law of quantification.

Among the objects of belief we need not always include a property or class. For example,

$$\text{'}X \text{ B}_E \text{ a,'a} = \text{a'},t\text{'}$$

expresses that X believes at t (according to E) of the object a that it is self-identical.

That the conditions of belief are regarded as more fundamental than the objects might be thought objectionable, particularly, perhaps, because (in the case of a belief without objects) acceptance and belief telescope into one. This circumstance may readily be circumvented, however, by regarding '$=$' as a *nonlogical* rather than a logical primitive. Which '$=$' should be regarded is not too clear anyhow, and there seem to be no compelling reasons for regarding it as one or the other. Thus, in place of (3) we might write

$$\text{'}X \text{ B}_E = \text{,'}(x)x = x\text{'},t\text{'},$$

Identity Law

NB

wherein an object of belief, the dyadic relation of identity, is forthcoming. All conditions of belief are then such as to involve objects. Hence in this second mode of treatment, conditions of belief are not regarded as more fundamental than their objects.

Leaving this special case aside, we should note a significant crucial difference between acceptance and belief on other grounds. Acceptance may be characterized without using any notions of semantics, whereas belief depends fundamentally upon designation (or some other semantical notion). On the other hand, both are notions of pragmatics, the one within a pragmatics presupposing only a syntax, the other within a pragmatics presupposing the fuller resources of a semantics. Acceptance, we might say, is a *pragmatico-syntactical* notion, belief a *pragmatico-semantical* one. The difference between syntax and semantics is thus at stake here for anyone who fails to note the difference between acceptance and belief. Moreover, acceptance is like direct quotation, believing and knowing being more like indirect quotation. (See Chapter IX, Section 4.)

Davidson would agree p 203

Ramsey's comments, noted in Chapter IV, Section 4, that belief may be handled as a many-place relation that "may . . . result from the combination of dual relations" is substantiated in part by the feasibility of definition (2). Although not strictly just a combination of "duals," a notation for belief is seen to be definable in terms of other specified relations. Acpt is not dyadic, but Des is. The remainder, needed for the definitions of 'DistPrimPredConLR' and 'DistPrimInConLR', are either dyadic or triadic.

6. Of Unicorns, Purple Cows, and Mermaids. Let 'U' ('unicorn') be a primitive predicate constant of *L,* and let the null class, Λ, be introduced as the class of all non-self-identical objects. 'U' is of course a primitive nonlogical predicate of *L,* 'Λ' being a defined logical one. *X* may then well believe of the class of unicorns U that all U's are U's without believing that all Λ's are Λ's, or without believing of U that all U's are Λ's or that all Λ's are U's.

Let 'P' be a primitive predicate of *L* designating the class of purple objects, and let 'C' be an additional one designating the class of cows. *X* may well believe of P and C that all P's that are C's, that is, all purple cows, are purple cows, without believing of P, C, and U that all P's that are C's are also U's, that is, that all purple cows are unicorns.

It is desirable that we have a full identity law within the logic of belief, an instance of which is as follows:

If $F = G$, then $X \, B_E \, F,a,t$ if and only if $X \, B_E \, G,a,t$.

Let 'M' ('mermaid') and 'S' ('swims in the sea') be further distinct primitive predicate constants. Then, of course, we should have that

(3)   If $M = U$, then $X\,B_E\,M,S,'(x)\,(\sim Mx \vee Sx)',t$ if and only if $X\,B_E\,U,S,'(x)\,(\sim Mx \vee Sx)',t$.

Now, clearly, X might well believe of the class of mermaids and of the class of things that swim in the sea, that all mermaids swim in the sea without believing of unicorns and of things that swim in the sea that all *unicorns* swim in the sea. However, note that law (3) does not require this to be otherwise. The second clause containing 'B' properly states only that X believes of U and of S that all M's are S's. Because U and M are in fact the same class, law (3) should be acceptable.

Still, the form

(4)   'X B_E U,S, '$(x)\,(\sim Mx \vee Sx)$',t'

seems a little strange. Clearly 'M' Des U, so that the form is meaningful according to the definition of 'B'. The reading 'X believes of unicorns and of things that swim that all mermaids swim', however, seems strange and unnatural, perhaps not even meaningful in ordinary language. The reading appears less unnatural, however, if we reflect that it is the *class* U of objects being referred to, and that as a matter of fact this class is null, and further that it is identical with the class of mermaids. After all, a rose by any other name is still a rose. Further, it should be remembered that it is the experimenter E who speaks the strange form (4) and that E presumably knows that U and M are the same class, even though X perhaps does not. The form (4) is thus not at all unnatural for E, nor is it for X, if X in fact also knows that $U = M$.

It seems, however, that forms such as (4) could be avoided altogether if we require that no two distinct primitive predicates of L designate the same class or relation. We then could not have two distinct primitives 'M' and 'U' designating the same class. In practice this requirement is desirable to avoid duplication among the primitive predicates.

Note that although the class of purple cows is in fact the same as the class of mermaids, it does not follow that whatever X believes of purple things and of cows, he believes also of mermaids. Here we should need the forms

(5)   'X B_E P,C,a,t'

as well as

(6)   '$X \, B_E \, M,a,t$'.

We cannot pass from one to the other of these, however, by any such
law as (3), for (5) involves two arguments, 'P' and 'C', whereas (6)
involves only one, 'M'. Thus for a given a, at least one of (5) or (6)
is meaningless, and in the law (3) each occurrence of 'B' must have the
same number of arguments. We recall that all the *primitive* predicate
constants occuring in the condition of the belief must be spelled out
in order to gain the maximum analysis, so that 'P,C' in (5) cannot
be replaced by an expression for the logical product of P and C if a
contains two primitive predicate constants. Nor could 'M' in (6) be
replaced by 'P,C' or by an expression for the logical product of P and
C if a contains only one primitive predicate constant.

What happens here to Ajdukiewicz' example about what Newton
knew? How can formulae of the form

'Newton knew that $x = 8$'

be handled? If we "develop" this as

'Newton knew of x and of 8 that $x = 8$',

a form results essentially like that suggested by Quine. Quine's 'believes
'. . . y . . .' satisfied by' becomes here 'knows '. . . y . . .' satisfied by'. This might be symbolized as

'$X \, K_E \, x,8,'x = 8',t$',

which in turn is of the form

'$X \, K_E \, x,8,a,t$',

where a is a sentential function containing at least one free variable.
This in turn might be analyzed by saying (roughly, and assuming for
the moment that '=' and '8' are primitive constants of L) that there
is a b, a c, and a d such that b Des x, c is a variable, a is a sentential
function consisting of c concatenated with '=' concatenated with '8',
d is a sentence consisting of b followed by '=' followed by '8', and
$X \, \text{Acpt}_E \, d,t$. However, there is a difficulty in this analysis. Suppose
that $x = y$ and that $X \, K_E \, x,8,a,t$. Then, by a well-entrenched law of
logic it should always follow that $X \, K_E \, y,8,a,t$. This, however, clearly

does *not* obtain, as we know from the example of Ajdukiewicz (Chapter IV, Section 8) about what Newton knew.[8] In the analysis suggested, where the condition of belief is a *sentence* rather than a sentential function containing a free variable, this difficulty does not arise.

In addition to the identity, extensionality, or replacement laws already mentioned, the following general forms may be noted:

Extensional Replacement

If $F_i = F_{n+1}$ and $X\ B_E\ F_1,...,F_i,...,F_n,x_1,...,x_k,a,t$, then $X\ B_E$ $F_1,...,F_{i-1},F_{n+1},F_{i+1}...,F_n,x_1,...,x_k,a,t$,

If $x_i = x_{k+1}$ and $X\ B_E\ F_1,...,F_n,x_1,...,x_{i-1},x_i,x_{i+1},...,x_k,a,t$ then $X\ B_E\ F_1,...,F_n,x_1,...,x_{i-1},x_{k+1},x_{i+1},...,x_k,a,t$,

If $a = b$ and $X\ B_E\ F_1,...,F_n,x_1,...,x_k,a,t$, then $X\ B_E\ F_1,..., F_n,x_1,...,x_k,b,t$.

Of course, analogous laws where '$X = Y$', '$t = t_1$', or '$E = E_1$' obtain as hypotheses. Corresponding laws with 'K' in place of 'B' also obtain.

It might be questioned whether full identity or extensionality laws of these kinds should hold. In fact some logicians have been willing to abandon them. That they should hold, however, is regarded here as a *sine qua non* of any adequate theory of belief. This point, it will be recalled, was raised in Chapter IV, Section 8. Why such laws should obtain everywhere else in logic and science but suddenly be abandoned in the discussion of belief, as some would have it, is by no means clear. The theory of belief should be of a piece with the rest of science. That it is not generally so regarded is an occasion for alarm. In any event, the abandonment of full identity laws in theories of belief surely requires an independent defense that has not been supplied.

7. On Knowing that One Knows. In separating sharply object and metalanguages, we cannot handle such forms as 'X knows (or believes) that X knows (or believes) that - - -' or 'X knows (or believes) that Y knows (or believes) that - - -', and so on, except by going up one level in the hierarchy of languages. Only in a similar vein can we handle the idiom 'it is true that it is true that - - -'. The need for the hierarchy of languages is forced upon us by the theory of truth in semantics, and it is doubtful that we can do any better in this respect

---

[8] It is not clear, incidentally, how Quine's 'believes '. . . y . . .' satisfied by' would be protected from this difficulty without giving up the principle of the substitutivity of identity, at least in its general form.

in the analysis of believing and knowing. Nor is it clear that we should wish to.

Simple statements to the effect that X believes so and so are thus sharply to be distinguished from statements to the effect that X believes that Y believes so and so. Consider

> 'X believes at t_1 that Y believes at t_2 that so and so'.

Here clearly *two* time parameters are needed. Also, X and Y may or may not be the same person. If this form is "developed" à la Ajdukiewicz, we would gain, as a first approximation, something of the following sort:

> 'X believes at t_1 of Y, of the relation of believing, and of t_2, that Y believes at t_2 of such and such objects that so and so.'

Hence, knowing that one knows is clearly a much more elaborate notion than mere knowing, and it thus will simply not do to assimilate it under the latter, as Hintikka does.[9] Strictly, we should distinguish the general form

> 'X knows (or believes) at t (according to E) of Y, of the relation of believing, of t', and of E', that Y knows (or believes) at t' (according to E') of such and such objects that so and so',

and then note several special cases of it.

From the point of view of natural language, especially interesting among these cases are those in which we part from the third person. Thus the idioms 'I know that I know - - -', 'I know that you know - - -', 'You know that I know - - -', and so on, will all have special and interesting properties. Much would depend here upon the handling of such words as 'I' and 'you'. Perhaps such words can be handled as elliptic Russellian descriptions. 'I' may be short for 'the speaker', 'you' for 'the person addressed', or for some other suitable descriptions. A discussion of this topic, however, would lead us afield, into natural language, or at least into a system considerably more complicated than the L's under consideration. (See Chapter XII, Section 10.)

[9] J. Hintikka, *Knowledge and Belief* (New York: Cornell University Press, Ithaca, 1962), especially pp. 103 ff. See Chapter XI, Section 9, below.

8. Normal Acceptance Patterns. In *Toward a Systematic Pragmatics,* several different kinds of patterns were put forward depending upon X's acceptances at a given time. Let us glance at a few of these preparatory to describing some similar patterns for belief.

Consider some class of sentences of L in which the experimenter E is especially interested. In particular E wishes to find out which sentences of this class X accepts or not at a given time. To determine this, E will experiment or observe under more or less controlled laboratory conditions. He will not wish to state his results *a priori* nor will he wish to impose answers upon X in advance.

Let the class (or *virtual* class, if one prefers—see the next chapter) of sentences under consideration be D. D in other words is the class (or virtual class) of all sentences a such that X Tst_E a,t. D may contain certain sentences together with their negations. Suppose this is the case. Suppose also that for all a, where both a and its negative are members of D, E finds that X accepts a at t if and only if X does *not* accept the negative of a. Under these circumstances E may say that D exhibits a *normal acceptance pattern* for the sign of negation '$\sim$' (relative of course to X at t). In other words, X's acceptances at t of members of D are in accord with the "logically correct" use of '$\sim$' to express negation.

Let us consider now the notion of a *normal acceptance* pattern for the sign '$\vee$' of disjunction. Suppose D contains some sentences a and b together with the disjunctions of such. Suppose also that for any such sentences a and b, X Acpt_E a,t or X Acpt_E b,t if and only if X accepts (according to E) the disjunction of a and b at t. We say then that D exhibits a *normal acceptance pattern* for '$\vee$' as the sign of disjunction for X at t.

It might be thought that this notion of a normal acceptance is not "normal" for the following reason. It might be thought normal for X to accept the disjunction of a sentence a with the negation of a (a form of the law of excluded middle, after all) without accepting either a or its negation. This objection, however, makes use of negation. Suppose D is such as to exhibit also a normal acceptance pattern for '$\sim$' relative to X at t. Surely it is then normal for X to accept a or not to accept a at t, and hence for him to accept a or to accept the negation of a. If the latter, then surely it is normal for him to accept the disjunction of a with its negation. Conversely, the situation appears more dubious. If, however, it is normal for X to accept a or not to accept a, then it is surely normal for him to do this if he accepts the disjunction of a with the negation of a. So at least where D exhibits a normal acceptance pattern with respect to '$\sim$', the suggested pattern for '$\vee$' seems normal also.

Logical theory as grounds of justification.

There are actually *three* patterns of normalcy for 'V' that should be distinguished here, not just one. By breaking up the 'if and only if' into two conditionals, two additional patterns are gained, the third being the one defined. Also, there are three patterns of normalcy for '~'.

In a similar vein let us go on to explore other normal patterns that X's acceptances might exhibit. They might exhibit patterns in accord with logical rules of inference such as *Modus Ponens*. X might also accept all the laws of logic (under test at the time) or all the laws of some science with which he is familiar. Many different kinds of patterns should be discriminated here, including some based upon the abbreviatory definitions within L, which would be of use in classifying X's acceptances.

Especially important among these patterns are some that depend on *equivalence* and *L-equivalence*. Following Carnap, we say that sentences a and b are equivalent if and only if they are both Tr or both false. Likewise, sentences a and b are L-equivalent (logically or analytically equivalent) if and only if the sentence consisting of '(' followed by a followed by '≡' (the sign for the biconditional) followed by b followed by ')' is itself *analytically* or *logically true*.

Let us consider now the following formulae:

(1)   If *a* is equivalent with *b* and X Acpt$_E$ a,t, then
           X Acpt$_E$ b,t.

see next page

(2)   If *a* is L-equivalent with *b* and X Acpt$_E$ a,t, then
           X Acpt$_E$ b,t.

Quite obviously (1) does not hold in general, although of course it may for special a, b, X, and t. It is surely *reasonable* for (1) to hold and if it does for a given X, for all a, b, and t, we should no doubt think that X's acceptances exhibited some degree of normalcy. Of any two equivalent sentences, if X accepts one he always accepts the other. Even if X is not familiar with the notion of equivalence, we should still regard his acceptances normal if they satisfied (1).

If (1) holds for all sentences a and b in some class of sentences D under consideration at the time, we shall say that D exhibits a *normal acceptance pattern for equivalence* relative to X and t.

(2) is perhaps a better candidate for a law, but of course it need not hold in general. Here again, if it were to hold, for all a, b, and t, we would think X eminently reasonable in this respect. We would no doubt think that X's acceptances are in some sense justified. Here again, X might not be explicitly familiar with the notion of

* Just because a sentence agrees with another in Truth Value, in accepting one (as true) it is reasonable to accept the other for we desire to enlarge the class of our true beliefs!

L-equivalence, but if his acceptances accorded with (2), we should recognize in them a certain pattern of normalcy. If (2) holds for all sentences a and b in some class D, we say that D exhibits a *normal acceptance pattern for L-equivalence,* relative to X at t.

This is important

In a way it is desirable that (1) and (2) hold, desirable both for X and for E and for us. It is desirable for X so that his acceptances may accord with the proper use of the notions of logic. It is also desirable for us, that is, for E also, who presumably know the syntactical and semantical rules of L and wish L to be used correctly. However, whether (1) or (2) do hold actually of X is of course quite another matter, one for observation or experiment to decide.

More interesting than (1) is perhaps the following:

NB

Yes!

(3)   If $X \, \mathrm{Acpt}_E \, c,t$, where c is the sentence expressing the equivalence of sentences a and b (that is, c is the sentence consisting of '(' followed by a followed by '$\equiv$' followed by b followed by ')'), and $X \, \mathrm{Acpt}_E \, a,t$, then $X \, \mathrm{Acpt}_E \, b,t$.

Surely if this holds, for all a, b, c, and t, we would, again, think X reasonable in this respect. Here provision is made for X explicitly to be familiar with the notion of equivalence.

To make provision for X explicitly to be familiar with the notion of L-equivalence requires going up one step in the hierarchy of languages. This, however, can be done without difficulty at any point if desired. (See Section 7 above.)

Finally let us consider again *Modus Ponens*. Let D contain some sentences a, b, and c where c is the sentence '(' followed by a followed by '$\supset$' for the material conditional followed by b followed by ')'. If for any such a, b, and c in D, if $X \, \mathrm{Acpt}_E \, a,t$ and $X \, \mathrm{Acpt}_E \, c,t$ then also $X \, \mathrm{Acpt}_E \, b,t$, then D exhibits a *normal acceptance pattern for Modus Ponens* relative to X and t. Under such a pattern, whenever X accepts

Interpretation of Pattern

the two premises of a *Modus Ponens* kind of inference he also accepts the logically correct conclusion. Even if X is not explicitly familiar with this logical rule, his acceptance behavior accords with it.

Or consider the relation of *logical consequence,* as based upon *Modus Ponens* and the Rule of Generalization in quantification theory. Let '$a \, \mathrm{LC} \, D$', where D is some class of sentences, express that a is a logical consequence of members of D, that is, that a is obtainable in a finite number of *Modus Ponens* or Generalization steps starting with members of D plus logical axioms. Another pattern of normalcy is to the effect that for all a and b, if $X \, \mathrm{Acpt}_E \, b,t$ and $a \, \mathrm{LC} \, \{b\}$, then $X \, \mathrm{Acpt}_E \, a,t$ also, where $\{b\}$ is the class whose only member is b.

Still another normalcy pattern is as follows. Let D now be some class of sentences of L accepted by X at t, and let D' be the class of all logical consequences of members of D. We require then also that X accept at t all members of D'. In other words we say that D' exhibits a *normal pattern for logical consequence upon the basis of D* for X at t (according to E) if and only if X Acpt_E a,t, for all a in D, for all b if $b\,\text{LC}\,D$ then X Acpt_E b,t, and D' is the class of logical consequences of D.

There is nothing especially sacrosanct about any of these patterns, and nothing depends upon the label given them. Some patterns no doubt exhibit desirable features or normalcy (or rationality), others do not. Our task here is simply to classify the most important patterns—although even so many will remain unmentioned—not to evaluate them. Before the tribunal of logic, all patterns are, as it were, on a par. It is the use we put them to that will determine the desirability of one over another.

We recall from Chapter IV, Section 4, that some of the patterns mentioned are akin to some suggested by Ramsey.

9. Some Patterns of Rational Belief. Using the notions of the preceding section as a guide, let us again turn to belief and attempt to define some patterns of *rational belief*.

First, consider the notion that a class of sentences D exhibits one of the rational belief patterns for *negation*. Clearly it will not suffice to characterize such a pattern without taking into account the *objects* of belief, that is, the individuals, classes, and relations, symbols for which occur in the condition of the belief. Let us define the locution

(1)   'D exhibits a rational belief pattern for negation relative to the person X and the time t',

in the strong sense in terms of 'if and only if'. To simplify, suppose that D contains only some atomic sentences and their negations and that the atomic sentences contain just one-place predicates. For each such atomic sentence a of D, and for every F and x, it is required that

X B_E F,x,a,t if and only if it is not the case that X B_E $F,x,(\text{`}{\sim}\text{'}{}^{\frown}a),t$,

where a consists of some b concatenated with some c, b designating F, and c designating x. This need not be stated more precisely, since the general intent is clear. If it is not required that D contain only atomic sentences and their negations, account must be taken of all of the objects of belief, symbols for which occur in the conditions of belief.

We may introduce in a similar vein the notion of a rational belief pattern for *disjunction* in any of the three senses. In these also there will be reference to the classes and individuals constituting the objects of belief. Again to simplify, consider the disjunctions of only atomic sentences, and let us the strong sense using 'if and only if'. *Let a* and *b* be atomic sentences, in some class *D. The* disjunction of *a* and *b*, that is, '(' concatenated with *a* concatenated with 'V' concatenated with *b* concatenated with ')', is also assumed to be in *D*. We may then say that *D* exhibits a rational belief pattern for disjunction relative to *X* and *t* if and only if for all such *a* and *b*, and for all d_1, d_2, e_1, e_2, F_1, F_2, x_1, and x_2,

$$X \ \text{B}_E \ F_1,x_1,a,t \text{ or } X \ \text{B}_E \ F_2,x_2,b,t, \text{ if and only if } X \ \text{B}_E \ F_1,F_2,$$
$$x_1,x_2,('('\!\!\urcorner a\urcorner'\text{V}'\urcorner b\urcorner')'),t,$$

where *a* is $(d_1\!\urcorner e_1)$, *b* is $(d_2\!\urcorner e_2)$, d_1 Des F_1, d_2 Des F_2, e_1 Des x_1, and e_2 Des x_2.

Note that patterns of *rational* belief are based upon patterns of *normal* acceptance. 'Rational' is thus used here as a pragmatico-semantical word, whereas 'normal' is the corresponding pragmatico-syntactical word. Normalcy has to do solely with acceptance, whereas in rational patterns of belief the objects of belief are brought in fundamentally. Among the patterns of rational belief, those that depend upon the laws of logic are especially important, rationality being so intimately intertwined with them. Here *X*'s acceptance of the laws of logic plays a fundamental role, as do the normal acceptance patterns with respect to logical rules of inference.

For example, consider again the rule of *Modus Ponens*. Suppose that if $X \ \text{B}_E \ F,x,a,t$ and $X \ \text{B}_E \ F,G,x,y,('('\!\!\urcorner a\urcorner'\supset'\urcorner b\urcorner')'),t$, then X $\text{B}_E \ G,y,b,t$, for all F, G, x, y, and for all *a* and *b* and $('('\!\!\urcorner a\urcorner'\supset'\urcorner b\urcorner')')$ in *D*. Then surely *D* exhibits a rational belief pattern for *Modus Ponens* relative to *X* and *t*.

We need not attempt here to characterize these various patterns in a more precise way. Also, there are many further patterns to be distinguished, some of them no doubt more interesting than others.

Let us reflect now a little more fully than above upon the axiomatic structure of the logic of belief. It is to be noted that very little has been postulated concerning the primitives 'Tst' and 'Acpt'. The axioms suggested are extremely weak. The development of the

* are there any that do not depend on them ?

** what does 'depend upon' mean here ?

logic of believing and knowing thus consists mainly, according to the method here, in defining suitable patterns for specific persons and perhaps for social groups, and then proving theorems *concerning these patterns*. Most of these theorems will be of the form of *conditionals* to the effect that such and such obtains *if* such and such patterns are exhibited. These patterns themselves are not to be imposed by *E*, who rather must observe and experiment in order to decide whether they are actually exhibited or not.

This procedure is in marked contrast to that often followed by statisticians and decision theorists, who speak as though there is *one* pattern of rationality to be imposed more or less by fiat. There is in some sense, according to them, a "best" pattern, on the basis of which statistics and probability and decision theory are to be founded. In the case of the logic of belief, the procedure suggested above is to define many alternative types of patterns and to draw out their consequences. However, no one pattern is, at this stage at least, intrinsically any "better" than any other, as far as the logic of belief is concerned.

The procedure suggested above also seems to be in marked contrast to that suggested by Church.[10] Church has not put forward any primtives for a logic of belief, and it is not clear just what kind or kinds he would wish to admit. Once he has selected them, however, he presumably wishes strong postulates to govern them. One must not, however, according to the attitude taken here, impose patterns of belief from on high. Rather one must patiently experiment and record, and explore the logical consequences of various patterns. The task of the logician of belief is to supply a suitable linguistic tool, not to lay down *ex cathedra logicae* patterns to which beliefs must conform.

In addition to the axioms governing 'Tst' and 'Acpt' here, of course, suitable axioms are assumed for the syntax and semantics of *L* as are some simple axioms concerning time flow. However, it is to be presumed that some such axioms would be required in any logic of belief in which the presuppositions are made explicit—as they most certainly should be anyhow.

From the study of rational patterns of belief we should turn to the characterization of rational patterns of *knowledge*. Most of these would be direct analogues of the foregoing. However, there will also be certain patterns intrinsic to knowledge with no analogues for belief, these involving in special ways the semantical truth concept.

[10] See A. Church, "Logic and Analysis."

10. Degree of Rational Belief. In *Intension and Decision* the attempt was made to characterize a notion of *quantitative acceptance* in terms essentially of the utility theory of von Neumann and Morgenstern. For present purposes we need not presuppose that or some allied notion explicitly. Instead, let us assume rather that 'Acpt' is given a quantitative meaning in whatever way seems most suitable. Thus,

(1)   'X Acpt$_E$ a,t,α'

may be presumed available, either primitively or defined, to express that X accepts the sentence a of L at time t *to degree* α. (1) can no doubt be interpreted in different ways, for example, in terms of X's willingness to *bet* on a at t or in terms of the utility (in some sense) that a has for X at t. Given such a quantitative notion of acceptance, a quantitative notion of *belief* should be forthcoming by a direct adaptation of (2) of Section 4 above.

The problem of how best to interpret (1) is a difficult one that need not concern us here. The full solution must await further experimental and theoretical work in decision theory, utility theory, and the like. Meanwhile, we merely note that a quantitative notion of belief is immediately forthcoming in terms of (1), provided (1) itself is suitably interpreted and characterized. Our main task would then be the study of *quantitative patterns* of acceptance, in the fashion of Section 8 and thence to quantitative patterns of belief, as in Section 9. The details need not concern us here, being more or less straightforward adaptations of the nonquantitative patterns.

We have by no means exhausted the study of patterns of rational belief. In fact, we have scarcely begun it. The subject quickly becomes highly technical, however, and we have been concerned here only with the philosophic foundations, more particularly, with the kind of linguistic framework needed.

11. Denotation and Belief. The forms suggested for 'K' and 'B' in Section 4 may be criticized on several grounds. For one thing, the readings of contexts containing them may be thought to be in some sense "unnatural," as far as predicates are concerned, whether for properties or relations.

First, consider just one-place predicates, and the context

(1)   'X B$_E$ P,Q,'$(x)(Px \lor Qx)$',t'.

The suggested reading of this formula is 'X believes (according to E) at t of the property (or class) P, and of the property (or class) Q

a problem

that for every *x*, *x* has P or *x* has Q'. This reading is unnatural and awkward in its reference to P and Q as objects of belief. Ordinary usage does not seem to condone phrases such as 'believes of P, of Q', 'believes of the properties P and Q', 'believes of the classes P and Q', and the like, as components of sentences expressing belief. Whether the phrases 'the property' or 'the class' occur seems not to matter. The important point is that in ordinary language we make reference to the *individuals* about which we believe so and so, but not to the properties or classes of such. A more natural reading of (1) seems to be '*X* believes at time *t* of P's and Q's that for all *x*, *x* is a P or *x* is a Q'. In fact, we have slipped unconsciously, as it were, into this mode of speaking at several points above. It seems natural to say that *X* believes *of males and females* that everybody is a male or a female, but not to say that *X* believes of the class of males and of the class of females that everybody is a male or a female.

NB

But not to variable individuals !

See below

As a sentence involving a two-place relation, consider again the example about Caesar, Rome, and so on. It was suggested that

(2)   'c B$_E$ r,S,t,'rSt',*t*'

be read 'Caesar believes at time *t* of Rome, of *the relation of being situated on*, and of the Tiber, that Rome is situated on the Tiber'. However, here too the phrase 'of the relation of . . .' occurs awkwardly. In its place we suggest 'of *x*'s and *y*'s such that *x* is situated on *y*'. To say that Caesar believed at *t* of Rome, of the individuals *x* and *y* (or of *x*'s and *y*'s) such that *x* is situated on *y*, and of the Tiber, that Rome is situated on the Tiber, seems less awkward, and closer to our ordinary ways of speech. Even this may involve some slight deviation from ordinary usage, but just enough to sharpen the reading of (2).

/ this is either ?

The foregoing argument is perhaps not very strong, but it does motivate us to seek definitions of 'B' and 'K' within a metalanguage in which classes and relations do not occur as values for variables. Thus let us seek a more or less quasi-nominalized version of the definition in a metalanguage in which the very phrases 'the relation so and so', 'the class such and such', and so on, are barred.

Under- statement !

Fortunately, such a metalanguage is immediately forthcoming, namely, that (as in Chapter II, Section 9) developed in terms of multiple denotation, rather than designation, taken as primitive. The relation of multiple denotation, we recall, holds between an expression for a class (or virtual class) and the objects in that class. For example, 'man' denotes severally each and every individual man, as previously noted. Let '*a* Den *x*' state that the expression *a* denotes the object *x*.

Let us suppose, for the moment, and merely to simplify, that L contains only one-place predicate constants, so that if a Den x, then a is a one-place (primitive or defined) predicate constant.

Let 'a PrNm x' state that the expression a is a *proper name* of x. This in fact may be defined in terms of 'Den'. To say that 'a' PrNm x is merely to say, where 'a' is an individual constant, that there is some expression b, for the class (or virtual class) whose only member is a, such that b denotes x. If a PrNm x then a of course must be an individual constant, so that only individual constants are regarded as proper names here. (Predicate constants are not names at all, although they do significantly denote.) To say that a is a proper name of x, is merely to say that such and such a virtual-class expression denotes x.[11]

We may now immediately alter the definition of 'B' in (V,D) as follows. Let 'P', with or without a numerical subscript, stand arbitrarily for any one-place primitive predicate constant of L. Consider first sentences a containing only one such constant and one individual constant. Then

(3)   'X B$_E$ P,x,a,t'

may abbreviate, for any P,

'a is a sentence of L in primitive notation; there are expressions b and c such that for all y b Den y if and only if Py, c PrNm x, b is the only primitive predicate constant and c the only primitive individual constant occurring in a; and X Acpt$_E$ a,t'.

The natural reading of the definiendum here for a given P, say 'P', is 'X believes (according to E) at t of P's and of x that a holds'.

Clearly this definition, or rather *definition schema,* may be generalized to provide any number of primitive predicate and individual constants to occur in a, and may be of any number of places. It might be thought that, if L contains a primitive two-place predicate constant, say d, the metalanguage should contain another denotation relation according to which we can say that d denotes x and y in this order; if a primitive three-place predicate constant, still another denotation relation enabling us to say that the predicate constant denotes x, y, and z in this order; and so on. That this is not the case, however, may be seen as follows. L may contain at most a fixed finite number

[11] For details, see *Truth and Denotation.*

of primitive two-place predicates. Suppose these are 'R_1', . . . , 'R_n'. Moreover, clearly a two-place predicate a is L-equivalent with another b provided the result of writing successively ')', 'x', ')', '(', 'y', ')', '(', a, 'x', 'y', '$\equiv$', b, 'x', 'y', and ')' is analytic in L. Then 'a Des R_1' may abbreviate 'a is L-equivalent to $\mathbf{R}$' where in place of '$\mathbf{R}$' we put in the structural-descriptive name of 'R_1'. And similarly for 'a Des R_2', and so on. Thus, where $\mathbf{Q}$ is any primitive two-place relational constant of L, in place of 'for all y b Des y if and only if $\mathbf{P}y$' we write 'b Des $\mathbf{Q}$'. And similarly for three-place relational constants, and so on. Thus the definition schema just given may easily be extended to sentences containing primitive relational constants.

A general relation for knowing may also be defined here in a fashion similar to that of Section 4.

Note that in a context in which a bold-face letter occurs, the single quotes enclosing that context are being used in the special sense of Quine's corners. A similar use is made throughout.[12]

A second advantage that acrues to these definitions, as contrasted with those of Section 4, is that the metalanguage in terms of denotation carries with it no ontic commitment to entities other than those that are values for the variables of L. The metalanguage of Section 4, it will be recalled, carries ontic commitment, in addition, to the classes or properties or relations designated by the primitive predicate constants of L. Moreover, all the other advantages of this simpler kind of semantics may also be invoked here. These many advantages then seem to recommend this second mode of analysis, within the more restricted metalanguage, as against that given above in the richer metalanguage.

Suppose it is required that no two distinct one-place primitive predicate constants denote the same objects, that no two distinct two-place predicate constants denote the same x's and y's, and so on. We then can never run into the rather awkward form such as (4) encountered in Chapter V, Section 6. Note that the requirement here must be stated in terms of denotation rather than designation as above.

We have not taken into account the use of the definitional abbreviations of L, either here or in Section 9 above. In particular, *defined* predicate constants or Russellian descriptions for individuals have not been considered. To do so would involve certain technicalities that need not concern us for the present. A person may or may not be familiar with the definitional abbreviations of L. He might well accept a sentence containing only primitives but not one containing

---

[12] W. V. Quine, *Mathematical Logic,* and the author's *Truth and Denotation,* pp. 34 ff.

a defined term or phrase. Here also various patterns of belief may be introduced, some of them depending upon the user's familiarity with the definitions of *L*.

Some readers might object that we have tarried too long over the forms for handling '*X* believes so and so'. The forms are crucial, pivotal forms in the logic of belief, however, and additional ones will be presented as we go on. The choice of a form here is determined to a large extent by one's philosophy of logic, and in turn determines to a large extent a whole philosophic view. Failure to be clear about the forms here, and to choose a satisfactory one, increases the likelihood of failure or confusion in other areas of philosophy.

[handwritten marginalia: Davdson would agree]

CHAPTER VI

The Philosophic Import of
Virtual Classes

There has been occasional reference in the above to virtual classes, and there will be further reference below, where fundamental use of them will be made. What are they, why are they philosophically interesting, and in particular, what role do they play in the logic of belief? In the present chapter the attempt is made to answer these questions to some extent.

Our language is not designed to speak of virtual classes, for there are no such entities. A virtual class in fact is a mere fiction; like the ghost of Hamlet's father, 'tis here, 'tis here, 'tis gone—mostly gone. Curiously, however, discourse concerning such entities, although a mere *manière de parler,* can be made as exact as one wishes and is subject to precise logical laws. Even more curiously, such discourse is not only useful but also conceptually of such interest that it may be viewed as constituting the very nerve of first-order logic. In fact we can almost go so far as to say that first-order logic *is* the theory of virtual classes and relations in a kind of notational disguise.

Virtual classes are not values for variables in any way, shape, or form, whereas real classes are. Here in sum is the difference. However, an enormous difference it is and one perhaps not sufficiently recognized either by logicians or analytic philosophers. Real classes are values for variables in some suitable class-theoretic formalism—and likewise for sets, if one wishes to distinguish in some way between sets and classes. Virtual classes, however, are never values for variables in any formalism whatsoever. Nor could any formalism be constructed in such a way that they could be. Virtual classes are classes *als ob,* and any attempt to make them real fundamentally alters their character.

The subject has been brought to the fore again in the introductory sections of Quine's *Set Theory and Its Logic.* There, attention centers upon virtual-class and virtual-relation theory only insofar as they are of interest for the subsequent "real thing." Later, Quine merges the two in a most skillful way. Virtual theory, however, is not merely a tool for mathematics, and the main motives for interest in it are surely philosophical. Quine notes only a few, but there are many more.

First let us sketch briefly the logic of virtual classes and relations in Section 1, and then reflect in Section 2 upon why it is thought to be of fundamental philosophic interest. In Section 3 a list of *useful notions* definable in terms of virtual classes is given. In Section 4 we reflect upon *virtual classes of virtual classes,* and the like. Some comments concerning real sets and classes are given in Section 5. Finally, in Section 6 we return to the logic of belief and, in terms now of virtual classes, an improved definition of 'B' is given.

Let us not worry about who first thought up virtual classes or, more precisely, formulated an exact notation for them with appropriate laws. The theory of virtual classes and relations was so called in Quine's lectures in Brazil in 1942.[1] It played a major role in the author's thesis of 1941 (published in 1943), written under the guidance of Frederic Fitch.[2] A full development of the theory was given in the author's Bonn lectures in 1960, similar to that suggested on pages 15–27 of *Set Theory and Its Logic.*

1. Notation. The theory of virtual classes and relations is primarily a matter of notation, so it is to notational matters that we should turn for a moment.

Let '(—x—)', as above, be some formula of L containing 'x' as its only free variable. The formulate of L are either atomic or (recursively) built up out of atomic formulae by means of '$\vee$', '$\sim$', '(x)', '(Ex)' and so on. Now the formula '(—x—)' may be either atomic or of any complexity. No matter which, it in effect predicates of the individual x such and such a property, or (equivalently) says that x is one among the individuals having that property. Let us collect *all* such individuals and form an expression for this collection. We can then use 'ϵ', the usual symbol for 'is a member of,' together with this expression, to say

---

[1] *O Sentido da nova lógica* (São Paulo: Martins, 1944), Section 51.
[2] "A Homogeneous System for Formal Logic," *The Journal of Symbolic Logic* 8 (1943), 1–23.

that x is one of this collection. In other words we can define the whole context

(1) $\qquad\qquad\qquad$ '$x \in y \ni (\text{---}y\text{---})$'

or, equivalently, essentially in Quine's notation,

(2) $\qquad\qquad\qquad$ '$x \in \{y:\text{---}y\text{---}\}$'.

(1) or (2) are defined as wholes, so that the '$\in$' here and the expressions '$y\ni(\text{---}y\text{---})$' or '$\{y:\text{---}y\text{---}\}$' have no meaning in isolation. With (1) or (2) as a definiendum, the required definicns is merely

$\qquad\qquad\qquad$ '$(\text{---}x\text{---})$',

where '$(\text{---}x\text{---})$' differs from '$(\text{---}y\text{---})$' appropriately.

Any expression of the form '$y\ni(\text{---}y\text{---})$' or '$\{y:\text{---}y\text{---}\}$' is called 'a one-place *abstract*'. The use of the inverted epsilon to form abstracts is akin to that of Peano. The colon here, on the other hand, is often preferred by mathematicians, and there are still other variant notations in common use.

One variant, specially to be recommended perhaps, may be given in which no use is made of '$\in$' and the abstract occurs to the left of the argument variable. Thus,

(3) $\qquad\qquad\qquad$ '$y\ni(\text{---}y\text{---})\ x$'

or

(4) $\qquad\qquad\qquad$ '$\{y:\text{---}y\text{---}\}x$'

may be used in place of (1) or (2). These notations have the advantage of exhibiting abstracts in the place of primitive predicates. Thus, where 'P' is a primitive one-place predicate of L, 'Px' and (3) or (4) have essentially the same form. (3) and (4) thus enable us to see clearly that formulae containing complex predicates may be given in effect the same form as atomic formulae containing only primitive predicates.

The notational legerdemain seemingly achieved by (1) or (2) (or by (3) or (4)) enables us to speak as though we were speaking of classes. Of course we are not. Everything ostensibly said in terms of classes is in fact said in terms merely of the primitive notation of L, which has only individuals as values for its variables.

The foregoing definition yields immediately the three logical principles:

(5)   '$x \in y \ni (—y—) \supset (—x—)$',

(6)   '$(—x—) \supset x \in y \ni (—y—)$',

and

(7)   '$x \in y \ni (—y—) \equiv (—x—)$'.

Quine calls (7) 'the *principle of concretion*', but it has frequently been called 'the *principle of abstraction*'. Actually (5) should perhaps more aptly be called 'the principle of concretion' because it enables us to pass, as it were, from an expression containing an abstract to one that does not. (6), on the other hand, enables us to pass from a concrete form, as it were, to a form containing an abstract, and hence is aptly a principle of abstraction.

Note that (1) and (2) are allowed to contain no free variable other than 'x'. Suppose '$(—y—)$' were allowed to contain some free occurrence of a variable 'z' other than 'y'. The resulting abstract '$y \ni (—y—)$', would no longer stand for a virtual class, but rather (by analogy with a set function) a virtual-class *function*. It is transformed into an expression for a virtual class by replacing all occurrences of 'z' by an individual constant (or a suitable Russellian description, if such is available).

In analogous fashion our notation may be extended to provide for virtual dyadic relations. Thus, we may define

$$x \, zw \ni (—z—w—)y \text{' or '} zw \ni (—z—w—)xy$$

$$x \, \{zw:—z—w—\} \, y \text{'   or   '} \{zw:—z—w—\} \, xy$$

merely as

$$(—x—y—),$$

where '$(—x—y—)$' is some formula of L containing 'x' and 'y' as its only free variables, 'z' and 'w' are any variables distinct from each other and from 'x' and 'y', and '$(—z—w—)$' differs from '$(—x—y—)$' appropriately. Similarly, we may go on to virtual triadic relations, and so on. The abstracts here are respectively of two and three places.

2. Why Bother? Why should we trouble ourselves about virtual classes and relations? First of all, we gain a "wealth of notation," as Quine puts it, "and we have seen how to define it in such a way as to recognize no such things as classes and relations at all except as a defined manner of speaking. A motive for talking thus ostensibly and eliminably of classes and relations is compactness of expression."[3] All the laws concerning virtual classes and relations turn out to be mere laws of the logic of quantification and identity in disguise, as we shall note in a moment. These laws are more compact, and often more intuitive, versions of the latter. Of course, "compactness of expression" is in general achieved by definitions in the real theory also. The more important motive here surely concerns ontic commitment. The various laws governing virtual entities in no way ontically commit us to such entities, whereas in the "real" formulation they do.

"Down the centuries," Quine notes, "a major motive, certainly, for assuming such objects as relations and classes or attributes has been this kind of [notational] convenience, and we now see that this kind of convenience can be served equally well by a virtual theory that assumes no such objects after all."[4] Also, there is little reason to think that down the centuries real classes and/or attributes were being aimed at any more than were virtual ones. For one thing, the very notion of being a value for a variable was not too clear. Of course one may have specific names for particular classes, relations, universals, patterns, forms, or whatever, without assuming that these names are in any way substitutable for variables. Thus one can often treat such objects virtually with impunity. Also, virtual classes of virtual classes can be introduced in various restricted ways—no doubt forms of forms, and so on. History should surely be viewed in the light of present knowledge. We have both the virtual and real theories now before us. A detailed argument from the text would no doubt be required to establish that any particular author (metaphysician, logician, or contemporary analyst) was aiming at the real, rather than the merely virtual, notion.

Another closely related point is that for philosophical purposes—especially in contemporary analytic philosophy—most of the reasons for having classes and relations at all seem served equally well by the virtual theory. Much philosophical writing is so inexact that the distinction between virtual and real seems premature. However, in more sophisticated writing, one speaks either of specific classes and relations or of classes and relations in general, where at most a large finite or a denumerable number is intended. Usually it is not clear

[3] *Set Theory and Its Logic*, p. 26.
[4] *Ibid.*, pp. 26–27.

which are to be regarded as primitive—expressions for them, that is—
and which are not. No matter. Such entities, whether expressions for
them are primitive or defined, need not be taken as values for variables,
and this is the key point. After all, philosophers tend to be interested
more in *specific* classes than in some general theory about all classes.
Also, they tend to be more concerned with the *members* of classes than
with the classes as such, and these latter in fact are usually thought of
as being uniquely determined by their members. Whatever classes are,
they are usually thought to be in some sense functions of, or at least
dependent upon, their members. Further, philosophers often regard
classes as the *extensions* of properties, in which case they are already in
effect virtual. Similar remarks presumably hold when we turn to classes
of classes.

   In view of the consistency of first-order logic, no inconsistency
can arise in the theory of virtual classes. Hence of course there is no
possibility of constructing embarrassing classes that might lead to con-
tradiction. Also, the virtual-class technique provides a very "natural"
way of going about constructing classes, getting them out of their
membership rather than, as it were, out of thin air.

   We have spoken here of ontic commitment only relative to an
object language. However, related comments apply to syntactical and
semantical metalanguages as well. The convenience of virtual classes
and relations can equally well be achieved in such metalanguages, where
use is made of virtual classes of and relations between individuals as
well as of or between expressions, and virtual relations between expressions and individuals. Here is an important matter that Quine
seems not to have noted sufficiently. The wholesale use of the virtual-
class technique makes possible the restricted semantical metalanguages
based on denotation.

   However, even if one does not wish to accept such metalanguages,
there is still a connection between virtual classes and denotation. What
kinds of terms can, in the most proper sense, be said to denote? According to the *Oxford English Dictionary*, *denotation* is "that which a word
denotes . . . ; the aggregate of objects of which a word may be predicated." The use of 'aggregate' here is suggestive. An aggregate is a
collection or agglomeration, or even a virtual class, but not of necessity
a real one. The "words" involved here are words that "may be predicated" of objects. Now, to say that a term is predicable of an object
is not to require that that term designate a real class; it is to require
that that term be such as to stand significantly in the position of a
predicate. Hence, that term can significantly be an expression for a
virtual class. Such expressions are significantly predicable of objects,

logical sum

just as expressions for real classes are, of course, but without the added commitment to existence, which is not involved in mere predication anyhow.

3. Some Useful Notions. Let us reflect, a little more fully than Quine does, upon the vast number of useful logical notions that may be construed virtually. Ordinarily it has been supposed that the definition of these notions presupposes the full resources of class or set theory. That this is not the case is occasion not only for some surprise but for rejoicing as well. For convenience in listing these ideas we shall use the terminology of *Principia Math∠matica*.

The *inclusion* and *identity* of virtual classes are clearly definable in the usual way. A given virtual class is included in a virtual class if and only if every member of the one is a member of the other. Identical virtual classes are then those that mutually include one another. The various Boolean notions are readily definable. The *logical sum* of two virtual classes is the virtual class of all *x*'s such that *x* is a member of one or the other, perhaps of both. Similarly the *logical product* of two virtual classes, the *negation* of a virtual class, the *universal* virtual class, and the *null* virtual class may be introduced. And similarly for relations. (See *20–*25 of *PM*.)

Russellian descriptions (*14), phrases of the form 'the one so-and-so', are of course definable without use of virtual classes or relations. *Descriptive functions* (*30), phrases of the form 'the one individual which bears *R* to *y*', are now definable where *R* is a given virtual dyadic relation. Given a virtual dyadic relation, its *converse* (*31) may be introduced. We may go on to *referents* and *relata* of a given term with respect to a given dyadic virtual relation (*32), to *domains, converse domains*, and *fields* of a virtual dyadic relation (*33), to the *relative product* of two dyadic virtual relations (*34), to dyadic virtual relations with *limited domains and converse domains* including *Cartesian products* (*35), to *plural descriptive functions* (*37), to the theory of *operations* (*38), to *unit classes and cardinal couples* (*51, *54), to *ordinal couples* (*55), to *one-many, many-one*, and *one-one* virtual dyadic relations (*71, *72, *74). The notions here are definable essentially as in *PM*, with some minor changes here or there, and most of the theorems given there are now provable for virtual classes and relations. The omitted notions and theorems are mainly of interest for the foundations of arithmetic and involve fundamentally higher logical types. Thus most of Volume I of *PM*, other than the material specifically concerned with mathematics, can readily be handled virtually.

We can press the theory of dyadic virtual relations still further, to include the notion of a *relation contained in diversity* (*200), of a *transitive, intransitive,* and *nontransitive relation* (*201), of a *symmetrical, asymmetrical,* and *nonsymmetrical* relation, of a *reflexive, irreflexive,* and *nonreflexive* relation, of a *connected* relation (*202), of a *serial* relation (*204), of a *partial ordering relation,* and of a *simple ordering relation.* No doubt there are other useful notions to be gained if we were to press further. This list is by no means complete, but let it suffice for the moment to convince us of the wealth of logical notions definable virtually.

If now we take into account the nonlogical primitive predicates of L, further notions are of course definable. As an example, suppose a relation of *discreteness* between individuals were available in L (either primitively or defined), in the sense that the individuals that are its arguments are spatio-temporal objects having no part in common.[5] Given a virtual class F of such entities, we say that an individual x is the *fusion* of F if and only if for every z, z is discrete from x if and only if z is discrete from every member of F. We say that the spatio-temporal individual x is a *part* of y if and only if every individual discrete from y is discrete from x. Then a spatio-temporal individual x is the *nucleus* of a virtual class F if and only if for every z, z is a part of x if and only if z is a part of every member of F. The theory of discreteness and attendant notions is contained in the so-called *calculus of individuals.* Strictly, the calculus concerns an uninterpreted relation of discreteness, whereas here we have been speaking of discreteness only as applied to spatio-temporal objects. The relation here is thus not strictly a relation of logic but presumably of the theory of space and time. In any event, the notions of fusion and nucleus are no doubt useful notions. And similarly for other virtually definable notions based on other nonlogical primitives.

4. Virtual Classes of Virtual Classes. Are there such things as virtual classes of virtual classes, or virtual classes of virtual relations, or virtual relations between virtual classes? Well, literally, no. However, a *manière de parler* for such can often be achieved in restricted contexts. We have noted above, for example, that the notion of a transitive virtual dyadic relation is definable. To say that R is transitive is merely to say that for any x, y, and z, if xRy and yRz then xRz. The very word 'transitive' here is in effect an expression for a virtual class of dyadic virtual relations. And similarly for many other virtual classes of or relations between or among virtual classes and/or relations.[6]

---

[5] See H. S. Leonard and N. Goodman, "The Calculus of Individuals and Its Uses," *The Journal of Symbolic Logic* 5 (1940), 45–55.

[6] Cf. again the methods used in "A Homogeneous System for Formal Logic."

We can explicitly introduce a notation for virtual classes of virtual classes by a straightforward adaptation of (1) or (2) of Section 1 above. Let 'F' and 'G' possibly with primes now be or abbreviate any one-place abstract. Pick out now some 'F' containing no free variables and let it function as a second-order variable of abstraction, so to speak. Then

$$\text{'}F \ni (\text{—}F\text{—})\ G\text{'}$$

or

$$\text{'}\{F\!:\!\text{—}F\text{—}\}\ G\text{'}$$

may now be regarded as expressing that the virtual class G is a member of the virtual class of all classes F such that (—F—). And similarly for virtual dyadic relations between virtual classes, for which

$$\text{'}G\ FF' \ni (\text{—}F\text{—}F'\text{—})\ G'' \text{ or } \text{'}FF' \ni (\text{—}F\text{—}F'\text{—})\ GG''$$

or

$$\text{'}G\ \{FF'\!:\!\text{—}F\text{—}F'\text{—}\}\ G'' \text{ or } \text{'}\{FF'\!:\!\text{—}F\text{—}F'\text{—}\}\ GG''$$

give us a suitable notation. These abstracts are *second-order* abstracts. Similarly there are second-order abstracts for triadic relations, and so on. For all of these abstracts there are also appropriate principles of concretion and abstraction.

Further, second-order abstracts for virtual classes of virtual relations, for virtual relations between or among virtual relations or between or among virtual classes and virtual relations, may be introduced in similar fashion. Of course, the use of all such abstracts introduces nothing essentially new that is not already contained in first-order logic.

The theory of virtual classes and relations and first-order logic, we see then, are in effect one and the same. Arithmetic, and therewith mathematics and/or set theory are something in addition, to be provided for by specific nonlogical primitives. And similarly for any other deductive discipline. On this meaning for 'logic' the logistic thesis, that all mathematics is reducible to logic, is of course false, just as is the corresponding thesis concerning, say, quantum mechanics. A key problem for the philosophy of mathematics is then what nonlogical primitive or primitives to adopt, and with what entities as arguments, and what best to postulate concerning them. The set-theoretic approach to arithmetic is merely one out of many, but not necessarily the most satisfactory.

Note, incidentally, that the phrase 'there exists a virtual class such that. . .', although strictly meaningless, may still be used occasionally or in restricted contexts. To say, for example, that there exists a universal virtual class is to say in effect that there exists an abstract of such and such a kind denoting all objects. To say that such and such a virtual class exists is to speak in a semantical metalanguage to the effect that such and such an expression denotes such and such objects.

It might be thought that our theory is intimately linked with nominalism, but this is not, it would seem, the case. Nominalists avoid assuming that there are such things as real classes or relations. Hence of course the virtual technique is serviceable to the nominalist. That it is also of interest to the set-theoretic realist is shown in Quine's book, for example, where a realist position as to the existence of sets is taken hand in hand with an extensive use of virtual classes.

Also it might be thought that virtual classes are linked in some way with finitism. It might be presumed that finite sets are virtually definable by complete enumeration, whereas infinite sets are not. To presume this is to miss the crucial point that virtual classes are not values for variables, whereas real sets, finite or infinite, are.

5. Sets and Classes. Finally, we should consider a terminological recommendation: hereafter to use 'class' solely for virtual classes and 'set' for the real thing. When philosophers speak of classes it is usually, or at least often, a virtual class that is meant—or if not, what is said can usually be rephrased appropriately so as to involve only a virtual class. Mathematicians generally seem to prefer the word 'set' to 'class'. Sets are real mathematical entities, as are sets of sets, and so on. However, in the usage being recommended, classes are not, and the very phrase 'class of classes' is already a little barbarous, and in fact is meaningless according to some set theorists.

Quine is usually—and indeed unusually—fastidious in his terminology, but in *Set Theory and Its Logic* he has perhaps missed the opportunity to straighten out this terminology once and for all. Quine uses 'set' and 'class' "almost interchangeably," as he puts it, but follows von Neumann in holding that not all classes are capable of being members of classes. Those that are, are sets, those that are not, are "ultimate classes," as Quine calls them. The word 'set' has more currency than 'class' in mathematical contexts, but Quine favors the word 'class' to 'set' except in calling the whole subject 'set theory'. Why not use 'set' for sets, 'class' for virtual classes, and then 'ultimate set' for those special entities incapable of being members but that may have members? (These special entities may in fact be virtual classes, as in Bernays' system of 1958, as Quine points out, or they may be values for a special sort of variable, as in Bernays' earlier system.)[7] This terminology would be unambiguous and would help to remind philosophers and mathematicians of their proper concern with virtual classes and with sets or other mathematical objects, respectively. That there may be various kinds of sets, some of them "ultimate," need occasion no surprise. Nonetheless, the notion of an ultimate set is surely *ad hoc*, introduced merely to help avoid contradictions, and its artificiality adds fuel to the arguments of those who are suspicious of the mathematical notion of set anyhow. A satisfactory account of the notion of a virtual class, however, may be given quite independently, as we have seen, an account that seems adequate for purposes other than those of founding mathematics. For this latter task we should perhaps look to notions other than that of set, so that even in mathematics the virtual technique may perhaps be made to suffice. This, however, is quite another topic.

Let us turn again to the topic of belief, with virtual classes now at hand.

6. Virtual Classes and Belief. It should be noted that in all the analyses of 'B' and 'K' given in the preceding chapters, B and K are regarded as $(n + k + 4)$-adic relations, depending on the number of arguments. One of these arguments, for the condition of belief, is a linguistic expression, and that this be the case is essential for all of the analyses thus far. It seems very difficult to see how the experimenter E can test X's beliefs completely other than by taking into account X's behavior as well as his reactions to certain sentences of some language L. Surely if beliefs are to be put to the test, as has been emphasized throughout, some such dependence on X's reactions to language seems essential. X may or may not know L, in which case his reactions are studied by E in some language known to X.

We have noted above that Church, who seems to advocate analyzing belief in terms of "propositions," wants beliefs to be empirically testable. However, X's belief concerning some proposition can be tested, it would seem, only by reference to some sentence that that proposition "expresses." In short, all analyses of belief seem to involve relativity in some fashion or other to the language in which the belief is formulated; the condition of belief must be expressed in some language or other as object language.

Let us consider now another handling of belief in which no

[7] P. Bernays, "A System of Axiomatic Set Theory," *The Journal of Symbolic Logic* 2 (1937), 65–77; 6 (1941), 1–17; 7 (1942), 65–89, 133–145; 8 (1943), 89–106; 13 (1948), 65–79; and 19 (1954), 81–96; and P. Bernays and A. A. Fraenkel, *Axiomatic Set Theory* (*Studies in Logic and the Foundations of Mathematics,* Amsterdam: North-Holland Publishing Co., 1958).

NB

relativization to language is explicitly indicated in the definiendum. In other words, a definition of 'B' will be proposed *with no sentence or sentential function as an argument* for the condition of belief, but rather a suitable virtual class. This does not mean that relativization to language is avoided in the sense that the relation Acpt with a sentence as one of its arguments plays no role in the definiens. To the contrary, here as elsewhere the experimenter tests X's belief by taking into account X's acceptance or rejection of some sentence.

Consider again the case of a sentence expressing X's belief that contains only one primitive predicate constant and only one primitive individual constant. Let '(—x—)' as above be some sentential function of L containing just one variable 'x'. We then let

$$\text{'}X\ \text{B}_E\ P,y,x\ni(\text{—}x\text{—}),t\text{'}$$

be short for

'There are expressions b, c, and d of L such that (1) for all z, b Den z if and only if Pz, (2) c PrNm y, (3) b is a primitive one-place predicate constant of L and the only such occurring in a, (4) c is the only primitive individual constant of L occurring in a, (5) d differs from a only in containing occurrences of the individual constant c wherever there are free occurrences of the variable 'x' in a, and (6) X Acpt$_E$ d,t',

where in place of 'a' we put in the structural-descriptive name of '(—x—)' and in place of 'P' any primitive one-place predicate constant.

This again is not a definition, but rather a definition schema covering as it were an infinity of definitions. For specific P and '(—x—)', say 'P' and '($Px \lor \sim Px$)', the definiens here may be read 'X believes at t (according to E) of P's and of y that y is a member of the virtual class $x\ni(Px \lor \sim Px)$'.

This definition schema may readily be generalized to sentences containing any finite number of primitive individual or predicate constants, as in Chapter V, Section 11.

The generalization of this definition schema as well as that of Chapter V, Section 11, are thought to be of especial interest. In fact, all the preceding analyses of 'B' may now be regarded merely as heuristics for these two. Of the two, the present one has the greater interest. It embodies completely the idea that only nonlinguistic entities be referred to in the definienda, even if only nominally so.

Suppose for the moment that X does not know L at all. Let us

The Translation Problem

be a little more explicit about this case than above. Suppose also that there is some L' that he does know, and which of course is known also to E. E then can test X's reactions to sentences of L'. To state these results, E here as above employs a metalanguage of L'. E may use a metalanguage constructed on the basis of L' so that it contains L' as a part, or it may be constructed so as to contain translations of the expressions of L'. In the former case, the definition schema just given would be altered by referring to L' in place of L. In the latter, we not only refer to L' in place of L, but also change the proviso as follows: '$(—x—)$' is now regarded as a sentential function of the translational part of the metalanguage (not of L' as before), and in place of 'a' we put in the structural-descriptive name of the translation of '$(—x—)$' into L'. In this way, then, E may express the results of his investigations concerning X's beliefs in a metalanguage containing a translation of a language that X is presumed to know.

E bilingual

Since X must accept d

The situation here is in contrast to that of Chapter V, Section 4 and 10, above, where the sentences constituting the conditions of belief were sentences within the object language presumed known to X. Here the '$(—x—)$' is a sentential function within the metalanguage within which the object language occurs as a part or is suitably translated.

The notion of translation employed here is esentially that of Tarski, in *Der Wahrheitsbegriff*. Even if one were to obejct to its use, this would not impair the foregoing analysis. It would merely limit E to employing a metalanguage constructed in such a way as to contain as a part a language known to X.

A similar definition schema may be given for 'K' in terms of the semantical truth concept. Of course these schemata may be generalized so that a may contain any fixed finite number of primitive constants.

Later, in Chapter IX, Section 9, the definition of 'B' just given will be further improved and generalized. Meanwhile it may be regarded as the most satisfactory yet, supplanting those of preceding chapters. We shall be able to do better later, however, after discussing intensions, facts, propositions, events, and related topics.

cf p.126 Specify the df of dyadic predicates

$$X \: B_E \: Q, x, y, \: \exists w \exists (—z—w), t$$

The English rendering of n-adic predicates seems most dubious. Try $X \: B_E \: Plato \: preceded \: Aristotle$

CHAPTER VII

Objective Intensions as Constructs

The use of intensions *sui generis* in philosophic analysis has been lamented throughout this work. It has been suggested, however, that intensions need not be viewed *sui generis,* but can instead be given a suitable analysis within the usual kind of extensional metalanguage. Let us reflect now upon what is needed if such an analysis is to be given.

In the first place, a well-articulated semantics including a syntax should be available. Surely nothing less than this is now acceptable. Because intensions are so intimately connected with both linguistic expressions and denotation or designation, the most natural logical underpinning is no doubt to be found in denotational or designational semantics.

Next a clear and acceptable notion of what intensions *are, a* clear ontic description of them, should be provided. One searches far and wide in the literature for this. (In the author's *Intension and Decision,* a theory of many kinds of intension was suggested. Certain defects, however, marred the theory there, but these we shall try to correct.) Intensions should emerge in a natural way, so we should contend, as certain kinds of entities already available in the underlying denotational semantics. The notion of *analytic truth* should play a fundamental role, supplanting the somewhat vague and unsatisfactory traditional use of 'necessary' or 'essential'. Also, intensions must be dissected into *parts* (or members) in some fashion, and are not to be regarded as indivisible wholes. There seem to be two historical lines of research concerning this. On the one hand there is the German tra-

137

dition, stemming no doubt from Kant, through Frege to Carnap. On the other, there is the English tradition to which Stuart Mill contributed notably. The key difference seems to be that in the German tradition intensions are regarded as *sui generis* and as indivisible wholes, whereas in the English, they are analyzed and dissected into components. On this crucial matter we side with the English, and will try to be as clear as possible as to precisely what these components are. Heretofore this has been left rather vague, as we have seen.

In Section 1 certain further *preliminary notions* are introduced, including in Section 2 a restricted notion of *L-designation.* In Section 3 several kinds of *objective intensions* are characterized. In Section 4 an important *objection* is overcome. In Section 5 several laws of *inverse variation* of extension and intension are given. The so-called *Whiteheadian intensions* are presented in Section 6, and in Section 7 we are concerned with *intensions of proper names.* In Section 8 some kinship again with *Russell* is noted. Some comments concerning *connoting* and *attributes* are given in Section 9. Finally, in Section 10, some tentative notions of *sense* and *synonymy* are discussed.

1. Some Preliminary Remarks. To designate is to be a proper name of, whether of an individual, a class, or a relation. To *denote* is to be a common name of an individual and of an individual only, as has been noted. Semantical rules concerning designation and denotation reflect both actual usage and convention, but are no doubt to be laid down in part by metalinguistic fiat.

There is a third notion, also of great semantical interest, that of *L-designation.* It is perhaps a more "natural" notion than either designation or denotation, simpler, and more closely reflecting actual usage. Relations akin to L-designation as construed here have occasionally been mentioned by Carnap, although they are very rarely used, even by him.[1] The relation here is definable, with certain desirable restrictions, in terms of denotation. Hence, an intensional semantics based on it shares the advantages enjoyed by the semantical metalanguages based upon denotation. It will also be useful to introduce a notion of *virtual-class L-designation.* The theory that emerges, with virtual classes used in place of real classes and L-designation in place of designation, represents an important improvement over the theory put forward in *Intension and Decision.*

Classes and sets are treacherous entities. They lead us astray in

----

[1] See R. Carnap, *Introduction to Semantics,* p. 81, and *Meaning and Necessity,* p. 163.

mathematics, and hence there is little reason to regard them as suitable tools in philosophy. In their favor is the circumstance that they are extensional entities and hence relatively clear. If they are rejected, it would not do to reinstate intensional entities in their place, entities such as properties or class concepts, relation concepts, individual concepts, or propositions. If we are to reject classes, we must do so *toto caelo* and reject intensional entities as well. Rejection here of course consists only of refusal to admit them as values for variables. If we can succeed in defining a suitable notation for such entities or somehow succeed in gaining the effect of such upon an acceptable foundation, this is all to the good. In fact, this is just what we hope to be able to do for the various kinds of intensions.

The philosophic importance attaching to the rejection of intensions as values for a special kind of variable has already been commented on and may be summarized as follows. First, there is the distrust of pseudo-entities. At best intensional entities are suspect and should not be multiplied beyond necessity. Then there is the complexity of the laws governing them. These are notoriously sticky and more complex than ordinary laws governing extensions. Also there is the further complexity of the whole metalanguage in which intensions *sui generis* can be accommodated. Extensional metalanguages are always considerably simpler, both in structure and in what is assumed. There is also the relevant thesis of the unity of science. Why should only extensional entities be required in certain parts of science and then all of a sudden abandoned when we turn to others? It is as though we were to condone here a fundamental severance similar to the alleged one between the *Natur-* and *Geisteswissenschaften*. Also there is the very considerable historical confusion that surrounds the subject of intensions. When properly viewed and analyzed, so we contend, the assumption of intensions *sui generis* is seen to be not only unnecessary but also positively harmful. The role of intensions, to a large extent at least, can be played instead by certain kinds of virtual constructs.

2. L-Designation. Let 'PredConOne *a*' express that *a* is a *primitive* one-place predicate constant of *L* or a one-place abstract containing no free variables. There will be concern primarily with one-place predicate constants, but we can pass on to two-place, three-place, and so on, predicate constants easily as desired.

Governing the primitive 'Den' for multiple denotation, we have the following two Rules. First, that for all *x*, *a* Den *x* if and only if (—*x*—), where (1) '*a*' is taken as the structural description of the abstract '*x*э(—*x*—)', '(—*x*—)' being a sentential function of *L* containing '*x*' as its only free variable, or (2) '**a**' is taken as the structural description of a primitive predicate constant and '(—*x*—)' consists of that predicate constant concatenated with '*x*'. Secondly, that for all *a* and for all *x*, if *a* Den *x* then PredConOne *a*. These two Rules fix the properties of Den. According to the first, certain PredConOne's denote certain objects, and according to the second, no expressions other than PredConOne's denote.[2]

In terms of 'Den' we may now define *virtual-class designation*. Thus, an expression *a* may be said to *designate* a virtual class *x*э(—*x*—) provided *a* is a PredConOne and for all *x*, *a* Den *x* if and only if (—*x*—). Thus,

(D1)   '*a* Des *x*э(—*x*—)'   abbreviates 'PredConOne *a*   and
                for all *x*, *a* Den *x* if and only if (—*x*—)', if (and so on.)

This 'Des' is of course to be distinguished from that of Chapter V, which is now no longer needed.

Let *L* contain 'M' (for men) and 'R' (for rational beings) as PredConOne's. According to this definition schema we may say that 'M' designates the virtual class of individuals who are men, '*x*э (M*x* · R*x*)' designates the virtual class of individuals who are both men and rational, and so on. Also, *a* here designates the virtual class *x*э(—*x*—), no matter what notation we use to refer to that class. Thus, if *x*э(—*x*—) = *x*э(- - *x* - -), then also *a* Des *x*э(- - *x* - -). After all, a rose by any other name. . . .

We may go on to virtual-class *L-designation* as follows. An expression *a* is said to *L-designate* a virtual class *x*э(—*x*—) if and only if *a* designates *x*э(—*x*—) and *a* = **a**, where in place of '**a**' we put in the structural-descriptive name of the abstract '*x*э(—*x*—)'. As a matter of fact, however, the clause concerning designation here may be dropped, for it follows from the other clause by one of the Rules of Denotation. Hence we are left with the especially simple definition,

(D2)   '*a* LDes *x*э(—*x*—)' for '*a* = **a**', where (and so on).

This definition, or rather definition schema, defines 'LDes' only in contexts in which '*a*' is the only free syntactical or expressional variable. The same is true, we note, of the definition schema (D1) for 'Des'. We have no variables for virtual classes, only abstracts, and hence we do not define 'Des' and 'LDes' in contexts wherein the

---

[2] See *Truth and Denotation*, pp. 99 ff., or *Intension and Decision*, p. 14.

second argument is a variable. Nor would it be desirable to do so where we are dealing with only virtual classes.

When we say that a LDes $x \ni (—x—)$, the notation we use to refer to $x \ni (—x—)$ is all-important. Here a rose by any other name differs remarkably, because the names themselves differ. L-designation is a matter primarily of the names, as it were, and only secondarily of what the names stand for. Thus 'M' L-designates $x \ni Mx$, but not $x \ni (Mx \cdot Rx)$, although the two virtual classes are the same. We see then that L-designation, strictly speaking, is a notion of syntax. Hence the virtual classes referred to in the definiendum of (D2) may be called 'syntactic or nominal virtual classes'. To say this, however, is misleading. It suggests that the virtual classes can be subdivided into those that are nominal and those that are not, but this is not correct. To be nominal is rather a property of the occurrence of a virtual-class expression. Although we gain the effect of speaking of a virtual class in the definiendum of (D2), this is merely an illusion, for strictly we are speaking only of a certain expression that L-designates it.

Although a virtual-class expression occurs in the definiendum of (D2), no such expression occurs in the definiens. The definiens merely stipulates that a be of such and such a shape. For a to L-designate is then merely for it to be of such and such a shape. However, as we have noted, any expression of such and such a shape does in fact designate such and such a virtual class in view of the Rules of Denotation. Hence, one and the same virtual class is, in a roundabout way, implicitly involved in the definiens as well as in the definiendum.

Note that the relation of L-designation here differs remarkably from that of Carnap. That of Carnap is of course a semantical relation, not one of syntax—and further, within the theory of meaning or intensions *sui generis* rather than within the theory of extension or reference. According to him, and in essentially his own words, an expression a L-designates an entity in L if and only if it can be shown that a designates that entity merely by using the semantical rules of L without any reference to facts.[3] For Carnap, the entity L-designated may be a real class, whereas here it can be only a virtual one. On the other hand, suppose we know that $a = a$, where in place of 'a' we put in the structural description of '$x \ni (—x—)$'. It then follows, merely by the Rules of Denotation, that a designates $x \ni (—x—)$, as we have already remarked. This circumstance seems sufficient to justify referring to the relation here as one of L-designation.

---

[3] *Meaning and Necessity*, p. 163.

Nominal virtual classes might also be referred to as '*thus-designated* virtual *classes*'. A natural reading of the definiendum of (D2) is the 'expression a stands for the virtual class $x\ni(——x——)$ as thus designated'. We may then, if we wish, speak of thus-designated virtual classes, although the terminology is perhaps a bit awkward. Nominal virtual classes might also be called 'virtual classes *in intension*'. They are not strictly intensions, but are merely "taken in intension," as the traditional phrase has it. We shall see in a moment that they may be *members* of intensions, entering into their inner constitution, as it were, but are not to be confused with intensions themselves. Also, using Quine's term, we may speak of occurrences of an expression for a nominal virtual class as being *opaque* rather than direct. In any event there is surely enough kinship here to justify the various terminologies.

3. Some Varieties of Objective Intension. Let us turn now to the various kinds of objective intensions.

An expression a is said to be *analytically included* in an expression b, in symbols 'a AnlytcInc b', provided the sentence that consists of '$(x)($' followed by (or concatenated with) a followed by '$x \supset$' followed by b followed by '$x)$', where a and b are one-place predicate constants, is an analytic sentence of L. Note that here we are merely spelling out the structural description of the given sentence. Suppose a is the predicate 'P' and b 'Q'. Then a is analytically included in b if and only if '$(x)(Px \supset Qx)$' is an analytic sentence of L.

Given a one-place predicate constant a, the members of its *objective analytic intension* are to be the nominal virtual classes L-*designated by one-place predicate constants b such that a is analytically included in b*. We cannot introduce the notion in just this fashion, but instead say that a given nominal virtual class $x\ni(——x——)$ is a *member of* the objective analytic intension of an expression a if and only if a is a one-place predicate constant of L and there exists a one-place predicate constant b that L-designates $x\ni(——x——)$ and such that a is analytically included in b. Thus we let

(D3)   '$x\ni(——x——)$ ϵ ObjAnlytcInt(a)' abbreviate 'PredCon-
              One a and there is a b such that b LDes $x\ni(——x——)$ and
              a AnlytcInc b'.

Of course the whole definiendum must be regarded as an indivisible unit. In other words, (D3) provides in effect a contextual definition of an expression for the entire phrase '$x\ni(——x——)$ is a member of the objective analytic intension of' and not of any part of this expression in isolation. Thus 'member of' is used here only by proxy, but there is enough similarity with class membership, or rather virtual-class membership, to justify the use. Likewise, 'the analytic intension of' is defined only as embedded in the given kind of context. Further contexts can be introduced as we go on.

Let us now turn to the classic example, *homo animal rationalis*. In accord with this, let 'M' be regarded as short for '$x_{\ni}(Rx \cdot Ax)$', where 'R' (for rationals) and 'A' (for animals) are likewise Pred-ConOne's. Let us assume that 'R' and 'A' are primitive. As members of the analytic intension of 'M' we have then the nominal virtual classes of rationals, of animals, and of men, together with any other nominal virtual classes in the L-designators of which 'M' is analytically included. Let 'F' (featherless) and 'B' (bipeds) be further primitive PredConOne's. Although

$$\text{'}(x)(Mx \supset (Fx \cdot Bx))\text{'},$$

which states roughly that every man is a featherless biped, is true in L, it is not analytically so. Hence the nominal virtual class of featherless bipeds as well as that of bipeds and that of featherless objects cannot be members of the analytic intension of 'M'. This is of course as we wish it and as it should be.

Let us say that *a* is *vertically* included in *b*, in symbols '*a* VerInc *b*', provided *a* and *b* are both PredConOne's and the sentence consisting of '(x)(' followed by *a* followed by '$x \supset$' followed by *b* followed by 'x)' is *true*. Veridical inclusion is like analytic inclusion, with 'Tr' for truth replacing 'Anlytc' in the appropriate definientia. Similarly, we go on to *theoremic* and *synthetic* (or *factual*) inclusion. '*a* ThmInc *b*' expresses that *a* is theoremically included in *b*, and '*a* SynthcInc *b*' that *a* is synthetically so. These relations prepare the way for other kinds of intensions.

We may introduce now objective *synthetic*, *veridical*, and *theoremic* intensions by replacing 'AnlytcInc' in the definiens of (D3) by 'SynthcInc', 'VerInc', and 'ThmInc' respectively. It is natural to think that these, together with analytic intensions, would constitute the four fundamental types, one corresponding to the semantical notion of being analytic, one to that of being synthetic, one to that of being true, and one to that of being a theorem. We let 'ObjSynthc-Int', 'ObjVerInt', and 'ObjThmInt', respectively, symbolize the notions.

Note that analytic intensions intimately depend upon the analytic truths of L. These in turn are merely the logical truths of L together with the results of abbreviating them by using the definitions. Nothing more elaborate is involved, so that the notion of being an Anlytc here is as well founded as that of being logically true.

4. An Objection Overruled. It is to be observed that the theory here does *not* allow that one and the same nominal virtual class can be a member of both the ObjAnlytcInt(a) and of the ObjSynthcInt(a). The *way in which the member is specified* or referred to makes all the difference. (Hence our concern with *nominal* virtual classes.) This may be seen as follows.

Let

(i) $x\ni(\text{---}x\text{---})\ \epsilon\ \text{ObjSynthcInt}(a)$

and let a L-designate some nominal virtual class N. Then N is a subclass of $x\ni(\text{---}x\text{---})$, and this synthetically. More precisely, we should say here that there is a b such that a SynthcInc b where b LDes $x\ni$ ($\text{---}x\text{---}$). However, N is also a subclass of the logical sum of N and $x\ni(\text{---}x\text{---})$, that is, of $x\ni(\text{N}x\ \vee\ \text{---}x\text{---})$, and this analytically. More precisely, there is a c such that a AnlytcInc c where c LDes $x\ni(\text{N}x\ \vee\ \text{---}x\text{---})$. Hence we have that

(ii) $x\ni(\text{N}x\ \vee\ \text{---}x\text{---})\ \epsilon\ \text{ObjAnlytcInt}(a),$

according to (D3). Although $x\ni(\text{---}x\text{---})$ and $x\ni(\text{N}x\ \vee\ \text{---}x\text{---})$ are in fact the same virtual class, N being a subclass of $x\ni(\text{---}x\text{---})$, they are *not* one and the same nominal virtual class. Therefore we are not allowed to interchange *salva veritate* the abstracts for them in either (i) or (ii). The way in which the member of an objective intension is referred to is crucial. Strictly, the members of an objective intension are merely nominal virtual classes, not virtual classes *simpliciter*, as we have noted.

(If objective intensions are regarded as real classes of real classes, in the manner of *Intension and Decision,* the situation just described raises difficulty. That every member of an analytic intension, in the sense of *Intension and Decision,* is also a member of the corresponding veridical one is immediate. The converse can be established by an argument similar to that of the preceding paragraph.[4] Hence, within that theory there seems to be no way of distinguishing properly the two kinds of intension. In the theory just sketched, however, in terms

[4] For essentially this argument the author is indebted to Evan Jobe. See his "R. M. Martin's System of Pragmatics," *Methodos* XV, 59–60 (1963), 313–330, and "A Note on Connotation and Attribute," *The Journal of Philosophy* LXII (1965), 325–328.

What is a meaning?

of Den, LDes, and nominal virtual classes, there is no such difficulty.)

Although the form of the definiens of (D3) is essentially the same as in the corresponding definition in *Intension and Decision*, with 'LDes' replacing 'Des', the definienda differ, as does the whole *ambiente*. In particular, objective intensions, as now conceived, are merely virtual classes of nominal virtual classes, no longer real classes of real classes. Therefore, expressions for them, as well as for their members, can occur only in suitably defined contexts. Also, strictly speaking, there are no such things as objective intensions at all. We cannot *quantify* over them nor over their members. However, it is not clear that we ever need to do this anyhow. An objective intension can be *specified* as having such and such *specified* nominal virtual classes as members. This is what, after all, we wish. A meaning or intension is nothing if not specified. If it is properly specified in some sense, nothing more should be needed. Thus, although it might seem that something important is sacrificed in the virtual treatment of intensions, it is by no means clear that this is the case.

It might be thought that in this theory extensionality is in some fashion abandoned. This, however, is not the case, as we have already in effect noted. Suitable extensionality laws hold for L-designation. To say that a LDes $x \ni (-x-)$ is merely to say that a is of such and such a shape. Because $x \ni (-x-)$ might be the same virtual class as $x \ni (..x..)$, by no means gives grounds for thinking that a LDes $x \ni (..x..)$ also. That a has one shape in fact rules out that it can have another. Clearly, however, if $a = a$ and such and such holds of a, then such and such holds of a likewise (where in place of 'a' we put in the structural description of a PredConOne). Too, if $a = b$ and a LDes $x \ni (-x-)$, then b LDes $x \ni (-x-)$ also. Finally, if a LDes $x \ni (-x-)$ and a LDes $x \ni (..x..)$, then not only is $x \ni (-x-)$ the same virtual class as $x \ni (..x..)$ but also $a = b$ where in place of 'a' and 'b' we put in, respectively, the structural descriptions of '$x \ni (-x-)$' and '$x \ni (..x..)$'). Thus we see that suitable extensionality laws hold for LDes without restriction.

Nominal virtual classes differ from ordinary virtual classes only in a *manière de parler*. There is no difference in ontology—in fact there is no ontology here at all, for, strictly, virtual classes do not exist in the sense of being values for variables. We speak, however, *as though* there were such things as nominal virtual classes and thus give the theory of intensions a kind of ontological flavor. Distinctions in intension thus seem to reflect an ontological difference, but actually are reducible to differences in the *manière de parler*. Strictly, there are no such things as virtual classes, nominal virtual classes, or intensions. They are mere forms of nonbeing.

The only contexts thus far introduced in which 'ObjAnlytcInt(a)' may occur significantly are of the form of the definiendum of (D3), in which a nominal virtual class is said to be a member of the ObjAnlytc-Int(a). Similarly for 'ObjVerInt(a)', 'ObjSynthcInt(a)', and 'ObjThm-Int(a)'. However, further contexts may be introduced definitionally, in particular, contexts in which we may say that one intension is *included* in another or that an intension is *identical* with an intension.

Various relations of inclusion as between one-place predicate constants have already been introduced. The following definitions introduce various relations of inclusion as between objective intensions.

'ObjAnlycInt(a) $\subset$ ObjAnlytcInt(b)' abbreviates 'Pred-ConOne a, PredConOne b, and for all c, if a AnlytcInc c then b AnlytcInc c',

'ObjAnlytcInt(a) $\subset$ ObjVerInt(b)' abbreviates 'Pred-ConOne a, PredConOne b, and for all c, if a AnlytcInc c then b VerInc c',

and so on, for all possible cases. There are sixteen in all. Identity for each case is merely mutual inclusion. Thus,

'ObjAnlytcInt(a) $=$ ObjAnlytcInt(b)' abbreviates 'Obj-AnlytcInt(a) $\subset$ ObjAnlytcInt(b) and ObjAnlytcInt(b) $\subset$ ObjAnlytcInt(a)',

and so on.

Also, we can introduce an existential operator for objective intensions. We let

'E!ObjAnlytcInt(a)' abbreviate 'There is a b such that a AnlytcInc b',

and so on.

We have immediately existence theorems, to the effect that if a is a PredConOne, then E!ObjAnlytcInt(a), E!ObjVerInt(a), and E!Obj-ThmInt(a). For synthetic or factual intensions, much depends upon the axioms of the object language, which in turn depend upon what the *facts* are, so to speak. Ordinarily we should be able to show that the objective synthetic intension of a PreConOne exists also, but it is not clear that this can always be done.

We have some interesting inclusional laws for intensions, as follows. If a is a PredConOne then the objective analytic intension of a

is included in the objective veridical intension of *a*. Similarly, if *a* is a PredConOne, its objective theoremic intension is included in its objective veridical intension, its objective analytic intension is included in its objective theoremic intension, and its objective synthetic intension is included in its veridical one.

Let '*F*', '*G*', and '*H*' be hereafter any PredConOne's. (Thus '*F*' and '*x*ɜ(—*x*—)', and so on, may be used pretty much interchangeably.) That analytic and synthetic intensions are properly distinguishable is shown by the following law. If the nominal virtual class *F* is a member of the objective synthetic intension of *a*, then *F* is not a member of its objective analytic intension. That they are properly combinable is shown by the following. *F* is a member of the objective veridical intension of *a* if and only if *F* is a member of its objective analytic intension or of its objective synthetic intension.

5. The Laws of Inverse Variation. A fundamental "principle" concerning intensions is the so-called law of inverse variation of extension and intension. There was much controversy over this law in the latter half of the nineteenth century, and its exact logical status was in doubt. The controversy seems never to have been settled, and the "law," if such it be, seems never to have been stated adequately. Although it has been occasionally mentioned by more recent writers, no one seems to have probed the logic, if there be such, underlying it. In particular, the law seems not to have been examined by such proponents of intensions as Carnap, Church, Fitch, or Frege. Yet, it has often been regarded as one of the fundamental laws concerning intensions. A clear and unobjectionable statement of it is necessary if the theory of intensions is to be given a secure modern footing.

Let us examine critically a little of the fascinating history of this law, preparatory to attempting to give it a more exact form. We shall not present a complete account but will merely select a few formulations of outstanding interest. If we start in the center, this will at least (in Bradley's phrase) get us into the heart of the matter.

Bradley in fact called the law "that preposterous article of orthodox logic [that] turned the course of our reasoning into senseless miracle."[5] However Bradley never formulated the law very clearly. "Extension and intension," he says almost mockingly, ". . . are related and must be related in a certain way. *The less you happen to have of the one, the more therefore you must have of the other* [italics added]. This statement has often passed itself off as both true and important.

[5] *The Principles of Logic*, 2d ed. (London: Oxford University Press; 1922), Vol. II, p. 486.

I confess that to me it has has always seemed false or frivolous."[6] Frivolous indeed, lacking clear and defensible definitions of 'intension', 'less', 'happen to have', 'must have', and, no doubt, other terms. Such definitions are not, it is to be feared, to be found anywhere in the annals of idealist logic.

For Bradley, as for others in the Hegelian tradition, the notion of intension is intimately bound up with the doctrine of the "concrete universal." There, however, 'intension' takes on a quite different meaning, in which extension and intension seem to coalesce. Hence naturally, on such a meaning, a law of inverse variation does not hold.[7]

As good a preliminary statement of the law as any—and better than most—is to be found in the fourth edition (1906) of Neville Keynes' *Formal Logic*.[8]

> (L)   In a series of common terms standing to one another
>   in a relation of subordination *the extension and intension*
>   *vary inversely*.

Keynes does not himself accept the law in this form but uses it merely as a basis for discussion.

Note first that this preliminary formulation of the law concerns *terms*, not what the terms designate or denote. Thus we see immediately that it is to be a law of syntax or semantics, not of some object language. However, the terms are *common*, that is, denotative, and they denote objects in common, so that the law is clearly a semantical law, not a syntactical one and not one of logic in a narrow sense. Further, the terms must be arranged in a series, although strictly this is an elaboration that is not needed. The relation of *subordination* between terms is presumably a semantical relation, analogous to class inclusion. A term *a* is subordinate to a term *b* if and only if every object denoted by *a* is also denoted by *b*.[9] The extension of a term *a* is presumably the class (or virtual class) of all objects denoted by *a*. So far so good, barring niceties.

The *extension* of a term, Keynes says (p. 22), "consists of objects

---

[6] *Op. cit.,* Vol. I, p. 170.

[7] See in particular B. Bosanquet, *Logic*, 2d ed. (London: Oxford University Press, 1911), Vol. I, pp. 64 and *passim*.

[8] (London: Macmillan, 1906), p. 35 ff. This book was termed "excellent" by C. S. Peirce (*Collected Papers*, 3.384), and has been called by Heinrich Scholz "the most perfect presentation of classical formal logic in general . . . [which] has been equally great and beneficent in its influence within Anglo-Saxon civilization." See his *Concise History of Logic,* tr. by K. Leidecker (New York: Philosophical Library, 1961), p. 48.

[9] See *Truth and Denotation*, p. 104.

of which the name can be predicated," whereas "its *intension* consists of properties which can be predicated of it," that is, of the extension. Intensions are of three kinds, *conventional, subjective,* and *objective.* The conventional intension, or *connotation,* of a class name consists of "those qualities which are essential to the class in the sense that the name implies them in its definition. Were any of this set of qualities absent the name would not be applicable. . . ." (How about *primitive* class names, not defined?) Perhaps Keynes's definition may be made a little more precise by regarding the connotation of a defined class name 'P' as the class of all "qualities" Q such that necessarily for all x, if x has P, then x has Q.

The subjective intension of a term depends upon the individual user of the term and is "less important from the logical standpoint."[10] Therefore, nothing more need be said about it here.

Finally, there "is the sum total of qualities actually possesed in common by all members of the class. These will include all the qualities included under the two preceding heads, and usually many others in addition." This sum total comprises the objective intension or *comprehension* of the class name. Perhaps a "sum total" is a logical sum of classes. Or is it rather a *set?* Keynes is not too explicit on this point, although, as we have seen, the word 'set' creeps surreptitiously into his explanation of the meaning of 'connotation'. However, a logical sum is not a set, and it is most important to know which is intended if we are to have here a clear meaning for 'connotation' and 'objective intension'.

Keynes speaks of "classes" as, presumably, the objects designated by class names. On the other hand, intensions are sum totals or sets of "qualities." His ontology is thus at best rather mixed.

Keynes distinguishes three laws of variation that "must together be substituted for the law of inverse variation between extension and intension in its usual form (L) if full precision of statement is desired." The first of these laws is (p. 37):

(K)   If the connotation of a term is arbitrarily enlarged or restricted, the denotation in an assigned universe of discourse will either remain unaltered or will change in the opposite direction.

The statement of (K) is surely clearer than that of (L). In particular, note that 'vary inversely' has been dropped. What is meant anyhow by 'inverse variation' in connection with the extension and

[10] See, however, *Intension and Decision,* Chapter II–IV.

intension of terms? We have no quantitative measure of terms, so that 'inverse variation' cannot mean here what it ordinarily means in physics.

Let 'M' be a class term. Let con('M') for the moment be the conventional intension or connotation of 'M'. What does it mean now to say that the connotation of 'M' is "arbitrarily enlarged or restricted?" Presumably by this—in accord with (L)—we are invited to consider the connotation of another class P in which M is properly included or which properly includes M. Let con('P') be the connotation of 'P'. In saying that the connotation of 'M' is enlarged, we are intended perhaps to consider that con('M') is properly *included* in or subordinate to con('P'). Of course we can say this only where con('M') and con('P') are themselves *sets* (or classes of some sort, perhaps classes of classes or of "qualities"), so that by 'inclusion' is mean set inclusion of the type appropriate to sets of "qualities." If, on the other hand, conventional intensions (or connotations) are to be construed as logical sums of classes, inclusion must be of the type appropriate to classes of individuals. Then two statements corresponding to (K) should be distinguished, depending upon whether con('P') and con('M') are taken as logical sums or as classes. Both of these statements, however, will have the form

(K')   If con('P') is properly included in con('M'), then M is properly included in or identical with P.

(K'), on the set meaning, although an improvement on (K), is still far from satisfactory. In particular there is implicit reference to "attributes" or "characteristics." It is doubtful that we need recognize a separate realm of attributes as distinguished from classes, for they are a dubious entity at best. A clear condition under which two attributes may be said to be identical is lacking, as Quine and others have repeatedly pointed out.[11] Also, the notion of connotation is not too clear. What are "those qualities which are essential to the class in the sense that the name implies them in its definition?" What is meant by 'essential' here? By 'implies'? Without acceptable answers to these questions we cannot claim to have put forward a clear theory of connotation at all.

It should be noted, incidentally, that Keynes is usually careful to distinguish between the use and mention of expressions, a care not shown by all writers on the subject. However, he vacillates between speaking of class names and of "properties" or "qualities" or "attributes"

[11] See, for example, *From a Logical Point of View* (Cambridge: Harvard University Press, 1953) and *Word and Object*.

or "characteristics," as we have noted. Many of his statements concerning class names are acceptable on the basis of modern syntax and semantics. When he speaks of "attributes" or "characteristics," in the wake no doubt of Aristotelian essentialism, he is less clear and not always defensible.

Keynes goes on to distinguish two other laws of variation, which, however, concern more special notions and are merely supplementary to (K).

Two further, but very different, formulations of the "law" are to be found in Cohen and Nagel's widely influential *An Introduction to Logic and Scientific Method*.[12] First:

(A)   *When a series of terms is arranged in order of subordination, the extension and intension vary inversely.*

Secondly:

(B)   *If a series of terms is arranged in order of increasing intension, the denotation of the terms will either remain the same or diminish.*

Cohen and Nagel criticize (A) but seem to condone (B) as a satisfactory law.

Although these two formulations appear similar to those of Neville Keynes, actually they are very different. In the first place, by 'a term' Cohen and Nagel do not understand an expression, but rather what the expression stands for. Propositions, according to them and following Aristotle,

either assert or deny something of something else. That about which the assertion is made is called the *subject*, and that which is asserted about the subject is called the *predicate*. The subject and the predicate [that is presumably, the things, not the expressions] are called the *terms* of the proposition. . . . A term may be viewed in two ways, [they continue,] either as a class of objects (which may have only one member), or as a set of attributes or characteristics which determine the objects. The first phase or aspect is called the *denotation* or *extension* of the term, while the second is called the *connotation* or *intension*. Thus the extension of the term "philosopher" is "Socrates," "Plato," "Thales," and the like; its intension is "lover of wisdom," "intelligent," and so on.

[12] (New York: Harcourt, Brace and Co., 1934), pp. 30–33.

It is interesting to note that Cohen and Nagel explicitly take the intension as a *set* of attributes or characteristics. They are perhaps the first to recognize explicitly that intensions are sets in some fashion, and this recognition constitutes an advance in the subject.

By 'the *conventional intension* or *connotation* of a term', Cohen and Nagel mean, more precisely, "the set of attributes which are essential to it." Thus the intension of the attribute P is presumably the set of all attributes A essential to P. By "essential," they say, "we mean the necessary and sufficient condition [in the singular, notice] for regarding any object as an element of the term." This definition is not too clear. Perhaps, according to it, we may say that attribute Q is essential to attribute P, if and only if necessarily every object which has P has Q, and conversely. The intension of P then becomes the set of all attributes A, such that necessarily every object which has P has A, and conversely. However, this is not the set intended, for presumably it would be a set with only one member, namely, P itself. Perhaps the intension of P here is to be only (i) the set of all attributes A such that necessarily every object that has P has A. Or perhaps (ii) the finite set of attributes $\{Q_1, \ldots, Q_n\}$ such that necessarily every x that has P has Q_1, has Q_2, . . . , has Q_n. This is all a little murky.

For the subordination of intensions Cohen and Nagel have a clear meaning, because intensions are certain kinds of sets, and hence subordination is merely class or set inclusion. Let for the moment 'int(P)' designate the intension of P in whatever sense they intend. If we disregard for the moment the unnecessary complication of bringing in the notion of a series, their formulation (A) seems to be:

(A′)   If P is subordinate to Q, then int(Q) is subordinate to int(P).

By 'subordinate' here is meant for the moment *properly subordinate* or *is properly included in*. (B) on the other hand would read:

(B′)   If int(Q) is subordinate to int(P), then P is subordinate to or identical with Q.

We do not claim that (A′) and (B′) are precisely what Cohen and Nagel intend by (A) and (B), but only that they are perhaps reasonably close approximations.

It should be noted that Cohen and Nagel's formulations are given as principles within an object language. However, for Keynes, as we have observed, these principles are metalinguistic, more precisely, semantical, principles. It is not altogether clear what is thought to be gained by their statement within an object language. Usually by 'a *term*' one understands an *expression* of such and such a kind. Keynes is explicit on this point. According to him, ". . . it seems better to start from the names. . . . Neglect to consider names in . . . connexion [with extension and intension] has been responsible for much confusion." Carnap and Frege also have emphasized the importance of regarding intensions as intensions of expressions. In fact, it is now almost universally recognized that the theory of extension, denotation, connotation, intension, and the like, belongs to semantics, and hence is to be formulated within a semantical metalanguage.

There is also the difficulty concerning 'necessary' in Cohen and Nagel's formulations. Is this to be construed in the sense of some modal operator? If so, the mixing of modal operators and quantifiers must be faced squarely. We do not wish to contend that this cannot be done satisfactorily, but only that there are grave difficulties here that must not be glossed over. Quine and others have pointed these out repeatedly. Surely we cannot expect a satisfactory formulation in the manner of Cohen and Nagel of the law or laws of inverse variation until these difficulties are overcome. Also closely connected with these is the dubious ontology of attributes, and so on, which we have already met in the formulations of Keynes.[13]

The reader may object that we are being excessively laborious as to logical detail. However, to borrow a phrase that Cohen and Nagel themselves use in another context, "it is necessary to . . . [be] so if we wish to avoid elementary confusions." In trying to avoid such confusions we must occasionally be allowed to refer to more advanced matters in modern logic, syntax, and semantics, as well as to pay strict attention to what might appear as minutiae. To refuse to allow this is often to refuse to let a subject grow or develop beyond its incipient (or textbook) stages. As logic itself, including now the theory of intensions, has developed enormously within recent years, it must carry its history along with it, subjecting it to fresh critical scrutiny in the light of present knowledge.

Let us try to do better now if we can with the law of inverse variation, in the light of the material of Sections 2 to 4 above.

Actually there are several such laws to be distinguished, a few of which are as follows: If a and b are both PredConOne's, then ObjAnlytcInt(a) $\subset$ ObjAnlytcInt(b) if and only if b AnlytcInc a. Simi-

all b's are a's

---

[13] Further, the Cohen and Nagel laws, if such they be, appear to presuppose fragments at least of some kind of modal set theory, which, it is to be feared, had not been adequately formulated at the time. See, however, F. B. Fitch, "A Complete and Consistent Modal Set Theory," *The Journal of Symbolic Logic* 32 (1967), 93–103.

larly, if a and b are PredConOne's, then $\text{ObjVerInt}(a) \subset \text{ObjVerInt}(b)$ if and only if $b\,\text{VerInc}\,a$. And likewise for objective theoremic intensions.

There are also several mixed laws of inverse variation, as follows: If a and b are PredConOne's and either $\text{OjbVerInt}(a) \subset \text{ObjAnlytc-Int}(b)$ or $\text{ObjThmInt}(a) \subset \text{ObjAnlytcInt}(b)$, then $b\,\text{AnlytcInc}\,a$. If a and b are PredConOne's, then either $\text{ObjAnlytcInt}(a) \subset \text{ObjVerInt}(b)$ or $\text{ObjThmInt}(a) \subset \text{ObjVerInt}(a)$ if and only if $b\,\text{VerInc}\,a$. If a and b are PredConOne's and either $\text{ObjAnlytcInt}(a) \subset \text{ObjThmInt}(a)$ or $\text{ObjVerInt}(a) \subset \text{ObjThmInt}(a)$, then $b\,\text{ThmInc}\,a$.

Various relations of equivalence as between PredConOne's may now be introduced as mutual inclusions. Thus *a* is *analytically equivalent* (AnlytcEquiv) with *b* where $a\,\text{AnlytcInc}\,b$ and $b\,\text{AnlytcInc}\,a$, and *a* is *synthetically* equivalent with *b* where $a\,\text{SynthcInc}\,b$ and $b\,\text{SynthcInc}\,a$, and so on.

As corollaries there are the following laws concerning the various kinds of equivalence: If a and b are PredConOne's, then $\text{ObjAnlytc-Int}(a) = \text{ObjAnlytcInt}(b)$ if and only if $a\,\text{AnlytcEquiv}\,b$. And similarly for objective veridical intensions relative to veridical equivalence and objective theoremic intensions relative to theoremic equivalence.

Let us say now that one *nominal virtual class* is *analytically included* in another if the expression that L-designates the first is analytically included in the expression that L-designates the second. Thus, where 'F' and 'G' are PredConOne's,

> '$F\,\text{AnlytcInc}\,G$'   abbreviates   'There is an a and a b such that $a\,\text{LDes}\,F$, $b\,\text{LDes}\,G$, and $a\,\text{AnlytcInc}\,b$'.

Also, we may introduce the relation of *analytical equivalence* as between nominal virtual classes. We let

> '$F\,\text{AnlytcEquiv}\,G$'   abbreviate   '$F\,\text{AnlytcInc}\,G$ and $G\,\text{AnlytcInc}\,F$'.

We now have some laws of inverse variation involving L-designation: If a and b are PredConOne's, $a\,\text{LDes}\,F$ and $b\,\text{LDes}\,G$, then $\text{ObjAnlytcInt}(a) \subset \text{ObjAnlytcInt}(b)$ if and only if $G\,\text{AnlytcInc}\,F$. Hence, if a and b are PredConOne's, $a\,\text{LDes}\,F$, and $b\,\text{LDes}\,G$, then $\text{ObjAnlytcInt}(a) = \text{ObjAnlytcInt}(b)$ if and only if $F\,\text{AnlytcEquiv}\,G$. And similarly for objective veridical intensions with respect to veridical inclusion and veridical equivalence.

We need not tarry with these technicalia further, the main line of development being clear enough.

6. Whiteheadian Intensions. Let us go on now to further kinds of intension, as suggested in *Intension and Decision*, refashioning them as needed. In particular, the so-called *Whiteheadian* intensions must be handled rather differently. Here there is no type theory by way of logical scaffolding, and hence the virtual theory must be made to suffice. Whiteheadian intensions will have as members nominal virtual classes of virtual classes.

The general definition for *Whiteheadian analytic intensions* is as follows. Here as above only contexts in which such and such a nominal virtual class (of higher type) is said to be a *member* of a Whiteheadian analytic intension of a PredConOne are introduced. It is presupposed that abstracts of higher type such as

$$\text{`}G\mathrm{ə}(\text{—}G\text{—})\text{'}$$

have been introduced contextually, and that

$$\text{`}b \text{ LDes } G\mathrm{ə}(\text{—}G\text{—})\text{'}$$

has been suitably defined. Then, without more ado

(D4)   '$G\mathrm{ə}(\text{—}G\text{—}) \in \text{WhtdAnlytcInt}(a)$' is to abbreviate 'PredConOne a and there is a b such that b LDes $G\mathrm{ə}$ (—G—) and Anlytc ($b\widehat{\ }a$)'.

The '$\widehat{\ }$' here is the sign of concatenation, we recall, so that ($b\widehat{\ }a$) is the string of symbols b followed by a.

And similarly for the other kinds of Whiteheadian intension, synthetic, veridical, and theoremic.

As an example, consider again the defined PredConOne 'M'. We note that '$(x)(Mx \supset Mx)$', '$(x)(Mx \supset (Rx \cdot Ax))$', '$(x)(Mx \supset Rx)$', '$(x)(Mx \supset Ax)$', and so on, are a few Anlytc's containing 'M'. As members of the WhtdAnlytcInt(a), where a LDes M, there are then the *nominal* virtual classes of virtual classes $G\in(x)(Mx \supset Gx)$, $G\mathrm{ə}(x)$ $(Gx \supset Mx)$, $G\mathrm{ə}(x)(Gx \supset Gx)$, $G\mathrm{ə}(x)(Gx \supset (Rx \cdot Ax))$, $G\mathrm{ə}(x)$ $(Gx \supset Rx)$, $G\mathrm{ə}(x)(Gx \supset Ax)$, and so on.

Enough has been said surely to indicate how the theory of Whiteheadian intensions for PredConOne's could be further developed.

That intensions turn out to be merely virtual, lends further support to the theory of virtual classes. And that intensions may be introduced within the semantical metalanguage based on 'Den' provides further ground for thinking that this metalanguage is adequate for philosophical purposes. To have used a metalanguage of higher order for the theory of intensions, as in *Intension and Decision*, was a step backward anyhow. To have employed essentially the whole of mathematics (contained in such a metalanguage) merely to develop so essentially simple a theory as the semantical theory of intensions is to have employed too much. The notions of intension are not notions of mathematics, and it is an anomaly to have supposed that they were. (By 'mathematics' here we mean, barring niceties, the theory of real classes and/or sets.) The inadequacy of the treatment in *Intension and Decision* results in part from having made too much of real classes rather than to have relied on their virtual counterparts. Here as elsewhere real classes lead us astray; virtual ones, on the other hand, are a sure guide.

7. Do Proper Names Connote? Mill says 'No'. Proper names, according to him, "denote the individuals who are called by them; but they do not indicate or imply any attribute as belonging to these individuals."[14] Hence proper names are "non-connotative." There is, however, according to Mill, "another kind of names, which, although they are individual names . . . are really connotative." Such names involve "some attribute, or some union of attributes, which, being possessed by no object but one, determines the name exclusively to that individual." As examples of such names Mill cites 'the sun', 'God' (as used by a Christian), 'the only son of John Stiles', 'the first emperor of Rome', 'the father of Socrates', 'the author of the *Iliad*', 'the murderer of Henri Quatre', and so on. Such connotative phrases convey some information, according to Mill, as contrasted with proper names, which convey none.

Carnap's *individual concepts* are closely allied with the connotations of proper names. (Recall Chapter III, Section 1.) "Now it seems to me a natural procedure," Carnap writes, "in the case of individual expressions, . . . to speak of concepts . . . of a particular type, namely, the individual type."[15] Thus, according to Carnap, the intension of a special individual constant 's' is the individual concept Walter Scott and the intension of the appropriate description is the individual concept The Author of *Waverley*. Individual concepts are thus a special kind of intension and share the *modus essendi* of intensions in general, which is that of (p. 21) "something objective that is found in nature." Beyond this we are not told very much, and the exact logic of individual concepts, it is to be feared, remains yet to be developed.[16] It is clear, however, that according to Carnap, both proper names and Russellian

[14] J. S. Mill, *A System of Logic* (many editions), Bk I, Chapter II, 5.
[15] R. Carnap, *Meaning and Necessity*, p. 41.
[16] See, however, Chapter XII, Section 5, below.

descriptions can significantly have both intensions and extensions, essentially as with Frege.

For Frege, in his own words, "it is natural . . . to think of there being connected with a sign . . . , besides that to which the sign refers, which may be called the *reference* of the sign, also what I should like to call the *sense* [*Sinn*] of the sign, wherein the mode of presentation [*Art des Gegebenseins*] is contained."[17] By 'a proper name' Frege understands a sign "which . . . has as its reference a definite object (this word taken in the widest range). . . . " Frege includes descriptive phrases among proper names, for he notes that "designations of a single object can also consist of several words or other signs." Precisely what a sense is for Frege does not emerge too clearly, however, as has already been suggested, but the matter need not be pondered further for the moment. (See Chapter X below.)

However this may be, it is interesting to note that the various kinds of Whiteheadian intension may be introduced for *individual* constants, and this in contrast to the other types of objective intension mentioned in Section 6.

By 'an *individual expression* of a first-order L' let us mean, as is more or less customary, either a primitive individual constant (proper name) or a Russellian description of an individual. Whether the latter are primitive or defined depends upon special features of L. Let us assume, mainly for convenience, that descriptions are taken as primitive terms of the system. Let 'InExp *a*' express that *a* is an individual expression. We may then for the moment let

(D5)   '$x\ni(\text{---}x\text{---}) \,\epsilon\, \text{WhtdAnlytcInt}(a)$' abbreviate 'InExp
         a and there is a *b* such that *b* LDes $x\ni(\text{---}x\text{---})$ and
         Anlytc $(b\frown a)$',

InCon (D5') see p. 159

preparatory to suggesting an improvement.

What are the analytic truths of L involving individual expressions (these latter being taken to include descriptions)? Actually they turn out to be rather dull. '$a = a$' is one where in place of '*a*' we put in any InExp. So is '$\sim a = b$' where in place of '*a*' and '*b*' we put in distinct InExp's. So is '$(x)Fx \supset Fa$' and the like. As members of the WhtdAnlytcInt of the specific InExp '*a*', we have then the nominal virtual classes $x\ni(x = a)$, $x\ni(\sim x = b)$, and so on, $x\ni((x)Fx \supset Fa)$, $x\ni(Fx \lor \sim Fx)$, $x\ni(x = x)$, and so on. $x\ni(x = a) \,\epsilon\, \text{WhtdAnlytcInt}('a')$ because '$x\ni(x = a)\, a$' is an Anlytc, that is, '*a* is a member of the virtual class of *x*'s such that $x = a$' is analytically true in L. Simi-

x §12

---

[17] *Translations from the Philosophical Writings of Gottlob Frege*, p. 57.

Information must include logical truths.

larly, '$x\ni(\sim x = b)$ a' is an Anlytc, and so on. This list just about exhausts the interesting cases. Roughly, the Whiteheadian analytic intension of 'a' consists of all universal nominal virtual classes (for strictly there are many) of the nominal virtual class of entities identical with a, of the nominal virtual class of entities distinct from b, from c, and so on.

We do not claim that there is anything wrong with the list, and in a way it does spell out some nominal virtual classes determinative of the intension of 'a'. The list does, in Mill's phrase, single out in effect "some attribute, or some union of attributes, which, being possessed by no object but one, determines the name exclusively to that individual."

Nonetheless, the notion of a Whiteheadian analytic intension seems more appropriate for primitive descriptions than for primitive individual constants. For the latter, the kinds of nominal virtual classes cited perhaps suffice. For descriptive phrases, however, more seems needed. Consider again 'the author of *Waverley*'. It might be thought that part of the intension of this phrase should be the very property of being the author of *Waverley*, and this even if *Waverley* had never been written. Another property its intension should have as a part, it might be maintained, is the property of being an author of something or other; and so on. For descriptive phrases, then, another definition recommends itself, incorporating these additional "properties."

Let '*inviota*' be the structural-descriptive name of the *inverted iota* '$\imath$', and '*ex*' of '*x*'. If c is then the structural-descriptive name of '(—*x*—)', then '(*inviota*⌢*ex*⌢*c*)' is the structural description of '($\imath x \cdot$ (—*x*—))'. Likewise, let '*invep*' be the structural-descriptive name of the *inverted epsilon* '$\ni$'. Finally, let 'SentFuncOne *a,b*' express that *a* is a sentential function of L containing *b* as its only free variable.

Now we may let

(D6)   '$x\ni(—x—) \epsilon$ WhtdAnlytcInt(*a*)' abbreviate 'There is a *b* and a *c* such that *b* LDes $x\ni(—x—)$, SentFunc-One *c,ex, a* = (*inviota*⌢*ex*⌢*c*), and (*ex*⌢*invep*⌢*c*) Anlytc-Inc *b*'.

(If some other variable is put in here in place of '*x*', the structural description of that variable is to supplant '*ex*'.)

Note that as members of the analytic intension of '($\imath x \cdot Axw$)' ('the author of *Waverley*'), we have now the following nominal virtual classes: $x\ni(Axw)$, $x\ni((Ey)Axy)$, $x\ni(x = x)$, $x\ni(Fx \lor \sim Fx)$, and any $x\ni(Fx)$ where '$(x)(Axw \supset Fx)$' is analytic. This gives us an interesting membership, namely, to speak loosely, the nominal virtual classes directly "determining the name [description] exclusively to that individual" together with all nominal virtual classes analytically entailed thereby.

Let (D5) be changed now to apply only to primitive individual constants. Also, let 'InCon a' express that a is a primitive individual constant. In the definiendum of (D5), 'InExp a' is now to be replaced by 'InCon a'. Let this result be (D5'). (D5') and the generalization of (D6) together then give a completely general definition for all individual expressions, that is, for all primitive individual constants and Russellian descriptions.

We may go on to the other types of objective intension, *synthetic, veridical,* and *theoremic,* by changing the clauses concerning analyticity in the definientia of (D5') and (D6) to corresponding clauses concerning being *synthetic,* being *true,* or being a *theorem.* Some of these further types of intension are perhaps not especially interesting on their own account, but they are there nonetheless.[18]

Mill thought that proper names were not connotative. This view is reflected in the dull array of nominal virtual classes that are members of the analytic intension of a primitive individual constant. It is interesting that Mill seems to have distinguished between proper names and descriptions rather more sharply in one respect than either Frege or Carnap, proper names being connotative for him, descriptions not. Neither Frege nor Carnap show how *Sinne* or individual concepts are built up, and hence they do not exhibit a difference in structure as between *Sinne* or individual concepts for the two kinds of individual expressions. Mill at least suggested a structure for the connotata of descriptions, but he did not characterize it too clearly. Here as often the English tradition triumphs over the Germanic one.

8. Russell on Meaning and Denoting. It will be of interest to compare very roughly the foregoing theory of intensions with some suggestions of Russell, with whom there is welcome kinship.

In his famous paper of 1905, "On Denoting," Russell makes the key point that "when we wish to speak about the *meaning* of a denoting phrase, as opposed to its *denotation,* the natural mode of doing so is by inverted commas."[19] Let C be some denoting phrase. Russell is interested in the relation between C and 'C'. ". . . [W]hen C occurs," he says, "it is the *denotation* that we are speaking about; but when 'C' occurs, it is the *meaning.*" We need not tarry over the details of Russell's discussion, which contains flashes of great insight

[18] See *Intension and Decision, passim.*
[19] B. Russell, *Logic and Knowledge* (London: Allen and Unwin, 1956), pp. 39–56.

amid a morass of confusion. The key point, which he is one of the first to have emphasized, is that discussion of meaning should take place in terms of discussion of signs. The meaning of a sign is thus to be found, in part at least, *in its mention*. Once this is granted, we can part from Russell widely on matters of detail.

Russell here differs remarkably from Frege. For Frege, the discussion of meaning is to take place in terms presumably of abstract postulated entities. Whatever Russell wishes to say about meaning, however, is to be said in terms of the signs. This view is echoed somewhat in the foregoing use of nominal virtual classes. However, because the theory of intensions above presupposes the notion of analytic truth, it is essentially a semantical theory, as with Frege, even though the semantical presuppositions involved differ remarkably.

In the theory put forward above, of course, 'denotation' is taken in a very different sense from that of Russell. Here only primitive or defined one-place predicate constants denote. Russell, on the other hand, in addition to descriptive phrases of the form 'the one so and so', regards phrases such as 'a man', 'all men', 'some man', and so on, as denoting. Apparently he had not, in 1905, straightened out completely the proper use of the quantifiers. Once this is done, what is left of Russell's theory concerns only descriptions.

Descriptive phrases have been explicitly introduced in the theory of intensions given above. However, there are of course alternative methods. Much depends upon whether descriptions are taken as primitive or defined in Russell's way. If the latter, there is then no need for a discussion of their meaning. If, on the other hand, they are taken as primitives, as with Frege or Carnap, and above, then of course there is. The distinction between primitive and defined signs, in general, is of the utmost methodological importance. Yet, curiously, little attention is paid to it by methodologists or analytic philosophers. Doubtless the reason is that the distinction seems irrelevant for natural language. We do not worry about what the primitives of a natural language are, although it is no doubt time that we did. However, for logic, the discussion of language systems, syntax, semantics, and the like, the distinction cannot be disregarded with impunity.

Russell is never too clear as to *precisely* what a meaning is. To say merely that "when '*C*' occurs, it is the *meaning*" we are speaking about, or that "the natural mode" of speaking about the meaning is by inverted commas, is not sufficient. Nonetheless, in these passages Russell is careful to distinguish between use and mention, a care unfortunately he does not always show. Also, he is careful there to distinguish between denotation and meaning, a care likewise that, unfortunately, he does not always show. In the theory developed above, meanings or intensions are explicitly identified with certain kinds of virtual classes and thus given an explicit ontological status.

Let us tarry with Russellian descriptions a little longer, particularly in connection with Frege's example concerning 'the morning star' and 'the evening star', so much discussed in the literature. These two phrases presumably stand for or designate the same object, but should have different meanings or analytic intensions.[20]

Within *L*, let 'S*x*' for the moment read '*x* is a star', 'M*x*', '*x* shines in the morning', and 'E*x*', '*x* shines in the evening'. As is customary, we disregard for the moment all astronomical matters and matters concerned with time, as well as more precise characterizations of 'M', 'E', and 'S'. Let Russellian descriptions be regarded as primitive terms of *L*. Let 'ms' and 'es' be distinct, *defined* individual constants, introduced in such a way that

$$\text{'ms} = (\imath x \cdot (Mx \cdot Sx))\text{'}$$

and

$$\text{'es} = (\imath x \cdot (Ex \cdot Sx))\text{'}$$

are analytic sentences of *L*. The Whiteheadian analytic intensions of 'ms' and 'es' then differ, as we wish them to intuitively, because we can find a nominal member of the one that is not a member of the other. Now clearly

$$\text{'}(x)((Mx \cdot Sx) \supset (Mx \cdot Sx))\text{'}$$

is analytic whereas

$$\text{'}(x)((Mx \cdot Sx) \supset (Ex \cdot Sx))\text{'},$$

although true in astronomy, is not. Hence,

$$x \ni (Mx \cdot Sx) \ \epsilon \ \text{WhtdAnlytcInt('ms')}$$

but

$$\sim x \ni (Mx \cdot Sx) \ \epsilon \ \text{WhtdAnlytcInt('es')} \cdot$$

And similarly for other cases. If, on the other hand, 'ms' and 'es' are primitive, defined individual constants, and where 'ms = es' is synthetically true, then clearly

---

[20] The following paragraph corrects pp. 124–125 of *Intension and Decision*.

$$x \ni (x = \mathrm{ms}) \; \epsilon \; \mathrm{WhtdAnlytcInt('ms')}$$

but

$$\sim x \ni (x = \mathrm{ms}) \; \epsilon \; \mathrm{WhtdAnlytcInt('es')} \cdot$$

9. On Connotation. The objective analytic intension of a PredConOne may be regarded as, if one wishes, its *connotation*.[21] Surely here again there is enough agreement with the traditional notion to justify the terminology. Traditionally, English logicians have preferred 'connotation' to the more Germanic 'intension'. At any event, it is convenient to speak here of a *relation* of connoting correlative with that of denoting. Actually the matter is very simple, for we may immediately introduce

'a Con F'   for   '$F \; \epsilon \; \mathrm{ObjAnlytcInt}(a)$'.

The definiendum may read 'a connotes the nominal virtual class F'.

More interesting is the notion of *virtual attribute* that emerges from the foregoing. To say now that an object x has the virtual *attribute associated* with a PredConOne is to say that x is a member of every nominal virtual class in the $\mathrm{ObjAnlytcInt}(a)$. This notion is not to be defined in this fashion, but rather as follows.

'x Att a'   abbreviates   'PredConOne a and there is a b such that b Des x and for all c, if PredConOne c and a Anlytc-Inc c, then Tr $(c \widehat{\ } b)$'.

Thus, very roughly, an individual x has the attribute associated with a given PredConOne, a, if x is truly a member of every virtual class in which the virtual class that a designates is analytically included.

Note that this roundabout definition achieves what we wish, lacking as we do quantifiers over nominal virtual classes. Note also that variables over attributes are not available. Attributes are *associated* rather with PredConOne's, one attribute corresponding with many, but analytically equivalent, PredConOne's. This association is reminiscent in some respects of Fitch's conception.[22]

An alternative notion of attribute suggests itself by merely regarding the attribute corresponding to a PredConOne a as the nominal virtual class L-designated by a. The attribute is then merely the virtual class taken in intension. This notion is clearly simpler than the fore-

---

[21] See the author's "On Connotation and Attribute," *The Journal of Philosophy* LXI (1964), 711–724.

[22] See F. B. Fitch, "Attribute and Class," in *Philosophic Thought in France and the United States,* ed. by Marvin Farber (Buffalo: University of Buffalo Publications in Philosophy, 1950), pp. 545–563.

going, and perhaps more natural. Given any virtual class, there are then many attributes corresponding to it; as many as there are distinct PredConOne's designating it. Of course some of these are equivalent with each other, or L-equivalent, and so on.

10. Sense and Synonymy. Carnap conveniently distinguishes between the intension of a term and its *sense*.[23] Intensions are related to analytic equivalence similar to the way in which senses are related to *synonymy*. Two terms that are analytically (or L-) equivalent have the same intension, just as two terms that are synonymous presumably have the same sense. Just what senses are, however, to say nothing of synonymy, remains rather obscure. The following suggestions toward providing an ontology for senses may not be without interest.

Let us say, for the moment, that a PredConOne *a* is *synonymous* with a PredConOne *b*, provided they are analytically equivalent and every primitive predicate or individual constant that occurs in one occurs in the other, with their left-to-right order preserved.

The three conditions seem reasonable. That analytic equivalence is a necessary condition for synonymy scarcely needs comment. That the two expressions contain precisely the same nonlogical constants rules out extraneous subject matter referred to in one and not in the other (even if only in analytic contexts).[24] For example, '$x \ni Mx$' is not synonymous with '$x \ni (Mx \cdot (Rx \lor \sim Rx))$', there being (in some sense) reference to R's in the second but not in the first. The preservation of the left-to-right order of occurrence is also desirable, assuring that the "movement of thought," as it were, is the same for the two expressions. Thus '$x \ni (Mx \cdot Rx)$' is not synonymous here with '$x \ni (Rx \cdot Mx)$'.[25] The emphasis is somehow different, it might be maintained, and this difference should be taken account of. Perhaps there are further conditions to be added. For example, we might wish to insist that the association within an abstract be the same, so that '$x \ni (Mx \cdot (Rx \cdot Fx))$' would not be regarded as synonymous with '$x \ni ((Mx \cdot Rx) \cdot Fx)$'. Here too there is a difference in the "movement of thought," it might be maintained, something more than a mere notational or logical difference.

Suppose for the moment that a satisfactory definition of synonymy were forthcoming in some such fashion. Let '*a* Syn *b*' express then

---

[23] See especially *The Philosophy of Rudolf Carnap* (in *The Library of Living Philosophers*, ed. by P. A. Schilpp, La Salle, Ill.: Open Court, 1963), pp. 897 ff.

[24] This suggestion is due apparently to C. I. Lewis.

[25] Carnap queries essentially this point in *The Philosophy of Rudolf Carnap*, p. 899.

that *a* and *b* are synonymous PredConOne's in some suitable sense. What then is a *sense*?

We have spoken only of synonymy, which arises out of analytical equivalence by suitable restrictions. What relation arises by appending these restrictions rather to the definition of analytical *inclusion*? Let us call it, for want of a better phrase, '*analytic entailment*'. Then, synonymy is mutual analytic entailment. Let '*a* AnlytcEnt *b*' express that the PredConOne *a* analytically entails the PredConOne *b* in some suitable way.

It seems natural now to think of a sense as arising from analytic entailment similar to the way in which an objective analytic intension arises from analytic inclusion. Thus, we might let

(D7)   '*F* ε Sns(*a*)'   abbreviate   'PredConOne *a* and there is
            a *b* such that *b* LDes *F* and *a* AnlytcEnt *b*'.

Again, this definition is put forward merely as a suggestion, worthy perhaps of further reflection. Other contexts involving 'Sns' can presumably be introduced in the fashion of Section 3 above.

The foregoing remarks provide a fairly complete sketch of an improved first-order theory of intensions, which is to supplant that of Chapter V of *Intension and Decision*. Although the key definition there, that of 'ObjAnlytcInt', was faulty and threw the whole chapter out of focus, we see now its value as a heuristic, using L-designation in place of designation and nominal virtual classes in place of real ones.[26]

We should emphasize again the extreme simplicity of the theory here. No complicated notions are used, in particular no notions depending upon higher-order quantifiers or in any way upon the mathematical theory of sets. This very simplicity is thought to recommend it for philosophic and linguistic use. We may conveniently distinguish *elementary* (or first-order) from *theoretical* semantics, just as mathematicians frequently distinguish between elementary and analytic number theory. In each case the elementary presupposes usually only a first-order logic. (This same distinction has been drawn in Chapter III, Section 6, as between philosophic and model-theoretic semantics.)

Theoretical semantics, comprising the theory of models, presupposes either a higher-order logic or some suitable set theory, as we

---

[26] The author wishes to thank Messrs. Hendry, Jobe, and Montague for their criticisms, which have helped pave the way for this improved formulation. See Herbert E. Hendry, "Professor Martin's Intensions," *The Journal of Philosophy* LXII (1965), 432–434, and Richard Montague's review of *Intension and Decision*, in *The Journal of Symbolic Logic* 31 (1966), 98–102.

have noted. In elementary semantics such high-powered tools are eschewed. Just as it is of interest in number theory to use only elementary procedures where possible, so also in semantics. We have attempted to show in this chapter that elementary procedures suffice for a semantical theory of intensions, and this heretofore, if we mistake not, has been thought possible.

Attention has been confined here wholly to PredConOne's. However, we can go on to two-place, and so on, predicate constants, constructing a theory of intensions for such by analogy with the foregoing. Perhaps here, as in relation theory generally, some interesting intrisincally relational notions would emerge, transcending the analogy with PredConOne's.

To summarize. The theory sketched in this chapter incorporates the following features. (1) We are concerned with *analyzed* intensions, not intensions *sui generis*, and in this analysis a multitude of kinds emerges that are not distinguished by advocates of the latter. (2) The theory is given within a *first-order* semantical metalanguage for any first-order system *L*. (3) Intensions are given only *virtual* existence, and at that only *nominally* so. (4) There is kinship with Russell in the suggestion that meanings are to be found primarily in the *mention* of expressions. (5) Intensions are dissected into *parts* or *members*, so that one can speak of such and such a nominal virtual class as being a member of such and such an intension. Such modes of speaking are apparently not available for intensions *sui generis*, usually regarded as in some sense indivisible or undissectible wholes. (6) Several laws of *inverse variation* are given in what is (hopefully) a satisfactory way. It is not clear that these laws have ever been adequately stated heretofore. (7) Suitable notions of *connotation* and *attribute* are forthcoming within the metalanguages discussed. (8) Some tentative suggestions are put forward toward characterizing notions of *sense* and *synonymy*.

Logic advances by slow, minute steps, but these we must not be afraid of, or disregard or condemn, if we wish to move forward and avoid "elementary confusions." The truth, it is said, is hid behind seventy thousand veils. If we succeed in lifting but one, we may consider ourselves fortunate.

CHAPTER VIII

Excursus on Facts

The word 'fact' is a seemingly harmless word in our philosophical vocabulary. We feel free to use it without subjecting it to analysis. The supposition is that there are no special difficulties with it, and therefore we should move on to more important matters. Facts are thought to be what true synthetic "propositions" or statements express. The facts are what we are said to believe when we believe truly. The facts are what we seek to have explained in empirical science. The totality of facts is everything that is the case. . . , and so on and on. These statements themselves, however, and their ilk, are far from clear and hence in need of explication. Insofar as particular philosophical positions depend upon them, these positions are themselves suspect and needful of clarification. It will thus not be idle to go to the very roots of the matter and attempt to determine the ontic status of the things (if such there be) that 'fact' is supposed to denote.

First let us examine very briefly in Section 1 some *significant* views on the subject, those of Russell, Ramsey, W. E. Johnson, and Wittgenstein. Two somewhat more technical theories concern us in Section 2, those of *Cohen and Nagel* and of *Carnap*. In Section 3 the *Austin-Strawson* controversy on the subject is discussed, and in Section 4, *Scheffler's* views concerning "explaining the facts." Some *conditions of adequacy* for an analysis of facts are suggested in Section 5.

A theory of facts in terms of *nominal virtual* entities is given in Section 6. The relation of *identity* as between facts concerns us in Section 7. Finally, in Section 8, *second-order* facts are distinguished from those of Section 6. Still more will be said in the next chapter.

167

1. Some Significant Views. Russell set the stage (in 1918) when he contended that there are

> particulars and qualities and relations of various orders, a whole hierarchy of different sorts of simples, but all of them. . . have in their various ways some kind of reality that does not belong to anything else. The only other sort of object you come across in the world is what we call *facts*, and facts are the sort of thing that are asserted or denied by propositions, and are not properly entities at all in the same sense in which their constituents are. This is shown by the fact that you cannot name them. You can only deny, or assert, or consider them, but you cannot name them because they are not there to be named. . . .[1]

In general there are two fundamental ways in which one can speak of a given entity, either by naming it or at least by having it as a value for a variable. Ordinarily, if it is named it is then also a value for a variable. To be sure, there are derivative ways of referring to it, for example, by Russellian descriptions, but to describe a thing is to presuppose already that it is a value for a variable. Unless facts then are either nameable or values for variables, it is not clear how we can speak of them at all.

Russell insists that we cannot name them. He is not clear as to whether they are admissible as values for variables. However, a moment's reflection should convince us that on his view they are not. Russell's ontology, at least in the Logical Atomism papers, consists of "particulars and qualities and relations of various orders" in accord with type theory. Presumably a fact is not a particular, nor a quality, nor a relation of any order, and hence cannot be a value for a variable. It is thus difficult to see how Russell can contend that facts are the "sort of thing you come across in the world." There is simply no room for them among the admissible furniture—or rather, there is no furniture for them in the admissible room.

We could tarry with Russell at length, for he returned to the subject of "facts" time and time again, but without, it is to be feared, arriving at an acceptable doctrine.

We might hope to find a gain in clarity in Ramsey's "Facts and Propositions" of 1927, already referred to in Chapter IV, Section 4. This paper seems mistitled, however, for it is concerned primarily with belief, and with facts and "propositions" only in their connection with belief. Of course philosophical interest in facts and propositions goes

---

[1] B. Russell, *Logic and Knowledge*, p. 270.

hand in hand with the analysis of belief. Propositions have traditionally been thought to be the objects of belief, and facts are what propositions, when true but not analytically so, express.

Ramsey agrees with Russell that 'the fact that so and so' is not to be regarded as a name. He also argues that it is not to be regarded as a description. We might reasonably be inclined to regard a phrase such as 'the death of Caesar' as a "description of an event." Such phrases should surely be analyzed and given an exact logic. (See Chapter IX, Section 2.) The first thing to note about them, however, is that they are not Russellian descriptions of the form 'the one so and so'. Event descriptions are something quite different. Ramsey tells us singularly little about them. Strictly, we should worry here as to what events are, as well as event descriptions. Whatever events and event descriptions may turn out to be, Ramsey insists rightly that they are *not* to be confused with facts and fact descriptions.

> The connection between the *event* which was the death of Caesar [Ramsey writes], and the *fact* that Caesar died [italics added] is, in my opinion, this: 'That Caesar died' is really an existential proposition, asserting the existence of an event of a certain sort, thus resembling 'Italy has a King', which asserts the existence of a man of a certain sort. The event which is of that sort is called 'the death of Caesar' [quotes added], and should no more be confused with the fact that Caesar died than the King of Italy should be confused with the fact that Italy has a King.

Perhaps so, but we cannot be very clear about this contention until we are much clearer as to whether existential propositions "really" assert "the existence of an event of a certain sort." Are these propositions of the form 'There exists an event E such that $—E—$', where '$—E—$' is a sentential function containing 'E' as its only free variable, 'E' ranging over events? Or are they of the form 'Such and such a *kind* of an event exists'? In either case, an ontology of events seems presupposed, and this very ontology itself is in need of analysis. Nonetheless, this passage is of interest in suggesting an important interconnection between fact and event talk, to which we shall return later.

Ramsey notes (pp. 141–2) that, because phrases beginning 'the fact that' are neither names nor descriptions, propositions "about 'the fact that aRb' must be analyzed into (1) the proposition aRb, (2) some further proposition about a, R, b, and other things; and an analysis of cognition in terms of relations to fact cannot be accepted as ultimate." In accord with this, 'X believes that aRb' is to be analyzed in terms of some polyadic relation having as arguments the person X, the proposition aRb, the thing a, the relation R, the thing b, and "other things" (we are not told what), perhaps a time *t*. The suggestion that belief sentences be so analyzed is of the highest importance, as has been noted above, but it is to be doubted that it throws much light on 'fact' or the ontic status of whatever it is supposed to denote (if at all).

In his *Logic*,[2] W. E. Johnson notes that "whereas a proposition is related subjectively to *assertion*, we shall find that it is related objectively to *fact*. Our conclusion, briefly expressed," he says, "is that any proposition *charcterizes* some fact, so that the relation of proposition to fact is the same as that of adjective to substantive." The relation of substantive to adjective corresponds for Johnson to that between particular and universal. "Ultimately [p. 11] a universal means an adjective that may characterize a particular, and a particular means a substantive that may be characterized by a universal." A proposition, or *assertum* or what is *assertible*, (p. xxxiv) is "analyzed by showing that the substantive alone can function as subject, and the adjective as predicate, and that these stand to one another in the relation of characterization."

That propositions are regarded as adjectival characterizations of facts is not so novel as it sounds. Bradley regarded propositions as ultimately characterizing Reality, and Bosanquet, as characterizing that portion of Reality immediately before us. Just as, given a substantive, Johnson notes, there is an indefinite number of adjectives truly predicable of it, so are there "many different propositions which truly characterize any given fact."

Try as we may, it would be difficult to substantiate, on the basis of modern semantics, the Johnsonian view that propositions are adjectival of facts, at least without a much deeper analysis of the latter. If *p* is a proposition and *f* a "fact," then the fundamental form of statement for Johnson would be

$$'pf',$$

which would be read '*p* characterizes *f*'. Unfortunately, Johnson tells us very little about 'characterizes' as used in this context, as a result of which we are scarcely better off than before we started. Of course he wishes to combine an epistemic analysis with some features of the Idealist logic. Hence his view seems primarily a backward glance.

A notion of fact—we say 'a' not 'the', for we do not know that there is just one—seems central to the ontology of Wittgenstein's *Tractatus*.[3] "The world is the totality of facts, not of things. . . . The facts

---

[2] W. E. Johnson, *Logic* (Cambridge: Cambridge University Press, 1921), Vol. I, p. 14.

[3] L. Wittgenstein, *Tractatus Logico-Philosophicus* (New York: Harcourt, Brace and Co., 1922).

in logical space are the world. . . . An atomic fact is a combination of objects (entities, things). It is essential to a thing that it be a constituent part of an atomic fact. . . ." These oft-quoted dicta do not, however, lead us to a clear notion of fact where others have failed. At best, as Max Black has suggested, "Wittgenstein has deliberately parted from the ordinary uses of 'fact' without providing instructions for the new uses."[4] If exact instructions had been given, these dicta would perhaps have lost much of their charm. A main advantage of clear philosophical writing, even if lacking in depth and charm, is that errors then become pellucid, whereas in the murky waters there is often only a seeming depth.

We need not comment at length upon the niceties of Wittgenstein's use of 'fact' in the *Tractatus*. Others have done this ably. Instead, we point out certain dicta for future reference. Especially interesting for such purposes are 2.03–2.032: "In the atomic facts objects hang one in another, like the members of a chain. In the atomic fact the objects are combined in a definite way. The way in which objects hang together in the atomic fact is the structure of the atomic fact."

2. Two Theories. In their *An Introduction to Logic and Scientific Method*,[5] Cohen and Nagel explicitly introduce 'fact' as a technical term. They distinguish four different senses for the word. (1) Facts are "certain discriminated elements in sense perception. That which is denoted by the expressions 'This band of color lies between those two bands', 'The end of this pointer coincides with that mark on the scale' are facts in this sense." Facts (2) are "propositions which *interpret* what is given to us in sense experience," or (3) are "propositions which truly assert an invariable sequence or conjunction of characters." Finally (4) facts are "those things existing in space or time, together with the relations between them, in virtue of which a proposition is true. Facts in this sense are neither true or false, they simply *are*: they can be apprehended by us in part through the senses; they may have a career in time, may push each other, destroy each other, grow, disappear; or they may be untouched by change. Facts in this fourth sense are distinct from the hypotheses we make about them. A hypothesis is true, and is a fact in the second or third sense, when it does state *what* the fact in this fourth sense is."

Senses (2) and (3) are obscure insofar as the notion of proposition itself is obscure. Wherein others have failed in characterizing what

4 Max Black, *A Companion to Wittgenstein's Tractatus* (Ithaca: Cornell University Press, 1964), p. 34.
5 *Op. cit.*, pp. 218 ff.

propositions are, it is not clear that Cohen and Nagel have succeeded. At any event, surely no analysis of 'fact' in terms of 'proposition', or conversely, is acceptable without an independent account of the other.

According to (1) facts are something or other "denoted" by certain kinds of declarative sentences containing the demonstratives 'this' or 'that'. What do such declarative sentences denote? According to Frege, declaratives denote a truth value, truth or falsity, but it is not clear how the presence of demonstratives would affect this doctrine. Declaratives containing 'this' are not to be regarded as either true or false, pending a specification of the semantics of 'this'. Perhaps here too we come back to facts regarded as certain kinds of propositions denoted by declarative sentences. If so, however, it is difficult to see how they are in any sense elements discriminated or even discriminable in sense perception. Perhaps physical objects are so discriminated, perhaps qualities of them, perhaps also even certain relations between or among them. However, declarative sentences (in particular, those containing the demonstratives 'this' or 'that') surely cannot in any reasonable sense be said to "denote" such perceptively discriminable elements.

Facts according to (4) are concrete physical objects, not just in isolation but *together with* the relations between them *in virtue of which* a proposition (which one?) is true. It is interesting that here we get into the healthy physical world with its actual things, as contrasted with a postulated realm of abstract propositions. The 'together with', however, is bothersome. In what sense are the facts "together with" certain relations between or among them? In the sense that they are all members of some class of higher order?

Take Jones, j, together with the relation O of being older than, and Smith, s. The proposition involved is presumably the one corresponding (in some obscure way about which we are told very little by those who carry on proposition talk) to the declarative sentence 'Jones is older than Smith' or 'Ojs'. What is the "fact" here? It is presumably Jones and Smith "together with" the relation O between them. However, what object is this? Is it the class whose only members are Jones, Smith, and the relation O? This would be a "heterogeneous" class in the sense of type theory. We might try to "homogenize" it, as it were, by taking instead the purported class whose only members are (i) the class whose only member is Jones, (ii) the class whose only member is Smith, and (iii) the relation O.

In type theory, however, there is no such class, since it would have classes of individuals and dyadic relations between individuals as members, so that this suggestion is not feasible. We might then go one step further and in place of Jones here speak of the ordered couple of Jones with himself. Our class then becomes the class of dyadic relations whose members are the ordered couple of Jones with himself, the relation O of being older than, and the unit relation of Smith to himself.

The difficulty with this kind of suggestion is that the "fact" in virtue of which 'Ojs' would be true would be the same fact in virtue of which 'Osj', 'Smith is older than Jones', would be true, an intolerable situation. Well, Cohen and Nagel do not go so deeply as this, with the result that 'fact' in the sense (4) is as obscure as in senses (1)–(3). Also, the key phrase 'in virtue of which a proposition is true' is never analyzed. It is not clear how one goes from the "fact" to the "proposition" to the corresponding declarative sentence, and conversely.

The difficulties with (4) do not end here, however. We are told that facts in sense (4) "can be apprehended by us in part through the senses." This is ambiguous. Are we to construe this as saying 'in part through the senses and in part in some other way', or as 'part of the fact can be apprehended through the senses', the part being one of the things or one of the relations? If the former, it would be of interest to know what kind of apprehension is involved in the "other way." If the latter, why should only a part be apprehended through the senses, and not all of the factors?

What can Cohen and Nagel mean literally when they claim or purport to claim that facts in the sense (4) "may have a career in time, may push each other, destroy each other," and so on? To substantiate this would involve a curious view indeed. It is not just physical objects that have a career, and so on, as in physics or common speech, but also the facts consisting of physical objects "together with" their relations. One and the same fact has a career in time, pushes another, destroys another, and so on. Surely our authors are not saying here what they mean.

Carnap, in *Meaning and Necessity*, is inclined to identify facts with a certain kind of proposition, taking propositions now in the "objective sense" as intensions of sentences. A proposition is thus (p. 27) not "a linguistic expression nor . . . a subjective, mental occurrence, but . . . something objective that may or may not be exemplified in nature." A fact for Carnap is not just any proposition, but rather one that is true, is factual or synthetic, and is "specific or complete in a certain sense." That a proposition (in Carnap's sense) should be both true and factual in order to be a fact is evident. False propositions clearly are not, nor are there facts corresponding to analytic or L-true propositions. The requirement of specificity is not so clear, however, and Carnap is less certain of it anyhow.

Carnap considers a true factual proposition p that a certain piece of paper is blue. "But the property Blue," he says, "has a wide range; it is not specific but includes many different shades of blue, say Blue$_1$,

Blue$_2$, etc." The given piece of paper, however, has only one of these shades, say Blue$_5$. The proposition q that it is Blue$_5$ is more specific than the proposition p that it is Blue. Hence, Carnap thinks, p should perhaps not be regarded as a fact. However, even Blue$_5$ may be further subdivided. If we suppose that it is not, however, q still may lack specificity with respect to other properties, for example, size, shape, and so on. If we go on in this way, Carnap suggests, and "require of a fact . . . [the] maximum degree of completeness (short of L-falsity), then there is only one fact, the totality of the actual world, past, present, and future."

There are several difficulties with this proposal, some of which no doubt Carnap would admit. For one thing, if there is only one fact, the sum total of the universal history of the actual world, there is not then much use for the term 'fact' at all. Further, we do use the word in the plural and such uses should surely be accommodated. There is also another matter, more important, that, curiously, Carnap does not discuss. When we speak of the "maximum degree of specificity," we should really add: relative to the language or language system being used. To speak of facts is to speak *in* a certain language or language system. There seems to be just no way of getting around this circumstance. Hence we can speak of a maximum degree of specificity only relative to the language or language system at hand, and therefore only relative to its vocabulary.

We can never hope to specify *all* the properties that the given piece of paper has. The best we can do is to specify those for which the language or language system at hand has expressions. Of course Carnap is speaking of propositions, not of sentences, and propostions are outside language. We get at propositions in his sense, however, by means of language, more particularly by means of the sentences that have them as their intensions, as Carnap puts it. The best we can hope for, in trying to indicate the degree of specificity of a fact in Carnap's sense, is by means of some declarative sentence in some language or language system. The notion of a maximum degree of specificity independent of language seems to be a myth.

Carnap agrees that there are enormous difficulties to be overcome before we can achieve a satisfactory notion of proposition. He is hopeful that this may be done, but presumably only within a kind of semantics that admits primitively intensions *sui generis* as values for variables. Thus it is doubtful, according to the view here, that a satisfactory theory of propositions, and hence of facts, along Carnap's lines can be achieved.

3. Austin and Strawson on Truth. In their Bristol symposium on "Truth" in 1950, Austin and Strawson agreed, for differing reasons, that it would be wrong to identify 'fact' and 'true statement'.[6] Austin is a bit cavalier, perhaps, concerning 'fact', and suggests no clear ontology for it. Strawson thinks (p. 133) that Austin fails to discriminate sufficiently among 'thing', 'event', 'situation', 'state of affairs', 'feature', and 'fact'. "All these are words," Strawson urges, "which should be handled with care." Surely—but let us go on to search for an exact (or even inexact) denotation for 'facts' in Strawson's comments.

> Facts are known, [he insists,] stated, learnt, forgotten, overlooked, commented on, communicated or noticed. . . . Facts are what statements (when true) state; they are not what statements are about. They are not, like things or happenings on the face of the globe, witnessed or heard or seen, broken or overturned, interrupted or prolonged, kicked, destroyed, mended, or noisy.

This passage suggests that facts may have certain epistemic properties, but otherwise it proceeds on the *via negativa*. However, we are no better off than we were before. It is to be feared that we cannot be very clear about 'Person X states fact f', 'Person X learns fact f', and so on, without some indication of what the f's are. Similarly, if facts are what true statements "state," we are left presumably with such forms as

'True statement a states the fact f',

or perhaps even

'True statement a states the facts $f_1, \ldots , f_m$',

dangling rather precariously without analysis. Resolute Oxford laymanship, to paraphrase Quine, presumably prevents the bringing in of strict logico-semantical or structural-linguistic considerations.

Perhaps Strawson regards facts as a kind of psedo-entity. However, even pseudo-entities, for example, virtual classes, have their proper dignity. If they are merely pseudo-entities to be discusesd in a *manière de parler,* it is truly "unfair to facts" not to give them their proper ontic status.

Are facts "things in the world," or not? Austin thinks so, but Strawson does not. Strawson is worried primarily about 'fact' as "wedded to that-clauses," whereas Austin contends that "to explain the meaning of 'fact' in terms of the expression 'fact that' is to invert the real order of things. . . . "[7] Curiously, Austin's "real" order turns out to be

---

[6] *Psychical Research, Ethics and Logic,* Aristotelian Society Supplementary Volume XXIV (London: Harrison and Sons, 1950), pp. 111–172.

[7] J. Austin, *Philosophical Papers* (Oxford: Clarendon Press, 1961), p. 112.

essentially the etymological order as given in the *O.E.D.* Originally, 'fact' stood for "something in the world," but later becomes embodied in 'fact that' as a "grammatical convenience." However, the "real order," whatever it is, is surely not to be identified with the etymological order. It might happen that they coincide, but one would not know this in advance. It is to be feared then that Austin has not made his point, commiting here some form of genetic fallacy.

It is surely a good admonition that we should "handle with care" such words as 'thing', 'event', 'situation', 'state of affairs', 'feature', and 'fact'. Possibly some of these might turn out to be equivalent to each other, in certain uses at least, but possibly not. Unfortunately, neither Austin nor Strawson has given us proper instructions for the careful handling of these fragile words.

We cannot tarry further with the quarrel between Austin and Strawson. That was their little affair anyhow and is now a thing of the past. Since neither looked beyond language to logic or metalogic, it would be miraculous if either of their views could have turned out satisfactorily. Without a proper logical underpinning, it would seem, there is not much hope for success in philosophic analysis. The use, implicit if not explicit, of a proper logic and metalogic gives a necessary condition surely for adequacy of analysis, although of course by no means a sufficient one. Good logic is "not enough," but it is surely necessary.

4. Scheffler on Explaining the Facts. A more sophisticated discussion of 'fact' is to be found in Scheffler's *The Anatomy of Inquiry*.[8] Attention is confined to contexts of the form 'explains-the-fact-that'. Scheffler, however, has not wedded facts to 'fact-that' clauses, for he takes full note of what is involved in the admission of a fact ontology. Such an admission he finds objectionable, and suggests two ways of handling 'explains-the-fact-that' that involve no such ontology.

If we say, as seems natural, that the aim of a scientific explanation is "to explain the facts," and seek to determine precisely, at the metalogical level, what such explanations are, we seem driven to admitting facts in some guise as explananda. The object of explanation is then not a "thing," that is (p. 59), is

> no longer the spatio-temporal individual chunk, but something of another sort associated with it, of which there are as many as there are logically independent descriptions of the chunk. These new entities (let us call them hereafter 'facts') [Scheffler writes,]

[8] (New York: Alfred A. Knopf, 1963), pp. 57 ff.

are not themselves spatio-temporal entities: they are neither dated nor bounded. Nor are they identified with the descriptions themselves. They are abstract ("logically intensional" [in Quine's phrase]) entities, intermediate between chunk and descriptions, each such entity corresponding to some class of logically equivalent (true) descriptions uniquely.

Scheffler does not tarry long with this "picture" of facts, but moves straightaway to avoid the dubious ontology involved. He suggests two methods. One requires fundamental use of 'EF' (for 'explains-the-fact-that'), the problem being to assure its proper syntactic behavior. Let 'Bk' express that the spatio-temporal chunk k is blue, and let g be a suitable class of premiss statements. (It is perhaps extraordinary for Scheffler, in the wake of Goodman's nominalism, to speak of a "class" of premisses. He should rather speak of a *virtual* class here or of a finitely long conjunction.) How, then, does the metalinguistic sign 'EF' behave? The metalinguisitic expression—Scheffler does not bring out clearly enough that he is operating within quite a complicated metalanguage, and hence the reiteration here of 'metalinguistic'—

(1)   '$g\,EF(Bk)$'

"is to be taken," we are told, "as consisting of the name 'g' and the one-place predicate 'EF(Bk)', formed by inserting 'Bk' into the second blank of '. . . EF—'. The whole statement thus applies a one-place predicate to the sentence-string [sic!] g. It does not relate g to anything else. . . ." A more perspicuous notation would be

(2)   '$EF(Bk)\ g$',

wherein, as in 'Bk' itself, the predicate is given first. If 'g' is the name of a finite conjunction of premisses, (1) or (2) seem acceptable locutions. However, if 'g' is a class word, which (on p. 66) Scheffler explicitly says it is, then (1) or (2) involve an abstract ontology, albeit a different one from that which he is trying to avoid. So regarded, (1) or (2) surely cannot be regarded as acceptable locutions to a presumed nominalist such as Scheffler.

We must now query the status of 'EF—', or rather of the 'EF—'s, for there is a vast multiplicity of them, within the whole metalogical system incorporating the desired explanation talk. Are they *primitive* predicates, each and every one? If so, what an extraordinarily excessive array, a different one needed for each different explanation! If they are not primitives, how are they defined? Some, somehow, in terms of

Levels of Language & Explanation

others? Scheffler gives no hint of an answer. We are told, however, that 'g EF(Bk)' "is true if and only if g fulfills the criteria of explanation with reference to 'Bk'." Now we may well ask what kind of a suggestion this is supposed to be. Is it a logical consequence of a definition of 'true in the metalanguage'? At any event, the statement itself appears to be one in the meta-metalanguage and hence cannot be an axiom of the metalanguage incorporating the explanation talk. The matter is of some consequence, for unless we are given axioms governing the EF(—)'s or unless they are characterized in some suitable alternative way, we are not told what the supposed theory concerning them really is.

Similar points were raised by Atlas in his essay on Toulmin but were misunderstood by Hempel.

Scheffler goes on to suggest a second method in order "to avoid the merest whisper of reference to facts." Here a sign 'W' is introduced as a "predicate-forming operator, producing a *one-place predicate of sentences* when its blank is filled by a sentence." Thus 'W(Bk)' is a one-place predicate applicable to sentences, and to say that a sentence is a W(Bk) is to say that that sentence is a why-k-is-blue sentence. The The why-k-is-blue sentences are just those logically equivalent to 'Bk'. Scheffler had earlier suggested that the fact-that-k-is-blue might be regarded as the class of sentences logically equivalent to 'Bk', but had rejected it because of the abstract ontology involved. (The *virtual* class of sentences logically equivalent to 'Bk', Scheffler fails to note, is not objectional in this way.) We gain the effect of talking of facts in essentially this sense, however, "if we construe 'W(Bk)' as a predicate applying to every logical equivalent of the sentence within the parentheses, inclusive of this sentence itself." Finally, to render this whole discussion "explicitly concrete," Scheffler regards sentences, and indeed expressions generally, as *inscriptions* or expression events rather than abstract shapes or expression designs, as is more customary.

Scheffler suggests no axioms concerning the 'W(—)'s, just as he had suggested none earlier concerning the 'EF(—)'s. Those needed for the 'W(—)'s would have to provide a kind of inscriptional account of logical or L-equivalence. It is a pity that Scheffler does not say anything about this, for no such account seems ever to have been given.[9] If we presuppose a syntax based on expression shapes, a syntax of the classical Carnap-Tarski kind, we may go on to a notion of L-truth or analyticity, using Platonistic devices, and thence to L-equivalence. To avoid this, and in order to presuppose only a syntax of inscriptions, Scheffler in effect takes L-equivalence (a special kind of analyticity) as a primitive in the form of a vast multiplicity of

---

[9] It is difficult enough to give a satisfactory account of L-equivalence within a first-order classical semantics, let alone an inscriptional one. See *The Notion of Analytic Truth*.

'W(—)'s. Whether this is a wise, or even really honest, logical procedure is to be doubted. It is simply packing too much into those 'W(—)'s that needs unpacking and analysis.

In the second method (that involving the 'W(—)'s) we have, it is true, lost all trace of reference to facts. However, in the first method too there is only the faintest lingering aroma of them, merely in the choice of 'F' in 'EF'. Scheffler could equally well have chosen 'T' for 'that' and written 'ET' for 'explains that'. We would not think we had therewith gained much illumination concerning a realm of *that's*. Of course the that's are eliminable, just as in his account the facts are. This, no doubt, is as it should be.

In the second method, that employing the 'W(--)'s, we seem to have lost all connection with explanation. Although the 'W' is supposed to read 'why', it is not clear that it should be, due to the use made of L-equivalence. That a sentence is L-equivalent to another is not in general a ground for regarding it as giving an answer to the question 'Why?'. In this second method we have lost sight of the explanatory premiss-string *g*. Further, it has often been suggested that a proposition, as we have noted above, may be regarded as a class or virtual class of L-equivalent sentences. Now 'W(—)' in effect functions as standing for just such a class. Hence, Scheffler is in effect identifying facts with propositions so regarded, surely an illicit identification.

5. Some Conditions of Adequacy. Although they are presumably eliminable, we need not conclude therewith that facts are uninteresting. Russellian descriptive phrases are eliminable, yet they are both interesting and worth defining. The question arises: can we construct a theory of facts, handling them not as an Austinian "something in the world," but rather as fictitious intensional or quasi-intensional entities, spoken of only in a *manière de parler* and within a proper kind of metalanguage in which the main uses of 'fact' may be accommodated? Let us attempt to answer this in the positive. First, however, another word about intensional entities, a word about the *manière de parler*, and a word about metalinguistic propriety.

That facts are intensional entities of some kind has perhaps not always been fully recognized. Of course, if they are identified with some sort of proposition, their intensional status comes out clearly. Even if propositions are not available, as here, we must still recognize the intensional status of facts. Scheffler brings this out conclusively. We cannot improve upon his presentation, and therefore refer the reader to pages 66–68 of his book.

The device of using a *manière de parler* is a familiar one since Russell's first writings on descriptions. Russell succeeded, it will be recalled, in defining in context phrases of the form 'the one and only x such that $(-x-)$', where in place of '$(-x-)$' we put in some sentential function containing 'x' as its only free variable. Such phrases are regarded as *manières de parler* within the wider sentential contexts in which they occur. They are not defined in isolation, but only within the wider contexts. Another use of the device of the *manière de parler* is in the notation for virtual classes. Virtual classes are not included among the values for variables, however, whereas the so and so, as introduced by Russell, is actually one of the objects so taken. There is this important difference between the two uses. However, there is the similarity in that the expressions for virtual classes also are defined only within the broader sentential contexts in which they occur.

Let us now attempt to construct a theory of facts within the metalanguages based on denotation. Of course certain heuristic principles must guide any such construction. Certain features that we wish the "facts" to have must be selected and others rejected. Concerning any such selection there is bound to be dispute. It is not clear that any one selection will give us the one and only true picture of the "facts." Rather, we must put forward a view and try to make it as adequate as we can. If we fail, there is then at least the possibility that it can be improved or rendered more adequate in this or that respect. However, one thing surely is clear at this late date: we cannot with impunity philosophize about facts in "resolute laymanship" and in disregard of the refined tools of modern semantics. To do so is to rely upon horse and buggy procedures, and to get only to the next town when we wish to go a great distance.

A few features concerning "facts" that the theory here will incorporate are the following:

(i) We shall speak of facts only relative to a language system L. It is fact *talk* that interests us, and facts only insofar as we can have fact talk about them. Given any L, there are no doubt always facts beyond the reach of the modes of expression of L. Of such facts there can then be no fact talk within L. Presumably we can always move on to a richer system L', which takes cognizance of these additional facts. Presumably also there is no richest system in which all facts, in some sense, can be accommodated. The very conception of such a system presupposes a notion of *all facts* independent of language. It is very doubtful that such a notion can be given any strict meaning. However this may be, we need here the relativization of fact talk to a specific and well-articulated L regarded as object language.

(ii) Facts are to be discussed only within a semantical metalanguage. In their analysis there is reference not only to the things of the object language but also to the expressions of that language. Now, semantics is the theory of how such things are brought into relation with such expressions, as has been noted above. Failure to realize the full semantic structure of facts has no doubt impeded previous writers on the subject. Perhaps an adequate notion of fact can be built up in some other than a semantical way, but this is doubtful, and at any event seems never to have been done.

(iii) Facts are eliminable in the sense that expressions for them are. More specifically, any metalinguistic sentence containing 'fact' is by definition a shorthand for a longer sentence, in the primitive notation of the metalanguage, in which neither that word nor any equivalent occurs. That facts are eliminable does not make them uninteresting or not worth bothering about, as we have already in effect remarked. The cardinal number two is eliminable (in the same sense) in the Zermelo set theory, for example, but we do not conclude from this that that number is somehow uninteresting or unimportant, or that there is then something the matter with that set theory. (There may well be something the matter with that theory, but not for this reason.)

(iv) Facts are "fictitious" entities in the sense that they are in no way values for variables within the metalanguage—or indeed in any language. Nor are they "named" in any sense by the primitive notation. Of course, expressions for them can be built up in context. However, such expressions are not named in any proper or strict sense. Just what kind or kinds of expressions are needed we shall note as we go on.

(v) Facts are most intimately bound up with the notation of L. In a certain sense, every metalinguistic sentence containing reference to a fact is reducible to a sentence describing the notation for that fact. In this respect facts are like nominal virtual classes. Although we speak of them as if they were legitimate objects, strictly our sentences refer instead to the notation.

(vi) Facts are intimately linked with the semantic notion of truth. Surely in the definiens of the definition of a sentence containing 'fact', 'true' will occur in a fundamental way. No matter what facts are, they are surely not independent of truth, and the notion of truth seems most efficiently handled in terms of the modern semantic notion. Many analytic philosophers think they can avoid bringing in the semantic concept, and that some rather vague, preanalytic notion will serve equally well. Well, perhaps so in the horse-and-buggy days. The view here is that the semantic notion cannot be avoided, and the sooner we get used to this the better for us all.

(vii) Facts are in some sense "logically intensional." This does not entail, however, that the metalanguage in which our fact talk is incorporated need be in any way an intensional metalanguage in the objectionable sense of having intensions *sui generis* as values for variables. The metalanguage rather is of the usual extensional kind, as above. Within it, a notion of logical or analytic truth may be defined, as we have noted, and hence also the notion of L-equivalence. Whether or not we decide to follow Scheffler in making fundamental use of L-equivalence, we shall surely need the notion of analytic or logical truth. However, all such notions—notions of what Carnap calls '*L-semantics*'— can be adequately accommodated within the purely extensional metalanguage, as has in effect been noted above.

(viii) Facts have an internal structure. In them objects are "combined in a definite way," this way being "the structure of the . . . fact." We can, if we like, distinguish between "atomic" and "molecular" facts, but not independently of the given language system *L*. This distinction thus loses the intrinsic ontic flavor that it had for Russell and Wittgenstein, and is hence unimportant here. The structure of facts, however, is significant, but again is not described ontically but rather in terms of the expressions used. The structure, in short, is a linguistic structure rather than an ontic one.

(ix) Facts, in the most fundamental sense at least, are concerned primarily with particular individuals, ascribing to them, as it were, a given property or relation. *General* facts, if there are such, are then to be mere congeries of facts about particulars. One might wish to condone general facts in some other sense, but this does not seem needed and at any event will not be done for the moment. (See, however, Section 8 below.) Carnap has emphasized this point, in his *Philosophical Foundations of Physics*,[10] when he notes that 'fact' is not to be applied exclusively to "singular, particular occurrences" and not to be correlated in some fashion with universal statements.

(x) Facts are intimately linked with the semantical notion of *factual* or synthetic truth, not just with that of truth. Nonetheless, facts are not just factual truths. They are a kind of pseudo-entity, so we shall maintain, sharply to be distinguished from linguistic expressions. However, more of this later.

6. Facts as Nominal Virtual Entities. The relation of virtual-class L-designation has been introduced above, as has the notion of a nominal virtual class. We wish now to be able to speak of the *L-designation of individuals* and of *nominal*, rather than real, individuals. Equivalently, we may speak here of individuals *taken in intension*. The roman letters 'a', 'b', and so on, are primitive individual constants. We then wish to affirm that 'a' L-designates the nominal individual a,

---

[10] (New York and London: Basic Books, Inc., 1966), p. 5.

'b' the nominal individual b, and so on. To make this exact, let us use (as we have been doing) the italic letters '*a*', '*b*', and so on, as variables of the metalanguage ranging over the expressions of *L*. We also introduce, in the metalanguage, an expression '*ay*' as the (structural-descriptive) name of '*a*', '*bee*' of '*b*', and so on. Then in general, we may let

$$\text{'a LDes a'} \quad \text{abbreviate} \quad \text{'}a = \mathbf{ay}\text{'},$$

where in place of '**a**' we put in an individual constant and in place of '**ay**' its structural-descriptive name. Hence, *a* LDes a if and only if *a* = '*a*', that is *a* = *ay*, *a* LDes b if and only if *a* = '*b*', that is, *a* = *bee*, and so on.

Let us use

(1)   '(**a** *in* x∍(—*x*—))-is-a-fact'

or

(2)   'Fct (**a** *in* x∍(—*x*—))'

as short for

'There are expressions *a* and *b* such that *a* LDes **a**, *b* LDes x∍(—*x*—), and (*b*⌢*a*) is true but not analytically so and is L-equivalent to no sentence not containing *a*',

where in place of '**a**' we put in an individual constant.

Note that we have here again a definition *schema*, not a definition. The schema stipulates an infinity (strictly, a double infinity) of definitions, one for each specific choice '**a**' and 'x∍(—*x*—)'. We may think of each instance of the schema as providing a definition.

Suppose the nominal individual a is a member of a suitable nominal virtual class x∍(—*x*—), truly but not analytically so. Then the nominal entity

(3)   (a *in* x∍(—*x*—))

is a fact according to this definition. It is a complex nominal entity consisting of a and x∍(—*x*—) combined in a certain way. The '*in*' here may be read (roughly) as 'as in', or the whole term (3) as 'a's *being in* x∍(—*x*—)' or as 'a's *being a member of* x∍(—*x*—)' or as '*that* a is *in* x∍(—*x*—)'. The effect of '*in*' as a technical semantical sign is to enable us to handle such phrases. Another reading is 'the actual *state of affairs* of a's being in x∍(*x*—)'. In using this reading we do not recognize a separate new realm of actual states of affairs or such like, but rather gain the effect of being able to talk about them within the semantics already at hand. Strictly the whole expression

(4)   '(a in $x\ni(\text{—}x\text{—})$))-is-a-fact' or 'Fct (a *in* $x\ni(\text{—}x\text{—})$)'

is defined as a unit and cannot be broken up. Strictly, we are not talking here about a state of affairs or about the individual a or the virtual class $x\ni(\text{—}x\text{—})$. Rather, as we see by glancing at the appropriate definiens, we are speaking of the *expression* 'a' and of the *expression* '$x\ni(\text{—}x\text{—})$'. Although it appears that we are speaking of the individual a and of the virtual class $x\ni(\text{—}x\text{—})$ in the definiendum, this is merely an illusion.

When we speak nominally of an individual a, we are only one step removed from a, as it were. We seem to be speaking of the individual a, but actually are speaking of the expression that L-designates a. When we are speaking nominally of a virtual class, however, we are two steps removed. The virtual class $x\ni(\text{—}x\text{—})$ itself is one, the expression that L-designates it, another. At the very best, we can say only that, in expressions of the form (4) we are speaking of a *quasi*-individual, a *quasi*-virtual class, and a certain *quasi*-connection of that quasi-individual with that quasi-virtual class!

Tenuous indeed then are facts, mere "trifles light as air." Nonetheless, whole expressions of the forms (1) or (2) or (4) are given a very concrete significance in the definientia. Also, the definientia are extremely simple, involving merely quantifiers over the expressions of L, defined notions of L-designation, and the semantical notions of truth and logical truth. Such minimal tools are required in almost all philosophical analysis anyhow. It is interesting to note that we can get along here with so little. It is as though God made logic, throwing in a little metalogic for good measure, and all the rest is the work of the philosopher.

The point of the clause concerning L-equivalence in the definiens should be remarked. The clause that the sentence consisting of *b* concatenated with *a* be L-equivalent to no sentence not containing *a* requires in effect that the variable 'x' of abstraction occurs in an essential way in '$(\text{—}x\text{—})$'. In other words, 'x' must occur in '$(\text{—}x\text{—})$' other than in merely analytic contexts.

The foregoing definition schema is not claimed to be a final one. Possibly upon further reflection we shall wish to emend it, perhaps by adding further conditions. Perhaps some requirement of specificity, as suggested by Carnap, would be desirable. This we need not decide for the present. As in philosophy and science generally, so here—we posit principles and definitions hypothetically as a basis for further exploration, hoping that they will turn out to be both convenient and fruitful for the purposes at hand.

One direction in which emendation might immediately seem called for, however, hovers around the distinction between *basic* (or *observational*) and *theoretical* predicates.[11] We might wish "facts" to be expressible wholly in terms of the former. This requirement is well brought out in the main item under 'fact' in the *O.E.D.*, namely, that a fact is "known by actual observation or authentic testimony, as opposed to what is merely inferred, or to a conjecture or fiction; a datum of experience, as distinguished from the conclusions that may be based upon it." Accordingly, we might require that expressions for facts contain only basic or observation predicates (and perhaps that the proper names involved as well as the range of the individual variables, be restricted to only certain kinds of concrete objects, excluding theoretical entities). We commonly speak of the facts of experience, after all, but only in a picaresque sense of the "facts" of, say, quantum mechanics.

7. Identity Between Facts. Introducing facts in the manner suggested embodies the features (i)–(x) put forward above as desiderata. We speak of facts only relative to the object language under discussion, and within an appropriate semantical metalanguage. Expressions for them are eliminable, and they are fictitious in an appropriate sense. The semantic notion of truth is needed in the definiens as well as the L-semantical notion of being factually true. Facts are "logically intensional" entities and have an internal structure. Let us explore these last two points a little more fully.

We have not incorporated L-equivalence into the notion of a fact here, as Scheffler does. However, if desired, we can build it into the notion of the *identity* of facts. Two facts are to be identical if and only if the corresponding factual sentences are L-equivalent. Thus we would have a definition schema for the identity of facts as follows.

'(**a** *in* $x\ni$(—x—)) = (**b** *in* $y\ni$(.. y ..))' abbreviates 'Fct (**a** *in* $x\ni$(—x—)), Fct (**b** *in* $y\ni$(.. y ..)), and ($c\,\hat{}\,a$) is L-equivalent to ($d\,\hat{}\,b$)',

---

[11] See especially R. Carnap, "The Methodological Character of Theoretical Concepts," in *Minnesota Studies in the Philosophy of Science*, Vol. I (Minneapolis: University of Minnesota Press, 1956), pp. 38–76; C. G. Hempel, *Aspects of Scientific Explanation*, especially pp. 173 ff.; *The Philosophy of Rudolf Carnap*, *passim*; and the author's "On Theoretical Constructs and Ramsey Constants," *Philosophy of Science* 33 (1966), 1–13, and "On Theoretical Entities," *Ratio* VIII (1966), 158–168.

where in place of '**a**' and '**b**' we put in either two individual constants or two descriptions, in place of '*a*' and '*b*' we put in the structural-descriptive names, respectively, of those constants or descriptions, and in place of '*c*' and '*d*' we put in the structural-descriptive names, respectively, of 'xэ(—x—)' and 'yэ(.. y ..)'. (The case where *a* is a primitive individual constant and *b* a description need not be admitted, for the individual constant could be introduced as an abbreviation for that description. Also for simplicity it is assumed that no two primitive individual constants designate the same individual.)

Let us consider an example. Suppose 'Scott' is a primitive individual constant and 'the author of *Waverley*' and 'the author of *Marmion*' are primitive descriptions (more properly 'the one x such that x is an author of *Waverley*' and 'the one x such that x is an author of *Marmion*'). These need not be symbolized more exactly. Then,

(1)   (Scott *in* xэ(x lived at Abbotsford)),   ~ is - a fact

(2)   (Scott *in* xэ($x =$ the author of *Waverley*)),

and so on, are facts. On the other hand,

(3)   (the author of *Waverley in* xэ($x =$ the author of *Waverley*)),

is not a fact, because of the analyticity of

'the author of *Waverley* $=$ the author of *Waverley*'.

Note that

'Scott $=$ the author of *Waverley*'

is true, but not analytically so. We cannot conclude from this that because (2) is a fact, (3) is then also. The reason is that 'Scott' and 'the author of *Waverley*' are used in (1)–(3) only nominally, that is, strictly they are not used at all, but only mentioned. Similarly,

(the author of *Waverley in* xэ(x lived in Abbotsford))

and

Marmion

(the author of ~~*Waverley*~~ *in* xэ(x lived in Abbotsford))

SIC

are distinct facts even though

(1') There are expressions *a* and *b* such that *a* L Des Scott , *b* L Des xэ(x lived at Abbotsford and (*b*⌐*a*) is true but not analytically so and is L-equivalent to no sentence not containing *a*.

'the author of *Waverley* = the author of *Marmion*'

is true (but not analytically so).

In addition to L-equivalence, there are of course various further semantical relations to consider here, as mentioned in Chapter VII, Section 10. Other stricter types of identity can be introduced and might well be preferable. The exact philosophical study of the plethora of semantical relations, based on L-equivalence with additional provisos in the manner of Chapter VII, Section 10, seems scarcely to have begun.

The internal structure of facts remains to be commented on. Of this both Russell and Wittgenstein made much. In failing to realize the intensional or quasi syntactical nature of facts, they in effect confused use and mention. Hence they sought in the world for a structure that is to be found only in language. The structure of a fact can be read off from the virtual-class expression constituting its second component. This may be of any complexity, atomic, disjunctive, implicative, negative. Are there then disjunctive, negative, and so on, facts? Yes, but only as special instances of the general schema. This seems harmless enough.

8. Second-Order Facts. Strictly, there is no need for introducing dyadic, triadic, and so on, facts, all of these being included in the general schema. We see this clearly by observing that relational sentences such as 'a is the father of b' may also be handled as virtual-class sentences of the form 'a is a member of the virtual class x (x is the father of b)'. Nonetheless, we may introduce dyadic, and so on, facts explicitly if desired. Thus,

$$\text{'(a,b } in \ xy \ni (\text{—}x\text{—}y\text{—}))\text{'}$$

would be the kind of expression needed for dyadic facts, and so on.

It might be advisable here also, for technical reasons, to exhibit all the arguments so that no individual constants are left occurring in the abstracts. Thus let us regard

$$\text{(a,b } in \ xy \ni (\text{—}x\text{—}y\text{—}))$$

as a fact only where are no occurrences of any individual constants in '(—x—y—)'. The reason for this will emerge later (in Chapter IX, Sections 4 and 5), when propositions and 'fact-that' clauses are considered. Meanwhile, we note that by explicitly exhibiting all the individual constants as arguments, we come close to giving something like a maximum analysis, as in Chapter IV, Section 9. Also we should perhaps exhibit as arguments the predicate constants as well. For this we use virtual classes and relations of higher order, as introduced in Chapter VI, Section 4.

In Chapter VI, Section 4 all the first-order abstracts introduced were *homogeneous* in the sense that the variables of abstraction were of the same order. Likewise, the second-order abstracts were homogeneous in the sense that the abstracts of abstraction, so to speak, were likewise of the same order. For the expression of facts, if the maximum analysis is to be achieved, *heterogeneous* abstracts must also be introduced. Thus we let, for a suitable *F*,

$$\text{‘}F x \ni (\text{—}F\text{—}x\text{—}) \ Gy\text{’}$$

now be significant and subject to appropriate laws of concretion and abstraction. The abstracts involved here are heterogeneous in an obvious sense. This is true also for heterogeneous abstracts of higher degree, involving several variables and abstracts of abstraction.

By 'a first-order fact' is meant one in which at least one individual constant is exhibited as an argument. All facts thus far considered are first-order facts in this sense. The notion of a *second-order* fact may be introduced now, by giving up requirement (ix) of Section 5, that all facts are somehow specific and concern only particular individuals. A second-order fact has then as its arguments, as it were, only predicate constants, and the abstracts are accordingly of second order and with no individual variables as variables of abstraction. In this way we gain the notion of a *general* fact. Presumably all general facts are of second-order, and conversely. As an example, the fact that the planetary orbits PO are ellipses E and not circles C may be expressed by using

$$\text{‘}(PO,E,C \ in \ FGH \ni (x) \ (Fx \supset (Gx \cdot \sim Hx)))\text{’}.$$

Earlier (in Chapter V, Section 3) a distinction was drawn between the "objects" and the "condition" of a belief. A similar distinction here is useful. The *condition* of a fact is now always the nominal abstract constituting its last component, the *objects* being the other nominal virtual classes, relations, or individuals involved. Thus, in the example just given, PO, E, and O are the (nominal) objects and $FGH \ni (x)$ $(Fx \supset (Gx \cdot \sim Hx))$ the (nominal) condition.

It might be objected that we have been tarrying too long with technicalia. Having found facts to be eliminable, fictitious, nominal entities, we might well wonder why we should bother about them at all. Quine suggests something similar. "We were able," he writes, "to abjure sakes, measures, unactualized possibles, and facts without a pang, having satisfied ourselves that to admit them would serve no good purpose."[12] Abjuration for Quine consists of not recognizing as values for variables. It need not consist in not recognizing as a *manière de parler*. Rather we should absorb or "paraphrase away" the various uses of the abjured words. Well, this is precisely what has been done here for 'fact' in the context 'so and so *is a fact*', by far the most fundamental. In this there is agreement (apparently) with Austin. We shall go on to 'fact that'-talk in easy and natural ways in the next chapter.

We have a choice before us now. We can forswear all uses of 'fact' with impunity, for they are all eliminable or paraphraseable anyhow. Or, alternatively, we can use 'fact' in various ways, subjecting each way to proper analysis, ultimately coming back hopefully to some such fundamental way as the one suggested. The view here is that it is not the aim of logical analysis to improverish our everyday modes of speech. Let us rejoice in the richness of its vocabulary and the enormous range of its expressive power. However, if it is a logical analysis that we want, nothing short of the deepest searching for fundamentals will suffice. For this we must have recourse almost always to a properly restricted and otherwise acceptable semantical metalanguage.

Even at the depth level, however, there is no need for 'fact' strictly. Instead, we can always go back to 'factually true sentence' if we wish, in less abbreviated notation. Thus in a sense, our whole enterprise comes to nought. If we have succeeded in reaching our goal, we have shown that we did not even have to start out in the first place. The Holy Grail is already to be found at our doorsteps.

---

[12] *Word and Object,* p. 248.

CHAPTER IX

On Events and Propositions

Facts are frequently confused with all manner of other things. Prominent among these are *events* and *propositions*. To give an exact semantical theory of what such entities are is by no means easy, and it is not clear that this has ever been done. Let us explore this matter a little in the present chapter on the basis of the foregoing.

In Section 1, some of *Hempel's* view's concerning events are examined by way of preamble. In Section 2, a theory of events regarded as virtual ordered *n*-tuples is given, with some *alternatives* in Section 3. Section 4 is devoted to *propositions* as contrasted with facts. In Section 5, a few remarks, promised in the last chapter, concerning 'fact-that' clauses are given. Finally, in Section 6, a few tentative *thoughts on thinking* are put forward.

1. Hempel on Events. In his *Aspects of Scientific Explanation*[1] Hempel distinguishes in a rough way between what he calls "sentential" and "concrete" events. A scientific explanation is regarded as "a potential answer to a question of the form 'why is it the case that *p*?', where the place of '*p*' is occupied by an empirical sentence detailing the facts to be explained." Such "facts" or events—Hempel does not distinguish them—are, for example "that the length of a given copper rod *r* increased during the time interval 9.00 to 9.01 A.M. or that a particular drawing *d* from a given urn produced a white ball." Such events, being described or describable by sentences, are called 'sentential'.

---

[1] Pp. 421 ff.

A "concrete" event, on the other hand, is not described or specified by a sentence but rather by "a noun phrase such as an individual name or a definite description as, for example, 'the first solar eclipse of the twentieth century', 'the eruption of Mt. Vesuvis in A.D. 79', 'the assassination of Leon Trotsky', 'the stock market crash of 1929'." Noun phrases of this kind let us hereafter call '*event descriptions*'.

By 'an individual name' Hempel presumably means a name of an individual, and by 'a definite description', presumably a Russellian description of the usual kind. Individual names are presumably either proper names or abbreviations for descriptions. In either case they name *individuals*, whatever the individuals of our discourse are. Let us assume, for present purposes at least, that they are either concrete, spatio-temporal chunks of matter (in accord with Carnap's *reism*), or physical objects in some sense (in accord with *physicalism*).[2] This seems the most natural assumption to make in the philosophy of science, or at least the most frequent, and one surely with which Hempel would not cavil.

The individuals might be taken instead as events in some sense, but just what events are, as contrasted with concrete or physical objects, is not too clear. In any case we should note that the "definite descriptions" and "individual names" Hempel mentions do not strictly stand for individuals in the sense of concrete or physical objects, but rather for events in some sense. A solar eclipse, whatever it is, is not a concrete or physical object, nor is the eruption of Mt. Vesuvius, nor the market crash of 1929. Nor for that matter is the increase in length of a copper rod or a drawing *d* of a ball from an urn. These are all events, in some vague sense at least.

The usual form of language system used above, employing a first-order logic with identity, seems well-suited to handle concrete or physical objects. How now can events be handled within them? How is time flow to be handled, for talk of time is surely endemic to event talk? Over and above events, we surely wish to admit physical or concrete objects anyhow. If so, precisely how are such objects related to events? It is, after all, the concrete or physical objects to which the events *happen*, as it were. Solar eclipses take place in time as between certain macroscopic objects; the eruption of Mt. Vesuvius is an event involving a certain geographic entity; an assassination is of a certain physical individual; and so on.

Perhaps the language in which there is talk of solar eclipses, for example, can be constructed in such a way as *not* to contain names

<hr>

[2] See especially *The Philosophy of Rudolf Carnap*, pp. 869 ff.

or variables for the macroscopic objects, sun, moon, earth, and so on, involved. It is not clear what would be gained in trying to avoid such reference, however, that is, in allowing our variables and names to refer *only* to events. The more natural course, as has been suggested, seems to be to admit concrete or physical objects as the fundamental ones and then try to build up events in some fashion as constructs. This seems never to have been done explicitly. The result is that phrases such as the event descriptions Hempel mentions seem never to have been analyzed *au fond* and given an exact logic. Let us attempt to analyze them within the framework of a reistic or physicalistic language.

First we should ask whether Hempel's distinction between two kinds of events, "sentential" and "concrete," can be maintained. Whatever *facts* are, they are not to be confused with events, as Ramsey was perhaps the first to point out. We recall his crucial comment on this, already quoted above: "The event which . . . is called 'the death of Caesar' [quotes added] . . . should no more be confused with the fact that Caesar died," he writes, "than the King of Italy [in 1927] should be confused with the fact that [in 1927] Italy has a King." 'The death of Caesar' is presumably an event description, just as 'the King of Italy in 1927' is an individual description. They are intimately related respectively with the "facts" given by the statements 'Caesar died' and 'Italy had a King in 1927'. Just as the King was a human person, not a fact, so is Caesar's death an event and not a fact. Hempel's "sentential" events thus seem best regarded as facts, and we are left with only his "concrete" events to worry about. It seems best to keep facts and events quite separate.

The very label 'sentential' suggests reference to language, whereas 'concrete' suggests reference to objects. The two labels are thus not on a par, as it were. Strictly, then, it seems we have only one kind of event but two ways of speaking of them. Further, it seems easy to pass from one way of speaking to another. For example, 'that the length of a given copper rod *r* increases during the time interval 9.00 to 9.01 A.M.' easily becomes the event description 'the increase of the length of the copper rod *r* during the interval 9.00 to 9.01 A.M.', and conversely. 'That Trotsky was assassinated' becomes 'the assassination of Trotsky' and conversely. It is thus not clear why Hempel thinks that we have two kinds of events rather than merely two ways of talking about them.

2. A Theory of Events. Let us go on to try to construct a theory of events within the familiar reistic or physicalistic object language.

The first item to note is that events involve time. An event is a happening *at a time*. The assassination of Trotsky took place at a time, and so on. Thus, some underlying theory of time flow seems needed here in the object language, just as it was needed above in the pragmatical metalanguage.[3]

That events involve time fundamentally has been well recognized. Broad brought this out clearly when he noted that an event is

> anything that endures at all, no matter how long it lasts or whether it be qualitatively alike or qualitatively different at adjacent stages of its history. [This he finds contrary to common usage], but common usage has nothing to recommend it in this matter. . . . [nor for that matter on most matters.] We usually call a flash of lightning or a motor accident an event, and refuse to apply this name to the history of the cliffs of Dover. Now the only relevant difference between the flash and the cliffs is that the former lasts for a short time and the latter for a long time. And the only relevant difference between the accident and the cliffs is that, if successive slices, each of one second long, be cut in the histories of both, the contents of a pair of adjacent slices may be very different in the first case and will be very similar in the second case. Such merely quantitative [qualitative?] differences as these give no good ground for calling one bit of history an event and refusing to call another bit of history by the same name.[4]

In accord with the familiar trichotomy of individuals (or objects), classes or virtual classes (or properties taken extensively), and relations or virtual relations (also taken extensively), let us distinguish three kinds of events, *object events, property events,* and *relation events.* This seems a reasonable trichotomy, and using it will help clarify the whole subject. These may be regarded as the most fundamental kinds of events. Other derivative kinds of events can then be built up in terms of them.

Object events are in effect enduring objects with the time of endurance made explicit. Thus the cliffs-of-Dover-at-time-t constitute an object event, as do the-cliffs-at-time-t_1, where t_1 is any continuous (nonscattered) part of t. The physical cliffs are the "content" of the events, and t or t_1 are their respective times. An object event is completely described in terms of its "content" (or object) and time. The longest object event whose content consists of the cliffs of Dover, is the-cliffs-of-Dover-at-t, where t is their whole temporal life span.

In his *Word and Object*, Quine has extolled the notion of an ordered pair (or unit relation) as a philosophical paradigm. In any

---

[3] See *Intension and Decision,* pp. 41 ff.
[4] C. D. Broad, *Scientific Thought* (London: Routledge and Kegan Paul, 1923), p. 54.

what order is that?

situation in which we have two entities in a given order and wish to consider them as one, the device of using the ordered pair recommends itself. Quine concerns himself with *real* ordered pairs in the sense that they are themselves values for variables. "A notion of ordered pair would fail of all purpose without ordered pairs as values of the variables of quantification," he writes. However, this is too strong. We can put *virtual* ordered pairs to work and get good service out of them. Likewise virtual ordered triples, and so on, should they be needed. Events are here to be regarded as virtual ordered pairs, triples, and so on, of a special kind. More particularly, object events are to be regarded as virtual ordered pairs, the first member of the pair being the "content," the second, the time.

Let 'x', 'y', and so on, be the individual variables, as above. Let

$$\langle x,t \rangle \text{ be defined as } 'yt_1 \ni (y = x \cdot t_1 = t)'.$$

The enduring object or object event x-throughout-t might then be regarded merely as $\langle x,t \rangle$. However, this would not quite do. For suppose that t were a time outside the life span of x. What kind of an "event" would this be? What sort of an event would

$$\langle \text{Leon Trotsky,A.D. } 79 \rangle$$

be? Possibly a *null* event? Well, it seems better to rule out such pairs by requiring that t be a *part* of x in the special sense in which times may be said to be parts of physical objects.[5] Let '$t\,P\,x$' express that the time t is a part in this sense of the physical object x. Then we may write

object event

$$\langle x,t \rangle^e \text{ for } 'yt_1 \ni (y = x \cdot t_1 = t \cdot t_1\,P\,y)'.$$

Such pairs are called 'virtual *event* pairs', and hence the superscript 'e'. The definiendum here provides a general notation for event descriptions of object events.

Let us turn now to the sort of events described by noun clauses such as 'the eruption of Mt. Vesuvius in A.D. 79', 'the assassination of Leon Trotsky', 'the death of Caesar', and so on, *property events*, so to speak. Each of them seems to involve not only a physical object and a time, but also a property or, more particularly, a

---

[5] See the author's "Of Time and the Null Individual," *The Journal of Philosophy* LXII (1965), 723–736. Note incidentally that for the handling of just object events, ordered pairs are not needed. Virtual *cardinal* couples would do equally well.

property as relativized to a time (whether the time is explicitly mentioned or not). The clause 'the eruption of Mt. Vesuvius in A.D. 79' involves not only Mt. Vesuvius and the time A.D. 79, but also the property of erupting. (Of course erupting here could be regarded as a relation between Mt. Vesuvius and a time, but we shall speak of it as a property instead.) 'The death of Caesar' involves Caesar, the property of dying, and a time.

Property events are not to be regarded merely as virtual ordered pairs, but rather as virtual ordered triples, one member of which is a property. However, even this will not quite do, for 'the death of Caesar at t'—the time is brought in for explicitness—does not describe an event unless Caesar actually died at t. Likewise 'the eruption of Mt. Vesuvius in A.D. 79' is not an event description unless Mt. Vesuvius actually erupted in A.D. 79, once and once only. So some provision must be made in handling this second kind of events to assure that the events described actually take place at the proper times, once and once only.

Let

$$'\langle x,F,t\rangle^{\mathrm{e}}'\quad\text{abbreviate}\quad 'yGt_1 \ni (y = x \cdot G = F \cdot t_1 = t \cdot Gyt_1)'.$$

The definiendum here provides a general notation for event descriptions of property events. The triple

$$\langle\mathrm{Caesar,dies},t\rangle^{\mathrm{e}}$$

is the event *the death of Caesar* provided Caesar actually died at t once and once only.

Of course we might wish to subdivide property events into various kinds, depending upon whether the relevant property is a quality, such as *red, green, warm,* and so on, an action property such as *walks, dies, accelerates,* and so on, or some other kind of property. Action properties seem to give rise to events in a very natural way; qualities, in a less natural way. Examples of action properties have already been met with in the examples considered. (See also Chapter XI below.) However, how about 'this leaf's being green at t'? Should this be regarded as a description of a property event?—provided, that is, that the leaf really is green. It seems better to handle phrases of this kind by means of the '*in*' of Chapter VIII, Section 7, as, namely, facts or propositions or state of affairs. (See Section 4 below.)

The "content" of a property event now consists not only of an individual but also of a property. Properties are taken here extensively, it will be recalled, so that neither intensionalism nor Platonism in any form need be involved in our reference to them.

To assure that an event description of a property event describes one and only one event, we must be sure that 'Gyt_1' is taken to express either that y has G throughout the entire time t_1 or that y has G during just one consecutive part of t_1. If Vesuvius erupts during the entirety of A.D. 79, then 'the eruption of Vesuvius in A.D. 79' is a unique event description. The case is similar, if Vesuvius erupts during some consecutive part of t_1 and at no other part. Caesar's death took place during some time span t, but at no proper part of t. Just how long did it take Caesar to die? Probably just a short time. Rasputin's death took longer. No matter. 'Caesar's death at t' describes an event uniquely, provided Caesar was dying during the whole of t. However, where t_1 is a proper part of t, and even though Caesar was dying during t_1, 'Caesar's death at t_1' does not describe the event of Caesar's death.

Strictly, we should be very clear here as to how 'Gyt_1' is to be construed. Without going too deeply into the matter we note merely that the following seems to hold, if not always, at least in a great many cases: namely, Gyt_1 if and only if (1) y has G continuously throughout t_1 (that is, at every part of t_1), or (2) y has G at one and only one proper consecutive part of t_1, or (3) y has G at t_1 but at no proper part of t_1.

Perhaps *momentary* events should be recognized as the ultimate constituents of events, a moment being a time slab of minimal duration. If it is assumed that there are such moments, then all events would be decomposable into a succession of momentary events. This need not be insisted upon here, for it would presuppose a rather special handling of time. However, the requirement does not seem unreasonable, if moments are admitted.

Just as properties give rise to property events, dyadic relations give rise to relation events. The event description 'the revolution of the earth around the sun at t', for example, clearly involves the relation of revolving with the two arguments 'the earth' and 'the sun'.[6] Here,

---

[6] Relational events should not be confused with the relations involved in those events. Russell apparently confuses these in "On Denoting" (*Logic and Knowledge*, pp. 53–54), where he regards 'the revolution of the earth around the sun' as the description of an "entity." "If 'aRb' stands for 'a has the relation R to b'," he writes, "then when aRb is true, there is such an entity as the relation R between a and b: when aRb is false there is no such entity. . . . E.g., it is true (at least we will suppose so) that the earth revolves around the sun and false that the sun revolves around the earth; hence 'the revolution of the earth around the sun' denotes an entity, while 'the revolution of the sun around the earth' does not denote an entity." Russell does not apparently distinguish here, as he should have, between the *relation* of revolving and the *event* consisting of the earth's revolving around the sun at some time. Instead of speaking here of the relation R between a and b as an entity, Russell should perhaps have spoken of the ordered quadruple among R, a, b, and a time, such ordered quadruples themselves being a kind of quadratic relation.

virtual ordered quadruples of a certain kind are needed. The "content" of a dyadic relation event must of course include the relevant relation as well as the relevant objects that stand in that relation. Also, a revolution of the earth around the sun requires a certain length of time t, and cannot take place fully at or during a proper part of t. Nor can one and only one revolution take place during a time twice the duration of t.

In a similar way we pass on to event descriptions involving triadic relations, and so on. 'John's giving a ring to Mary', for example, involves the triadic relation of giving. 'X's selling y to Z in recompense for w dollars' involves a quadratic relation, and so on.

Greater sophistication in the handling of time would no doubt be required if we were to consider more closely the actual language of physics. It is not clear that this would require any fundamental change. The simple topology of time used here seems common to all theories of time, absolute, relative, epochal, or whatever, in the sense that it can be built up within them. If a metric for time is introduced, this would merely complicate the treatment rather than alter it fundamentally. Also, the class of object languages here is so wide that the presumption seems justified that any domain of knowledge however complex can be accommodated within them. Although we have stuck to rough, more or less common, examples, as is customary, this does not render the mode of treatment necessarily inadequate as applied to more sophisticated material.

It need not be claimed that the kinds of events discriminated, object, property, and relation events, are the only basic kinds, but this does seem likely. Each kind can be subdivided in various ways, as desired. Also, events in any one kind can be combined to form longer or more complex ones in appropriate ways.

Let us consider the motor accident, of which Broad speaks. This may perhaps be analyzed as a succession of property events involving the same object, but with differing properties. Without oversimplifying too much let us assume the motor accident involves just the four successive times, t_1, . . . , t_4. At t_1 the motor car is running along smoothly. At t_2, it skids, at t_3 it hits the embankment, at t_4, it overturns. Here there is a succession of property events, with the respective properties of running along smoothly, skidding, hitting the embankment, and overturning. (We recall that an individual x stands in the logical product $(R \frown S)$ of two virtual dyadic relations R and S to y if and only if x bears R to y and also x bears S to y.[7] And similarly for triadic virtual relations, and for virtual relations in which one of

[7] See *Principia Mathematica*, *23.02.

the relata is itself a virtual class.) The accident then may be regarded as the logical product of the four property events mentioned. Let us call such a product the *successive product* of the property events concerned. Let D, S, H, and O be the respective properties here, and let m be the motor vehicle. Then, the respective property events are $\langle m,D,t_1\rangle^e$, $\langle m,S,t_2\rangle^e$, $\langle m,H,t_3\rangle^e$, and $\langle m,O,t_4\rangle^e$. Their successive product, the motor accident under review, is then

$$(\langle m,D,t_1\rangle^e {}^\frown \langle m,S,t_2\rangle^e {}^\frown \langle m,H,t_3\rangle^e {}^\frown \langle m,O,t_4\rangle^e).$$

There is enormous freedom, of course, in building up successive products of property events. Presumably, any successive product with the same object is a property event. The most interesting cases are those in which there is a significant or unusual change in the properties involved. These constitute the "events" of common speech. Similar remarks apply to relation events. Object events, on the other hand, are presumably not recognized as "events" in our common language.

Hempel remarks in a footnote that he is not certain as to how a necessary and sufficient condition for the *identity* of "concrete" events is to be formulated. If events are assimilated to "facts," there is a real problem here, for the latter are in some sense intensional entities. The condition under which two "facts" are to be regarded as identical is controversial, as we have noted. We have been urging, however, that events are not to be regarded as intensional entities. Hence a clear-cut notion of identity between events ought to be forthcoming. It is in the virtual treatment, namely, merely as identity between the virtual entities involved. The event should not be confused with the event description. We may vary the description without varying the event. One and the same event may have alternative event descriptions, just as one and the same individual may have alternative Russellian descriptions. In the case of object events there seems no problem. $\langle x,t\rangle^e$ is identical with $\langle y,t_1\rangle^e$ just in case $x = y$ and $t = t_1$.

Turning now to property or relation events, we might be puzzled as to the condition of identity. It is not clear, however, that such puzzlement would be fruitful. Puzzles ought not to be multiplied beyond necessity. If F and G are one and the same property or virtual class, surely $\langle x,F,t\rangle^e$ and $\langle x,G,t\rangle^e$ are one and the same property event. To be sure, we *describe* it differently. However, here likewise we must not confuse the event, the actual going on in nature, with the terms we use to describe it.

Of course there are other relations between events to be noted, in particular, various relations of *part-to-whole*. A full theory of these is surely needed.

The phrase 'occurrence of an event' is frequently used by philosophers of science without analysis and in ways that are logically jarring. In discussions of causal explanation, for example, it is frequently alleged that "there are general laws . . . in virtue of which the occurrence of the causal antecedent . . . is a sufficient condition for the occurrence of the explanandum event." It might be argued that we all know well enough what this says, and hence there is no need for analysis of the key phrases. However, the step from using 'occurrence of an event' to 'existence of a thing' is a short one, and it may be that similar confusions attach to each. No sophisticated philosopher would use 'existence of a thing' without qualms. The same, we wish to urge, should hold for 'occurrence of an event'. Of course events occur, there is nothing else for them to do. What are nonoccurring events? Like nonexistent individuals, no doubt. To say of an event that it occurs is merely to say that it contains a time factor, and this is always true. The phrase is thus at best periphrastic. To say that an event occurs is like saying that an object exists, bad philosophical grammar no doubt being involved in both cases.

An event description is taken in such a way as always to describe an event. A kind of "existence" condition, as it were, is built into the definientia. In the case of object events, the existence condition is that the time involved be a part of the object constituting the "content." If this existence condition fails, the virtual ordered couple is merely the appropriate null virtual dyadic relation. In the case of property events, the existence condition is that the object involved has the relevant property at the time. Likewise, if the condition fails, the triple is merely the appropriate null virtual triadic relation. And similarly for relation events. Also, a kind of unicity condition, that there is *at most one* event being described, is implicit in the uniqueness of the respective objects, properties, relations, and times and in the way in which these are interrelated.

Note that events are sharply to be distinguished from facts, not because of the virtuality involved but because events are not spoken of nominally. Facts are to be regarded as nominal entities having an intensional structure, and hence can be referred to only indirectly. Events, on the other hand, are referred to directly. Events are not regarded as real things in the world, although their "contents" are. However, this circumstance is surely sufficient to give them enough reality and concreteness. Further, we note that talk of events can take place within the physicalistic or reistic object language, provided it contains a theory of temporal flow. Talk of facts is metalinguistic through and through. Events are temporally dated, facts are not. Events are clear-cut extensional entities, facts are intensional constructs. Both, however, are fictitious in the sense of being handled only virtually.

Throughout, the *virtual* treatment of properties, relations, and hence of ordered *n*-tuples, has been used. However, nothing of a technical nature hinges fundamentally upon this, so far as the treatment of events is concerned. We may, if we wish, regard events as the corresponding *real* ordered *n*-tuples, involving *real* classes and relations, presupposing now some kind of set or type theory as the basic logic. We would thus gain a theory of events within the richer resources of a reistic or physicalistic object language built upon a set or type theory, such richer languages being widely preferred to the narrower ones utilizing only the virtual theory of classes.[8]

It should be emphasized that, by admitting the variables '*t*', and so on, over stretches of time, we are not thereby committed to any special theory of time in physics, psychology, or wherever. Instead, we are merely introducing a little logic of tenses, so to speak. The problem remains as to how this theory relates to the various theories of time in physics, absolute, relativistic, epochal, and so on. Just how is the theory of temporal flow here to be built up in any of these theories? This of course is an interesting question. However, it need not be answered here as a prerequisite for using such a theory. A similar question arises concerning the *other* types of variables admitted. How are macroscopic physical objects construed in relativity theory, and so on? How human persons? There seems to be no special problem with regard to time. We have similar problems with regard to *all* kinds of entities admitted as values for variables, and indeed with regard to all properties and relations admitted as well.

Finally, we should consider whether there are such things as negative events, disjunctive events, and so on. That we need recognize such entities seems doubtful. It has been suggested that restrictions should be placed upon the properties or relations allowed to give rise to corresponding kinds of events. Clearly only *primitive* properties should be allowed to do so, and perhaps only primitives of a certain kind, for example, action properties (see Chapter XI), motion properties, and the like. Those properties and relations that hold at certain times and not at others and over short intervals, seem to give rise naturally to events. This is a difficult matter that we need not decide for the present, other than to note that some restrictions seem reasonable here, lest events be multiplied beyond necessity.

3. Some Alternatives. Two or three alternative ways of handling events will now be suggested.

---

[8] See Chapter XII, Section 6, below. See also J. Kim, "On the Psycho-Physical Identity Theory," *American Philosophical Quarterly* 3 (1966), 1–9, and R. Brandt and J. Kim, "The Logic of the Identity Theory," *The Journal of Philosophy* LXIV (1967), 515–537.

Rather than introduce events directly as certain ordered couples, triples, and so on, we could introduce a general predicate 'is an object event', 'is a property event', and so on. Conceivably there might be some advantages in such a treatment. We need not therewith recognize a realm of nonevents. Rather we would have predicates for singling out expressions for those ordered pairs, triples, and so on, that do describe events from those that do not.

Let

$$\text{'ObjEv } R\text{' abbreviate '}(Ex)(Et)(R = \langle x,t \rangle \cdot x \text{ P } t)\text{'}.$$

To say that a dyadic virtual relation R *is an object event* is then to say that there is an x and a t such that R is the virtual ordered pair $\langle x,t \rangle$ and x P t. Similarly,

$$\text{'PrpEv } Q_F\text{' abbreviates '}(Ex)(Et)(Q = \langle x,F,t \rangle \cdot Fxt)\text{'}.$$

A triadic virtual relation Q (involving the property F in a certain way) *is an event determined by the property F,* provided there is an x and a t such that Q is the virtual triple $\langle x,F,t \rangle$ where Fxt. (Note that because we cannot quantify over properties or virtual classes, the 'F' must occur in the definiendum as a parameter.) And similarly for relation events.

Certain restrictions upon quantifiers over events should be noted. Concerning object events, there is no problem. Quantification over them is achieved by quantifying the respective variables for individuals and times. In the case of property and relation events, the expressions for virtual classes and virtual relations cannot be quantified. Nonetheless, schemata may be given, with the individual and time variables directly quantified, which give substantially the effect of quantifiers. Thus, some general principle concerning property events, for example, could be written as a schema thus:

$$\text{'}(x)(t)(\text{PrpEv } \langle x,F,t \rangle \supset (-\langle x,F,t \rangle -))\text{'},$$

for all predicate constants F. The effect of having universal quantifiers over property events is achieved to some extent in this way. Of course the use of schemata does not give the full effect of quantifiers, but at least it suffices for many purposes.

Similar remarks, *mutatis mutandis*, should be made concerning quantifiers over events in the method of Section 2.

Still another alternative is to be remarked, in which events are allowed to be values for variables. For this the time parameters and variables are dropped altogether. Event descriptions then become descriptions of *event kinds* or *types*. Carnap has noted[9] that it is "very important to distinguish clearly between *kinds of events* (war, birth, death, throw of a die, throw of this die, throw of this die yielding an ace, etc.) and *events* (Caesar's death, the throw of this die made yesterday at 10:00 A.M., the series of all throws of this die past and future)."

Expressions for event kinds would now be admitted as predicates. New variables for events would then be introduced to which these predicates could be applied, as would suitable relations of identity and of part-to-whole. Where 'e' is an event variable, we would have, for example,

$$\text{'}\langle c, \text{dies}\rangle^e e\text{'}$$

expressing that e is an event of the kind *Caesar's death*,

$$\text{'}\langle m, S\rangle^e e\text{'},$$

that e is an event of the kind *the skidding of the motor car* m, and so on. The full syntax and semantics in which events are handled in this fashion remain to be worked out.[10]

Let us now turn to "propositions."

4. Propositions. In this book, and *a fortiori* in this and the last chapter, we have not accepted the—or any, if there is more than one—traditional notion of proposition. Propositions, regarded as whatever it is that declarative sentences state or "express," are surely as obscure as facts. Hence it will not do to presuppose them in the analysis of the latter. The two go hand in hand, and both are in need of analysis. It we can succeed in straightening out one, the suspicion is that we shall have gone a long way toward straightening out the other as well.

What now are propositions? Is there a notion of proposition concomitant with the treatment of facts in the preceding chapter? Yes. In the definientia of the general definition schema of Chapter VIII, Section 6, we merely drop 'true but not analytically so and'. The last clause then reads merely 'and the result of writing b followed by a is L-equivalent to no sentence not containing a'. Propositions are then like facts in being nominal, eliminable, intensional entities referred to only in a *manière de parler*.

[9] *Logical Foundations of Probability*, p. 35.
[10] See the author's "On Events and the Calculus of Individuals," presented at the XIV International Congress of Philosophy in Vienna, September, 1968, and "On Events, Histories, and Physical Objects," presented at a meeting of the Western Division of the American Philosophical Association at St. Louis, May, 1968.

Propositions are, we might say loosely, *states of affairs* (not just actual ones) that are facts when an appropriate sentence is factually true. Nonactual propositions are like mere "possibilities," as it were. They are nominally there, but not realized. However, this is loose talk indeed, and what is meant by it is fully spelled out in the definition.

Consider again the example of Ajdukiewicz. What is the "proposition" that Rome is situated on the Tiber? Consider again Rome, r, the Tiber, t, and the relation of being situated on O. 'Ort' is a sentence, hence the nominal entity $(O,r,t \; in \; Fxy \ni (Fxy))$ is the corresponding proposition. And similarly for any other atomic sentence.

In general, for molecular sentences we can always exhibit as argument all the primitive predicate and individual constants that occur. Then for the corresponding propositions, we should have such forms as

$$'(P,a,Q,b,c \; in \; FxGyz \ni (-F-x-G-y-z-))',$$

and so on. The abstract may be either homogeneous or heterogeneous, and if homogeneous may stand for a virtual relation among individuals only (if of first order) or for a virtual relation among virtual classes and/or relations (if of second order).

That propositions thus conceived *really do what they should do* in connection with belief may be seen by embedding propositions now in belief contexts. Consider again the generalized definition of 'B' suggested in Chapter VII, Section 6. Suppose then that

(1) $'X \; B_E \; P_1,...,P_n,a_1,...,a_m,F_1...F_nx_1...x_m \ni (-F_1,...,F_n,x_1,..., x_m-),t'$

is suitably defined, reading 'X believes (according to E) of the virtual classes or relations $P_1, \; . \; . \; . \; , P_n$ and of the individuals $a_1, \; . \; . \; . \; , a_m$ that $(-P_1,..., \; P_n,a_1,...,a_m-)$ at t'. Although actually there is no explicit mention of a proposition here, all the ingredients are present. (1) can easily be rewritten in propositional terms. We assume that

$$'(P_1,...,P_n,a_1,...,a_m \; in \; F_1...F_nx_1...x_m \ni (-F_1,...,F_n,x_1,...,x_m-))-$$
is-a-proposition' or 'Prp $(-)$'

is properly defined, in the manner of (2) of Chapter VIII, Section 6. Then

(2) $'X \; B_E \; (P_1,...,P_n,a_1,...,a_m \; in \; F_1...F_nx_1...x_m \ni (-F_1,...,F_n,x_1, ...,x_m-)),t'$ may abbreviate 'Prp $(P_1,...,P_n,a_1,...,a_m \; in \; F_1... F_nx_1...x_m \ni (-F_1,...,F_n,x_1,...,x_m-))$ and (etc., as needed)'.

The schema (2) ties together the analysis of belief of Chapter VI, Section 6, with the doctrine that propositions are nominal entities. The only significant difference is that now in (2), the *objects* as well as the *conditions* of belief are nominalized, so to speak. On the basis of (2), we have succeeded in making some sense of the doctrine that propositions are the entities believed, and this wholly within an extensional metalanguage.

The "identity" of propositions may be handled as in Chapter VIII, Section 8, on the identity of facts. Here likewise many further semantical relations are of interest, as in Chapter VII, Section 10.

In *Intension and Decision* it was suggested that a proposition corresponding to a given sentence is to be built up from the intensions of the constituent terms, so to speak. Given the plethora of types of intension, there would then be a great variety of kinds of propositions to be distinguished. We could do something similar here on the basis of the theory of objective intensions of Chapter VII. Propositions so conceived would seem rather remote, however, and it is not clear just what use could be made of them. However, propositions in the sense in which we are now regarding them are of immediate interest in connection with the analysis of belief, knowing, and so on. In fact, (1)—that of Chapter VI, Section 6—and (2) here give what are regarded as the most satisfactory analysis of 'B'. The others in the preceding chapters have served their purpose as heuristics and may now be dropped.

Note that extensionality is by no means abandoned if (2) is used in place of (1). Of course we do not have substitutivity laws for the constituent terms of propositions in belief contexts, the objects involved being nominal. For example, we might wish to say that

(3)   If $P = Q$ and $X\,B_E$ (P,a *in* $Fx\ni(Fx)$),t, then $X\,B_E$
         (Q,a *in* $Fx\ni(Fx)$),t.

Such a formula is significant, but whether it holds or not in a specific instance is to be decided by studying X's patterns of belief at the time. However, as we know from Chapter V, the failure of (3) and allied forms to hold in general gives no grounds whatsoever for abandoning extensionality. (Note that the two occurrences of 'P', as well as of 'Q', in (3) are of different kinds. The first is direct, whereas the second is nominal or opaque.)

Just as we distinguished second-order facts, so now we note that there may be second-order propositions, and these as termini of beliefs.

The question remains as to how propositions, in the sense in which we have been discussing them, relate to the objective intensions of Chapter VII. The answer is not difficult. Propositions are nominal entities consisting in a certain way of (nominal) individuals, virtual classes and virtual relations. Moreover, a proposition "corresponds," as it were, to a certain sentence, but is in abstracted form. For example,

$$(P, a \ in \ Fx \ni (Fx))$$

corresponds to the sentence 'Pa'. Propositions are thus in effect what we might call sentences *taken in intension*. Also, they are like the members of the objective intensions of predicate constants, not like those intensions themselves.

There are objective intensions of *sentences*, however, as we may see by using essentially the methods of Chapter VII, Section 3. Let 'Sent *a*' express that *a* is a sentence of *L* and let '*a* LImp *b*' express that *a* *L-implies b* (in essentially Carnap's sense), that is, that the sentence consisting of '(' followed by the sentence *a* followed by '⊃' followed by the sentence *b* followed by ')' is an Anlytc. Clearly we may then let

'$(P_1,...,P_n,a_1,...,a_m \ in \ F_1...F_n x_1...x_m \ni (—F_1,...,F_n,x_1,...,x_m,—))$' ∈ ObjAnlytcInt($a$)', abbreviate 'Sent a and there is a b_1, a b_2, . . . , a b_n, a c_1, . . . , a c_m, and a d such that b_1 LDes P_1 (etc.) and c_1 LDes a_1 (etc.) and d LDes $F_1...F_n x_1...x_m \ni (—F_1, ...,F_n,x_1,...,x_m—))$ and a LImp $(d \cap b_1 \cap . . . \cap b_n \cap c_1 \cap . . . \cap c_m)$'.

And similarly for the other kinds of objective intensions, synthetic, veridical, and theoremic. We could also go on to the notion of the *sense* of a sentence, essentially as in Chapter VII, Section 10.

The objective intensions of sentences, as well as of the terms contained in them, are useful in spelling out certain further normal acceptance patterns as well as patterns of rational belief. Thus, for example, suppose a person believes a proposition corresponding to the sentence *a*. Then it is rational for him to believe also any proposition which is a member of the objective analytic intension of *a*. It is also rational, but in a different sense, for him to believe any proposition which is a member of *a*'s objective veridical intension. Also, in still another sense, it is rational for him to believe any member of the sense of *a*. There are many other types of patterns to be distinguished in terms of some variation in the nominal entities constituting the objects of the propositions. The analysis of patterns of rational belief quickly becomes technical, however, as noted in Chapter V, Section 10, and will not be discussed further here.

Note again that sentences taken in intension are very different from the intensions of sentences, just as a suitable nominal virtual class is very different from the intension of a PredConOne.

It might be thought that this discussion of propositions is all sound and fury signifying nothing. In a way of course it is, for propositions are fully eliminable in the way facts, and intensions in general, are. Everything we wish to say about a proposition can be said semantically in terms of some declarative sentence. Like facts, propositions are nominal, intensional entities, and hence wholly dispensable in the primitive notation. The sound and fury is merely to have shown this, and their connection with belief, in suitable detail. It is interesting that so much can only be gotten out of so little, with the presupposition of only the most elementary logical framework.

It might be objected that both propositions and facts should be regarded as extralinguistic, or at least interlinguistic, whereas the treatment of them here is intralinguistic. Perhaps further senses of 'fact' and 'proposition' can be built up, on the basis of the present ones, taking into account other languages. Unfortunately, however, very little sound comparative semantics has yet been developed, so that there is at the moment little groundwork for such construction. Also it is thought to be a merit of the present proposal that these notions can be accommodated within the semantics of a single language and without bringing in the complexities of interlinguistic comparison.

It was mentioned in Chapter V, Section 5, that acceptance is like direct quotation, and that believing and knowing are more like indirect quotation. The comparison is now clear in view of the nominal or opaque treatment of propositions. 'Proposition-that' clauses are handled nominally, whereas acceptance clauses are quoted directly.

Another argument for the intralinguistic treatment of propositions is that statements of indirect quotation are couched always in a single language. To assume, with the interlinguists, so to call them, that propositions require for their analysis a host of languages with translatability and perhaps synonymy relations among them, is to assume more than is needed as well as much that is highly dubious. In such a statement as 'Copernicus believed that the earth is not the center of the solar system' there is surely no even disguised reference to a multiplicity of languages, and to suppose that there is seems somewhat quixotic. No doubt indirect quotation is best to be handled within the metalanguage of a single language. Once clear about the single language, we can move on to interlinguistic comparison on a firm footing.

The identity of propositions may be handled like the identity of facts—in terms of L-equivalence, if we follow Scheffler.

5. 'Fact-That' Clauses. In the preceding chapter we were concerned with "facts" as entities and sought to determine their ontological status. Let us now consider facts as "wedded to 'fact-that' clauses."

The clue for the handling of 'fact-that' is to be found in the preceding section. 'Fact-that' clauses are akin to 'proposition-that' clauses. (2) of Section 4 can after all be read 'X believes at t the proposition that so and so'. Similarly now with 'fact-that'. We can let

$$\text{`}X\,B^t_E\,(P_1,...,P_n,a_1,...,a_m \ in \ F_1...F_nx_1...x_m \ni (—F_1,...,F_n,x_1,... x_m—)),t\text{'}$$

abbreviate '$Fct\,(P_1,...,P_n,a_1,...,a_m \ in \ F_1...F_nx_1...x_m \ni (—F_1,...,F_n,x_1,...,x_m—))$ and so on, as needed)'.

A good reading of the definiendum here is to the effect that X believes the fact that so and so (at t according to E).

A limitation here upon the handling of both facts and propositions is that quantifiers over them are not directly available. Some of the effect of achieving quantifiers over them could be achieved by the use of schemata, as in Section 3. Another method would be to try to make quantifiers over sentences, and factual sentences, suffice. Thus, where 'Synthc a' expresses that a is a synthetic or factual sentence of L,

$$\text{`}(a)\,(\text{Synthc } a \supset —a—)\text{'},$$

where '$—a—$' is a suitable context about facts corresponding with a, in effect yields universal quantification over facts. And similarly

$$\text{`}(a)\,(\text{Sent } a \supset —a—)\text{'}$$

yields universal quantification over propositions, for a suitable '$—a—$'. To be sure, some of the laws governing these quantifiers would have to be stated in very special ways, but there seems no essential difficulty involved in doing this.

Note that in contexts containing 'fact-that' or 'proposition-that' clauses, the phrasing must be given *in just the way intended*. The 'that' clause must be given *in just those words*. The phrase 'in just those words' is borrowed from Quine, who urges us to

> begin by picturing us at home in our language, with all its predicates and auxiliary devices. This vocabulary includes 'rabbit', 'rabbit part', 'rabbit stage', 'formula', 'number', 'ox', 'cattle'; also the two-place predicates of identity and difference, and other logical particles. In these terms we can say in so many words that this is a formula and that a number, this a rabbit and that a rabbit

Thinking

part, and this and that different parts. *In just those words.* This network of terms and predicates and auxiliary devices is, in relativity jargon, our frame of reference, our coordinate system. Relative to *it* we can and do talk meaningfully and distinctively of rabbits and parts, numbers and formulas.[11]

Quine is speaking here primarily of reference, not of meaning. 'In just those words', however, is appropriate only for meaning. Other words will do equally well for reference. This phrase raises a most important point, of which, unfortunately, Quine makes little. 'This is a rabbit' can be said in any equivalent way so long as the same object is referred to. If, however, 'rabbit' occurs in a 'that' clause, it is to be referred to in just this way. For example,

'Quine believes that this is a rabbit'

must be said in just this or some cointensive way. (Cf. Frege's *Art des Gegebenseins*, discussed in Chapter X, Section 3, below.)

6. Some Thoughts on Thinking. The foregoing analyses of knowing and believing, and of facts and propositions are given within metalanguages in which there are *no specifically epistemological objects*, so to speak, as values for variables. That is to say, no objects such as sense data, percepts, thoughts, ideas, or such like. In their place certain *relations* between users and expressions (and times) are admitted primitively. The interesting problem arises as to whether this mode of treatment may be made to suffice for epistemology generally. Because belief is so fundamental a notion, if the foregoing *kind* of analysis is adequate, the supposition is that we can perhaps *always* dispense with specifically epistemological objects in favor of certain well-chosen relations. These relations are not taken as values for variables within the metalanguage and hence are in no way a part of its fundamental ontology. If there are no specifically epistemological objects, what has traditionally been regarded as epistemology becomes absorbed in the study of certain relations, the exact character of which is to be found in the logico-behavioristic study of language.

In their correspondence concerning "Intentionality and the Mental,"[12] Sellars and Chisholm have discussed the problem as to whether

---

[11] This is the key passage in Quine's second John Dewey Lecture. See his "Ontological Relativity," *The Journal of Philosophy* LXV (1968), 185–212, esp. p. 200.

[12] In *Minnesota Studies in the Philosophy of Science*, Vol. II (Minneapolis: University of Minnesota Press, 1958), pp. 507–539.

(1)   '. . .' means p

is to be analyzed as

(2)   '. . .' expresses t and t is about p,

where t is a *thought* and p a proposition of ordinary language. Sellars does not regard thoughts as theoretical entities or constructs. "We have direct (non-inferential) knowledge, on occasion, of what we are thinking," he notes, "just as we have direct (non-inferential) knowledge of such non-theoretical states of affairs as the bouncing of tennis balls." Presumably we have, according to him, direct (non-inferential) knowledge of thoughts, more specifically of thought t_1, of thought t_2, and so on. In order to make this statement, we must have either *proper names* for thoughts or *variables* ranging over them.

Ordinarily when one admits proper names for a kind of entity, one also admits variables ranging over them, as we have noted. At any event, it is not unreasonable to think that both Sellars and Chisholm need both names of, and variables for, some kind of mental entity. Otherwise (2) would be difficult to construe—indeed, it is difficult to construe anyhow without a good deal of clarification concerning 'expresses' and 'about', as both Sellars and Chisholm recognize.

The question arises then as to whether a domain of objects called 'thoughts' should be admitted in the metalanguage or whether the effect of having such can be achieved in terms of suitable relations. This is a difficult matter not casually to be settled one way or the other, and it in no way affects the foregoing logic of belief, if adequate.

Of course, the admission of mental entities in some form or another as values for variables ushers in difficult theoretical problems. Under what circumstances is thought t_1 *identical with* thought t_2? Presumably, as a first attempt at an answer, one might say: when t_1 is *about* the same object or objects as t_2. This, of course, will not do. We can surely have distinct thoughts about one and the same object. We should then anlyze thoughts into constituents, if possible, and require that every constituent of t_1 be also a constituent of t_2, and conversely. However, what constituents are is not very clear. A first and very fundamental problem in the admission of thoughts as values for variables is the condition of identity and the determination of constituents, for they go hand in hand. A similar difficulty has plagued the logic of intension, as developed at least in the fashion of Church, as noted in Chapter IV, Section 6.

Perhaps we may identify thoughts, in the objective sense, with propositions in the sense of Section 4. (See Chapter X, Section 4, below.)

For handling *thinking*, some new epistemic relation should perhaps be introduced. To be thinking of a proposition is of course not necessarily to be accepting the corresponding sentence; rather it is merely to *apprehend* or to be aware of it without assent. We could let

$$\text{'}X \text{ Apprh}_E\, a,t\text{'}$$

express that X apprehends the sentence a at t in this sense according to E. Where E is X himself, we have self-conscious awareness. To *précisé* this relation would of course, as in the case of Acpt, require a good deal of further discussion. For the present, it is merely suggested that a "logic of thoughts" would make fundamental use of some relation such as Apprh just as the logic of belief does that of Acpt.

Notions of *utterance* and *assertion* are perhaps to be handled in similar vein. Let

$$\text{'}X \text{ Utt}_E\, a,t\text{'}$$

express that X *utters* the sentence a at t in the sense of actually exhibiting for E at t some audible or visible (or even tactile) inscription of a under circumstances taken to be normal. Then, assertion of a proposition may perhaps be defined in terms of the simultaneous utterance and acceptance of the same corresponding sentence. For example, we could let

$$\text{'}X \text{ Asrt}_E\, (P, a \text{ } in \text{ } Fx\ni(Fx)),t\text{'} \quad \text{abbreviate} \quad \text{'}(P, a \text{ } in \text{ } Fx\ni$$
$(Fx))$-is-a-proposition, $X \text{ Acpt}_E\, a,t$, and $X \text{ Utt}_E\, a,t\text{'}$,

where 'a' is taken as 'Pa'.

If these suggestions are sound, at least in principle, we should have suitable kinds of linguistic forms for the development of a rather full logic of epistemic relations. On this topic more will be said in Chapter XII below.

Incidentally, one can, if one wishes, drop at any point the abstracted form for facts and propositions in favor of the concrete form without abstracts. To do so would be to lose sight of the intuitive distinction between objects and conditions, however, and hence of the notion of a maximal analysis à la Ajdukiewicz. Further, there is nothing at all complicated about the abstracted form, once one gets used to it.

CHAPTER X

On Frege's Sinne

Frege's doctrine of *Sinne*, of "propositions," and the like, has been mentioned above as a doctrine of Platonic intensions *sui generis*. However, was Frege really a "thoroughgoing Platonic realist," in this respect, as Church contends? Well, one can say so, and no doubt passages in Frege will echo in reply. Other echoes, however, may also be heard. Surely a less realist interpretation is consonant with some at least of Frege's text, and anyhow may be espoused on other grounds.

In any event let us examine freshly Frege's most important passages on the subject from the point of vantage of the material above. Frege's remarks are not all above obscurity. We must do the best we can to fathom them, trying always to be as clear as possible in suggesting an interpretation that fits more or less. The fit is never exact anyhow and the best we can do is to approximate. At the same time we must not be afraid to let a subject grow and to realize that the work of the past must continually be scrutinized in the light of what is now known. Those commentators who follow Frege too literally have perhaps failed to take adequately into account more recent developments.

We shall try to follow Frege literally, but if we fail here or there to do full justice to the very letter of what he says, there need be no grief. What we wish to do is, primarily, to suggest an interpretation hinted at surely by Frege's text, one that seems very important indeed, but which has perhaps not been emphasized sufficiently by previous commentators. Other than this, along the way various

213

textual points may be illuminated, especially those on matters relevant
to the material of this book.

In Section 1 Frege's introductory remarks on *identity* are commented on. In Section 2 the notion of *Sinn* is discussed literally in
the way in which Frege actually introduces it. Especially important
here is the notion of the *Art des Gegebenseins*, which is then discussed further in Section 3. Section 4 is devoted to "thoughts" or
"propositions," the *Sinne* of declarative sentences. Finally, Section 5
is concerned with the relations between *indirect discourse* and *belief*.

Attention is confined here almost entirely to "Über Sinn und
Bedeutung," without our attempting to consider all relevant significant
passages in the rest of the Frege *corpus*. To undertake this latter
would take us too far afield and would not alter, fundamentally at
least, the points to be presented.

1. Identity. At the beginning of "Über Sinn and Bedeutung,"
Frege is concerned, it will be recalled, with the proper interpretation
of the identity sign. This leads him directly to the distinction between
sense (or meaning) and designation (or reference). "Equality [or
identity]," he notes, [p. 56], "gives rise to challenging questions
which are not altogether easy to answer. Is it a relation? A relation
between objects, or between names or signs of objects?" In other
words, Frege urges that we distinguish between the formula

(1)   'a = b'

and

(2)   ' 'a' = 'b' '.

To state (1) is to state that the object a, whatever it is, is the *same
object* as b. To state (2), which is, incidentally, a falsehood, is to
state that the sign or symbol 'a' is *the same sign* or symbol as 'b'.
Frege notes these two meanings, but decides that identity is most
properly a relation between objects, not signs. (1) is interpreted to
mean that the object designated by 'a' is the same object as that
designated by 'b'. The same object here is designated by different
signs. In (2), on the other hand, identity is, as we would now say,
a purely syntactical relation, one holding only between signs and not
between the nonlinguistic object or objects that the sign or signs
designate. We need not throw out forms such as (2), but should
rather retain them in their proper place. In any case, (2) is merely a
special case of (1), where our "objects" are themselves signs.

Frege goes on to say that "it is natural . . . to think of their being connected with a sign . . ., besides that to which the sign refers, which may be called the *reference (Bedeutung)* [*or designatum*] of the sign, also what I should like to call the *sense (Sinn)* of the sign, *wherein the mode of presentation is contained* [italics added] . . . ." Let a, b, and c be the lines connecting the vertices of a triangle with the midpoints of the opposite sides, in a Euclidean space of two dimensions. The point of intersection of a and b is then the same as the point of intersection of b and c. So, one and the same point is designated *in different ways*. The distinct phrases 'the point of intersection of a and b' and 'the point of intersection of b and c' designate the same point by means of different modes of presentation, Frege would say. In other words they have the same reference but different senses. Similarly, the phrase 'the morning star' designates the same object, namely, such and such a planet [Venus], as does the phrase 'the evening star'. Nonetheless, these phrases clearly have different senses or meanings. (We recall Chapter VII, Section 7 here.)

Although he does not say so explicitly, Frege has often been interpreted here as in effect postulating a new realm of abstract entities called '*senses*'. To each expression of such and such a kind, of the language at hand, is presumably associated a corresponding sense. (Recall Chapter III, Section 6.) However, precisely what these senses are, and how they are interrelated with each other and with other objects, we are not told.

Frege's remarks lead us to distinguish a third meaning for identity, the meaning in which we wish to say that the sense of the sign 'a' is identical with the sense of the sign 'b'. Let 's(a)' stand for the moment for sense of 'a', and similarly 's(b)' for the sense of 'b', as in Chapter III, Section 6. We then have formulae of the form

(3)   's(a) $=$ s(b)'.

To say (3) is to say in effect that 'a' and 'b' are *synonyms* or *mean the same*. The problem is to give equations of this form a sharp meaning, and this is not easy, as we know from Chapter VII, Section 10. We would say nowadays that the equation (1) is an equation of logic proper, (2) of syntax, and (3) of intensional semantics.

We have been speaking only of identity between "objects." An object for Frege (p. 57) is something "definite," "but not a concept or a relation . . . ." Let us go along with this restriction *pro tem* and speak of objects only in the sense of *individuals*, although much of what is said can be said of classes and relations as well. We need not tarry with Frege's "concepts" here, for classes and relations, even virtual ones, will do equally well for present purposes.

The "meaning" that Frege gives to (1) is in effect that 'a' designates whatever 'b' does, and conversely. So stated, we have a relation in a semantical metalanguage, '*codesignation*' we might call it. 'a' is codesignative with 'b', we might say, if and only if for all x, 'a' designates x if and only if 'b' does. Strictly, this is a very different relation from that of (1), which is presumably object linguistic. (1) is perhaps best to be introduced in terms of a primitive '$=$' or else defined via a suitable adaptation of Leibniz's definition.

Still another notion emerges if we consider *denotation* rather than designation. Thus 'a' may be said to be *codenotative* (or *coextensive*) with 'b' if and only if for all x 'a' denotes x if and only if 'b' does. Codesignation and codenotation are very different relations, but of course closely related in a suitable semantical metalanguage. Codenotation would not be a relation between signs for individuals but rather a relation between signs for virtual classes or relations.

Strictly under (2) we should distinguish two syntactical relations of identity, one as between sign designs or types, the other as between sign events or tokens, a distinction already met with above.

For Frege, a term is regarded as having one and only one intension or *Sinn*—we need not distinguish them for the moment—just as it is regarded as having one and only one designatum. This point of view has obscured the important fact that there are many different kinds of intensions to be discriminated. That Frege failed to make such discrimination is probably due in part to the fact that he gives no clear condition under which two intensions differ or are the same. Each term (of the proper kind) has a unique intension, but precisely how this intension differs from the intension of some other term is not clearly indicated. In other words, Frege gives us no really clear analysis of equations of the form (3). He does not tell us how or in what respect the sense of the phrase 'the morning star' differs from the sense of the phrase 'the evening star'. He merely tells us, in a rather unilluminating way, it would seem, that they are different. Also, intensions are usually regarded, at least by Fregeans if not by Frege himself, as in some sense *sui generis*, and hence how they involve or consist of or are generated out of other kinds of entities is not considered.

2. Sinne and Signs. How are *Sinne* related to signs?

By 'a proper name' Frege understands a sign or phrase consisting of several words or signs designating an object. "The sense of a proper name," Frege writes, "is grasped by everybody who is sufficiently familiar with the language or totality of designating expressions to which it [the proper name] belongs." Perhaps the sense of a proper name is to be gained somehow or "understood" by taking into account the signs of the language. The sense is to be read off, as it were, from the signs somehow and in some manner depends upon them. In any event, if we wish to find out what the sense of a proper name is, it is to the signs we must look, it would seem, and not to some separate realm of hypostatized entities, as some would have it.

"Comprehensive knowledge of the reference [or referent of a proper name] would require us to be able to say whether any given sense belongs to it [the proper name]. To such knowledge we never attain." A sense, it is to be noted, is of a sign only. We do not speak of the sense of an object. Objects may be green or blue, hot or cold, but they do not significantly have a sense. A person omniscient of object x as designated by proper name a—notice that the 'as designated' phrase is needed here—would be able to say of any given sense α whether or not α "belongs to" a. Such omniscience is never attained, but it still may be invoked here as a kind of "theoretical construct." To this topic of omniscience we shall return in a moment.

Frege distinguishes in admirable fashion (p. 59) between the reference and sense of a proper name, on the one hand, and its "associated idea," on the other. Ideas vary from person to person, as we say, and even from time to time. "The idea is subjective: one man's idea is not that of another." "The same sense is not always connected, even in the same man, with the same idea." A sign's sense "may be the common property [possession] of many and therefore is not a part of a mode of the individual mind." Ideas are similar in these respects with what elsewhere have been called '*subjective intensions*'. Subjective intensions common to all men at all times seem very like senses. "For one can hardly deny that mankind has a common store of thoughts which is transmitted from one generation to another." Hence, Frege adds, "one need have no scruples in speaking simply of *the* sense, whereas in the case of an idea one must, strictly speaking, add to whom it belongs and at what time."

Frege's comments here concerning the interconnection between the idea and the sense suggest that it is from the "common store of thoughts" of mankind somehow that we garner the sense. The sense of a term somehow is what is common to the associated ideas when they are stripped of anything depending upon the particular person or the particular time. It would be of interest to know precisely how this is achieved. Unfortunately Frege is not very clear about this. Nor is he any clearer as to what an idea *is* than he is as to what a sense is. "If the referent of a sign [p. 59] is an object perceivable by the senses,

my idea of it is an *internal image* [italics added]. . . . Such an idea is
saturated with feeling; the clarity of its separate parts varies and oscil-
lates. The same sense is not always connected, even in the same man,
with the same idea." At least one subclass of ideas consists presumably
of mental images and these are "connected" somehow with senses. Concerning other sorts of ideas we are told nothing, nor about their "connection" with senses.

Between subjective and objective intensions there is a definite interrelationship that we can get at through their respective parts or members. Ideas and senses, however, seem to occupy different realms of
being altogether. To build the appropriate bridges between the two, on
Fregean grounds, would thus not be easy.

"The regular connection between a sign, its sense, and its referent
is of such a kind that to the sign there corresponds a definite sense
and to that in turn a definite referent, while to a given referent there
does not belong only a single sign." However, not all expressions that
have a sense need have a referent. 'The celestial body most distant
from the Earth' has a sense, but it is very doubtful that it has a reference. An omniscient being would know. 'The least rapidly convergent
series' has a sense, Frege says, but is known to have no reference. Both
of these examples are, of course, descriptive phrases in the sense of
Russell, which may fail to stand for one and only one object but still
have a sense, this sense to be read off somehow from the constituent
words.

It is most interesting to observe that in all of these comments there
is no suggestion that senses, as conceived by Frege, need be regarded
as occupying a separate realm in some Platonic hierarchy of abstract
objects. Those who have so suggested have perhaps done Frege a dis-
service. On the contrary, one might contend, one should be able to
bring senses somehow closer to language itself. A sense is "grasped by
everybody who is sufficiently familiar with the language" and not in-
tuited only by those endowed with a special faculty for discerning
Platonic archetypes. If we know enough about a referent of a proper
name we would know whether a given sense is the sense of that proper
name or not. Senses are connected with mankind's "common store of
thoughts." All of these comments can be interpreted surely in a more
Aristotelian fashion, if you like, than is usually done. To this let us
now proceed.

3. The Art des Gegebenseins. An important point to note, and
one rather neglected (if we mistake not) by commentators on Frege,
is the *Art des Gegebenseins*. A key passage is that (p. 57) in which
the "cognitive value" of 'a = a' is contrasted with that of 'a = b', where

"the sign 'a' is distinguished from the sign 'b' . . . by means of its shape, . . . not by the manner in which it designates," that is, not by having different designata. "A difference can arise," Frege continues, "only if the difference between the signs corresponds to a difference in the mode of presentation of that which is designated." In accord with this we are perhaps to regard a difference in sense, not so much as a difference, somehow, between abstract hypostatized entities, but as a difference depending in some fashion upon the notational difference between the two signs involved. Signs are presumably merely shapes anyhow, so that we may speak equally here of a difference in the *Art des Gegebenseins* as given by a difference in the shapes involved. A clear view as to what senses are would perhaps emerge if we were really to take the *Art des Gegebenseins* seriously.

Now a nominal virtual class, in the sense previously discussed, may be regarded as a virtual class *in a fixed mode of presentation*, the mode of presentation being explicitly given. Where the members of one nominal virtual class are precisely the members of another, there may still be a difference in the modes of presentation, that is, in the expressions L-designating them. Differences in intension, in other words, may be reflected by differences in the modes of presentation. It is most interesting that Frege speaks immediately of the *Art des Gegebenseins* in the very first sentence wherein he speaks of a sense. It is the sense of a sign "wherein the mode of presentation is contained." The sense is not identical with the mode of presentation, but the latter must be "contained" in it and we should be shown explicitly how.

Nominal virtual classes might also be called '*thus-designated* virtual classes', as has been suggested in Chapter VII, Section 2. To be thus designated is to be expressed in the given mode of presentation. Frege speaks of an object a as designated by such and such a proper name, and this is perhaps what is meant by an object a in a given mode of presentation. Surely there is sufficient kinship here to think that the use made of nominal virtual classes incorporates an essential feature of what Frege seems to mean by 'a mode of presentation'. Also, we have been explicit in Chapter VII in attempting to show *how* the mode of presentation is incorporated in the notion of an intension. We have also tried to be "as clear as possible," in Moore's phrase, as to what *else* is involved, in particular, various notions of syntax and semantics.

When are two modes of presentation the same? Well, first there is the sheer syntactic identity of the expressions involved. 'a' is identical with 'a' in this sense. Then there is L-equivalence as between suitable signs. For example, if '$(x)((—x—) \equiv (\ldots x \ldots))$' is analytic, then '$(\imath x \cdot (—x—))$' is appropriately L-equivalent with '$(\imath x \cdot (\ldots x \ldots))$'. There are further relations here also, connected with analytic entailment and synonymy (Chapter VII, Section 10), although their precise character remains controversial, as we have noted.

It has been remarked that there are several universal nominal virtual classes and that two nominal virtual classes may differ in their modes of presentation even though identical in membership. Thus, the use of nominal virtual classes truly reflects differences in intension, as we wish it to. Whether it reflects them correctly, so to speak, depends upon the condition laid down for one nominal virtual class to be identical-in-intension with another. Out of the plethora of relations mentioned in the preceding paragraph (harking back to those of Chapter VII, Section 10), one surely can be found to reflect whatever differences in intension we wish, however subtle.

Barring niceties, we suggest that analytic intensions and senses as construed in Chapter VII are the legitimate heirs of Frege's senses. Surely the family resemblance, the fit, is close enough, as close perhaps as for the alternatives. And it is surely not above all dispute that the more Platonic fit is the only one or even the preferred one.

Frege has commented, it will be recalled, that "comprehensive knowledge of the referent [of a proper name] would require us to be able to say whether any given sense belongs to it [the proper name]. To such knowledge we never attain." The phrase 'any given sense' here does suggest that senses are somehow spread out before us and that comprehensive knowledge would be required in order to know which one is the sense of a given proper name. We need not attach too much importance to this phrase, or sentence either. Equally well, had senses been distinguished into parts or members, as we have suggested should be done, one could say that comprehensive knowledge of a referent is required to enable us to say *whether such and such a nominal class is a member of the sense of its proper name.*

Now it is interesting to note that our notation is such that we do not specify the class of all the nominal classes that are members of an analytic intension. We do not even form an expression for a finite subclass of these classes. We can specify them one by one. We can say that

F_1 is a member of the analytic intension of a,

F_2 is a member of the analytic intension of a,

and so on. However we do not collect together all of these F's, or even a finite number, into an expression such as

$$'\{F_1, \ldots, F_n\}'.$$

Such an expression is meaningless, the *F's* being only nominal. When we refer nominally to a class in a definiendum, this class is referred to in the corresponding definiens in a context only of L-designation, and no such context seems to be forthcoming for '$\{F_1, \ldots, F_n\}$'. The result is that we do not, and perhaps never can, specify the full sense of a proper name. Only omniscience can.

4. "Thoughts." The foregoing is merely the preface to Frege's doctrine, concerned with proper names. The real content appears with his comments concerning direct quotation and indirect quotation.

"We now [p. 62] inquire concerning the sense and reference for an entire declarative sentence." Frege regards the truth value of a sentence as its reference, where "by the truth value of a sentence I understand the circumstance that it is true or false. . . . For brevity I call the one the True, the other the False." Frege speaks of the True and of the False as "objects," but comments that this "may appear to be an arbitrary fancy or perhaps a mere play upon words, from which no profound consequences could be drawn."

To state that a sentence "designates" the True or has the True as its reference is merely to state the circumstance that the sentence is true, nothing more and nothing less. No special mystique need be read into 'the True' not contained in 'is true' as a predicate. Thus without loss, it would seem, on Frege's own grounds (in "Über Sinn und Bedeutung"), we can properly say '*a* is true' in place of '*a* designates the True', where *a* is a declarative sentence. So much for our Aristotelian, versus the Platonic, interpretation of Frege's comments on truth.

The "thought" is the "object content" of a sentence, "which is capable of being the common property of several thinkers." The thought "must be considered as the sense." We shall return to this in a moment, after a word or so about indirect discourse.

> [A] word standing between quotation marks must not be taken as having its ordinary reference . . . , [Frege notes, pp. 59–60]. In reported speech one talks about the sense . . . of another's remarks. It is quite clear that in this way of speaking words do not have their customary reference but designate what is usually their sense. . . . In reported speech, words are used *indirectly* or have their indirect reference. We distinguish accordingly the *customary* from the indirect reference of a word; and its *customary* sense from its *indirect* sense. *The indirect reference of a word is accordingly its customary sense* [italics added]. [And similarly, p. 65] in direct quotation a sentence designates another sentence, and in indirect quotation a thought [or proposition].

ie its customary sense & indirect reference

The italicized sentence here is of course remarkable. The customary sense of a word is merely its indirect reference, which is somehow given in reported speech, that is, in speech standing between quotation marks. The sense thus seems to be given in the *way* in which the speech is reported, in the *Art des Gegebenseins*. It is a pity that Frege does not tell us more here. At any event, the italicized sentence surely underscores the point that senses need not be regarded as hypostatized entities but rather are to be linked somehow more directly to the actual uses of language.

5. Indirect Discourse and Belief. It is interesting to note that Frege does not again mention the *Art des Gegebenseins* when he speaks (in "Uber Sinn und Bedeutung") of thoughts or propositions. The *Art des Gegebenseins* is "contained in" the sense of a proper name. However, is not an *Art des Gegebenseins* "contained in" the sense of a sentence as well? If we take it seriously here, we shall be able to construe thoughts as propositions in the manner of Chapter X, Section 4.

Let us consider Frege's example,

'Copernicus believed that the planetary orbits are circles',

although any similar one would do equally well. Here, 'that the planetary orbits are circles' is presumably to have a thought as its sense. Clearly this thought will be a second-order proposition in the sense of Chapter IX, Section 4. Let 'PO' and 'C' be as in Chapter VIII, Section 8. Our second-order proposition is then

$$(PO,C \ in \ FG\ni(x)(Fx \supset Gx)),$$

and it is this that Copernicus believed at a certain time. That Caesar believed at *t* Rome to be situated on the Tiber involves the first-order proposition

$$(O,r,t \ in \ Fxy\ni(Fxy)),$$

and it is this that Caesar believed at *t*. We end up then essentially with the doctrine of Chapter IX, Section 5, as regards belief. Of course we are not saying here that this is Frege's doctrine, but only that it seems a natural development of his remarks, if the *Art des Gegebenseins* is taken seriously.

Evidently for Frege beliefs are to be handled in the manner of reported speech, as in the method above. The typical form is '*X* believes so and so at *t*', where the so and so is a proposition with its condition or mode of presentation a kind of reported speech. It is interesting to note that there is no reference here to the *sense* of a word in reported speech but only to the *concept*—taking concepts here as nominal virtual classes or nominal individuals. Accordingly, the indirect reference of a word is *not* its customary sense, as with Frege, but rather the appropriate nominal virtual class or nominal individual. Fregean senses thus seem to be of no interest in the analysis of belief and other propositional attitudes, as has been so widely thought. Rather, nominal individual and virtual classes are of such interest, and these only insofar as they form constituents of propositions. Senses remain useful in the way in which intensions or connotations do, when, namely, we wish to spell out, as it were, the various items determining that sense or to construct various patterns of rational belief.

The remainder of Frege's discussion contains nothing essential to the analysis of belief that has not already been referred to. In much of the discussion he is struggling with sentences that we should now handle by means of quantifiers. For example (p. 69),

> 'Whoever discovered the elliptic form of the planetary orbits died in agony' $(x)($ $)$

seems best handled now by means of a quantifier in the usual way. The phrase 'whoever discovered . . .' need not be regarded as a designating or descriptive phrase.

It is most interesting to note that, according to Frege (p. 71), "places, instants, stretches of time, are, logically considered, objects; hence the linguistic designation of a definite place, a definite instant, or a stretch of time is to be regarded as a proper name." A rather similar view has been suggested above in Chapter X, Section 2. Peirce likewise seems to have taken this view. It is certainly a natural one in helping to gain logical forms for many kinds of sentences.

It should be emphasized again that here and throughout it is not *literally* Frege's doctrine that we are speaking of—for no one seems quite sure just what that doctrine is. It is rather a certain interpretation we are concerned with, to which some of Frege's suggestions seem naturally to give rise. Of course, all talk of virtual classes, nominal entities, and the like, is quite foreign to Frege.

Fascinating as Frege's comments are, they need not detain us further. A tragedy of some Frege scholarship is that the commentators will not let the subject grow. They fail to view Frege's work in the light of recent research in set theory (including type theory), on the one hand, or in semantics, on the other. The result is sterile preoccupation with items that have long been cleared up. It is no credit to Frege not to confront him with what is now known. On the contrary, his true greatness is perhaps best seen by noting how extraordinarily well he measures up.

CHAPTER XI

Performance, Purpose, and Permission

In this chapter an attempt is made to formulate logical foundations for a theory of *actions* or *performance*. Human beings act in various ways, and their actions are intimately interrelated with their use of language. However, precisely how these are interrelated is not too clear. One reason is perhaps that we have no precise vocabulary in terms of which such interrelations may be handled. There is need for developing a systematic theory in which different kinds of actions may be discussed, contrasted, and compared. Then, the various interrelations between actions and linguistic usage may perhaps be discussed more carefully and thoroughly than has been done heretofore.

Although much important preliminary work has been done in the analysis of actions, no one, it seems, has attempted to develop a strict logical theory for such analysis. A few tentative and programmatic steps were taken in *Toward a Systematic Pragmatics*. Let us attempt here to improve these and take yet a few more. Any first attempts of this kind are of course fraught with difficulties. There inevitably will be some oversimplification or some overelaboration. Ultimately of course we are interested in interrelating performance with various notions from syntax, semantics, and pragmatics. However, this is not easy, and only a few tentative suggestions toward such a development can be given here.

In Section 1, the distinction between *action kinds* and *action events* is drawn, and the character of the primitive or primitives needed for the theory of performance is discussed. In Section 2 some *further notions* are then defined. Certain *Rules of Performance* are suggested

225

in Section 3. In Section 4 the fundamental notions required for *Parsons* and *Shils'* theory of *social action* is discussed briefiy. In Section 5 we attempt to define the two basic notions required in *Leonard's* recent papers concerning *authorship* and *purpose*. In Section 6 we examine critically an alternative account of actions (and events) due to *Davidson*. In Section 7, the theory of performance is interrelated with *von Wright's deontic logic*, in which such notions as *permission* and *obligation* are accommodated. Finally, in Section 8, certain fundamental features of von Wright's *method* are critically examined, as are those of *Hintikka* in Section 9.

Some of the notions introduced here have been touched upon in the discussion of events in Chapter IX. The theory here is in effect a special case of the theory of that chapter. Nonetheless, because the topic of action is so fundamental for the behavioral sciences, it will do no harm to look at the subject afresh and from its own point of view, as it were, rather than from that of the more general theory.

1. Action Kinds and Performance. The distinction between sign designs and sign events, it will be recalled, is a familiar one in logical syntax. An analogous distinction can be introduced between *action kinds* or *types* and *action events*. By 'an action kind' is meant, roughly, a specific class of similar actions, such as the lighting of cigarettes, or the submerging of a given object or of given objects in a chemical solution, or noting that a pointer is opposite such and such a numeral on such and such a dial. Action kinds have *instances* performed *by* human beings *on* specific objects *at* specific times. These instances are mere *action events*. All action events of a given kind are of course sufficiently "similar" to each other in certain respects.

In an extended treatment, one would presumably wish to take account of both action events and action kinds, just as in an extended treatment of syntax and semantics one would wish to consider both sign designs and sign events. As a matter of fact, however, no such detailed treatment of syntax and semantics has yet been given. These subjects were first developed with expressions construed exclusively as sign designs. A similar method ought, presumably, to be followed in developing a general theory of performance. In this first attempt we shall probably do well then to take into account primarily action kinds, although action events need not as a result be neglected, as we shall see. In similar vein, the syntax of sign designs has been used throughout rather than the more complicated one of sign events.

Some action kinds or the expressions designating them, may be said to be *monadic*, some *dyadic*, some *triadic*, and so on. If an action kind is monadic, we may say that an expression for it has *degree one*;

if dyadic, of *degree two*, and so on. Often there is a choice as to the degree of an expression for an action kind. For example, 'lighting a cigarette' may be taken in the monadic sense according to which we say that person X lights a cigarette x at time t. It might also be taken as involving a match, a lighter, or so on. In this second dyadic sense, we would say that X performs the lighting *on* the cigarette x *with* the match or lighter y at time t. The specific purpose at hand would presumably dictate which kind of analysis is preferable, the monadic or the dyadic. In the general theory to be suggested, each action kind considered is to have its degree uniquely specified.

How best to analyze or explicate a given action kind is not the concern of the general theory. Often there will be alternative ways, and it will not always be clear that one way is necessarily "better" than another. It might be that these alternative ways will not exclude each other. The situation is similar to that often met with in the analysis or explication of other notions. For example, the word 'father' may be regarded as a class word on some occasions, but on others it may be better to regard it as a dyadic-relation word. The alternative analyses need not exclude each other, however, and 'father' is in fact correctly used in both ways.

To simplify, let us consider for the present only monadic action kinds. The general theory to be suggested, however, can easily be extended to action kinds of higher or even of zero degree, as we shall see. A zero-adic (medadic) action type takes no explicit account of an object of action and is often expressed by intransitive verbs. For example, swimming, sleeping, bathing, and so on, are presumably medadic. Of course one swims *at* some place, but there is no direct object of one's swimming.

Let 'f', 'f$_1$', 'f$_2$', and so on, 'g', 'g$_1$', and so on, and perhaps 'h', and so on, now be constants, that is, names designating distinct monadic action kinds. In the *general* theory of performance, little more need be said concerning them. In any specific application of the theory, of course, specific properties of each action kind should be laid down. For example, if 'f' names the monadic action kind *the lighting of cigarettes,* then an axiom should be laid down that whenever f is performed on x by someone, x is in fact a cigarette. (See Section 3 below.) *Variables* also will be needed, ranging over action kinds. Let these be the *italicized* letters '*f*', '*g*', and '*h*', with or without numerical subscripts. (The *roman* letters 'f', and so on, as above, are constants.)

To accommodate action kinds and to develop a theory concerning them, a general relation of *performance* is introduced as follows. Let 'Prfm' be a primitive and let it occur significantly in contexts of the form

(1)   '$X \text{ Prfm}_E f,x,t$'.

The subscript 'E' brings in our old friend the experimenter. Surely no harm can come from his reappearance here, and there is gain in explicitness. Occasionally mention of him may be omitted, but he is to be assumed present nonetheless. In studying human behavior, including acceptances, it seems desirable to bring out explicitly the relativization to the experimenter. Often there is doubt as to whether X *really* accepts *a,* or really performs f at such and such a time. In bringing in the subscript 'E' responsibility is thrust upon the experimenter. Of course there may also be doubt in physics as to whether physical object x has such and such a property. In this case, however, there is usually greater agreement, and to bring in the relativization to the experimenter seems less apt. In physics the idiom 'physical object X has such and such a property according to E' is rarely needed. In the study of human behavior, however, it seems not inappropriate to bring in the additional clause 'according to E', thereby making explicit an important pragmatic factor often neglected.

The first argument place of (1) must be occupied by a variable (or name) for *persons* (or *users*), the second by a variable (or name) for *action kinds,* the third by a variable (or name) for an *individual,* and the fourth by a variable (or name) for a *time stretch* (1) may be read 'Person X performs an action of type f *on* the individual x *at* time t according to E'.

Let us assume now that expressions of the form (1) are admitted *within the object language L,* where L is one of the usual logical systems of first order, as above. The theory of performance and action kinds is not a theory about linguistic expressions, and hence it seems appropriate to develop it within an object language and therewith independent of syntax, semantics, and pragmatics. Then, in the next chapter, the theory of performance may be interrelated with these, and various notions connecting performance with semantical or pragmatical notions may be defined.

Note that (1) above is significant only where in place of 'f' there is a name or variable for a *monadic* action type. For a *dyadic* action type, say g, 'Prfm' is also regarded as significant in the context

'$X \text{ Prfm}_E g,x,y,t$',

read 'X performs (according to E) on x with y at t', with perhaps some other appropriate preposition in place of 'with'. And similarly for action types of higher degree. As has already been remarked, for the present only monadic action kinds and hence 'Prfm' only in contexts of the form (1) need be considered.

Let us think of 'Prfm' throughout in a very concrete sense involving only the simplest kind of physical action types, action types consisting of physical motions or physico-chemical processes. Further, the objects upon which the actions are performed are to be thought of as physical or physico-chemical objects. These restrictions are not strictly needed, but they help to facilitate the intuitive model. Later, actions upon other *users* of the language may be admitted as well, so that (1) will be significant if in place of 'x' a variable or name for a human being is inserted. However, first let us develop the outline of the theory in the simplest way. Later it can be extended step by step in various directions as may be needed.

When X Prfm_E f,x,t, the relevant action event of the type f is to be thought of as being carried on continuously through the whole of t, so that when t ceases the action event does also. Perhaps the phrase 'during t' suggests this rather better than 'at t'. To say that X performs f on x during t suggests that X does so continuously. We shall use the phrase 'at t', however, bearing in mind specifically what is intended.

The analysis of action kinds should be of particular interest for the philosophy and methodology of empirical science, especially perhaps for the analysis of the notion of a scientific *experiment*. Experiments consist of actions performed upon specific objects by certain persons at certain times. Curious as it may seem, the notion of an experiment has never received the attention it merits. It is surely one of the most important concepts in the philosophy of science and there is need for its adequate analysis and explication. It would seem that such an explication would involve fundamentally a theory of actions and performance.

Note that action kinds or types are admitted as values for variables, not action events. The effect of talking about action events is, however, achieved by formulae of the form (1), that is, 'X Prfm_E f,x,t'. To say that X performs f on x at t is in effect to relativize f to X, x, and t. Presumably X cannot perform two instances of the same action kind on the same object at the same time. Nor can two persons perform the same action event upon the same object at the same time. Nor, indeed, can a person perform the same action event on two distinct objects at the same or at different times. In fact an action event should be regarded as uniquely specified by a sentence of the form (1). Thus, action events may be thought of as being *virtual ordered quadruples* of a suitable kind, essentially as in Chapter IX, Section 2. Let

(2)   '$\langle X,f,x,t \rangle_E$' be short for '$Ygyt_1 \ni (Y = X \cdot g = f \cdot y$
     $= x \cdot t_1 = t \cdot X \text{Prfm}_E f,x,t)$'.

where abstracts of this kind are assumed appropriately defined by the methods of Chapter VI. An action event of a given kind may then in effect be designated by an expression of the form (2) with appropriate constants in place of the free variables. It is doubtful, however, that such expressions will be needed in the sequel, the effect of such being achieved well enough in contexts of the form (1). (A predicate for being an action event could also be introduced in the fashion of Chapter IX, Section 3.)

Monadic action types are in effect a certain kind of triadic relation, with their domains, middle domains, and converse domains suitably restricted. To say that X performs f on x at t is to say that X stands in a certain triadic relation R to x at t. The theory of monadic action types is thus in effect a branch of the theory of triadic relations. Hence one might suppose that action events could be thought of as triples rather than quadruples. For example,

(3) $\langle X, x, t \rangle$

might be thought of as an action event. The objection to this is that any triple of this kind would then be an action event, without a specification of the action type. The triple consisting of Theaetetus, a certain chair, and a certain time would then be an action event, even if the time t is not within Theaetetus' life span or even if the chair x is a fine Chippendale of the eighteenth century. Further, expressions of the form (3) would require that there be one and only one action event involving X, x, and t. There might, however, clearly be two or more action events involving these three, or perhaps none at all. We should surely wish to be able to differentiate between Theaetetus' sitting on the chair x at t and his *making* say, the chair x at t, surely quite different action events. The notation involving quadruples enables us to bring this out clearly. For distinct action kinds f and g,

$$\langle X, f, x, t \rangle_E$$

and

$$\langle X, g, x, t \rangle_E$$

are distinct action events, as we should surely wish them to be.

Note that the time parameter 't' is used explicitly throughout, as in the treatment of events in general in Chapter IX. Surely we should wish to be able to say that Theaetetus sits on the chair x at one time but not at another. With the time factor explicitly brought out, such statements may easily be made. However, note that no *spatial* factors or coordinates are needed, nor for that matter any coordinates for temperature or other physical properties. Why should the time factor then be given so privileged a status? The objects x are regarded here as enduring physical objects upon which certain actions may be performed during their life span. A person X may perform an action of a given type upon x at one time during its life span but not at a later one. The time factor is needed to differentiate between these explicitly. Spatial and other physical factors, on the other hand, are implicitly involved in x itself. In general, it seems, these need not be mentioned unless the specific context requires it.

The admission of the variables 'f', and so on, ontically commits us to action kinds. Such variables are admitted for convenience, just as variables over sign designs have been admitted throughout. A pure nominalist may object to this and, if desired, variables of both types may be dropped without too much change. A syntax and semantics based on sign events or inscriptions would then be needed in place of the simpler one actually presupposed. However, no new variables for action events would be needed. We should have to make more use of schemata instead, as has been done above. No really essential changes, however, would have to be made in the material of this chapter.

A distinction between *acts* and *actions* is sometimes made, actions being consciously performed or intended on the part of the agent. The forms (1), and so on, here include both. Intending, however, is to be handled by means of a special predicate. (See form [16] in Chapter XII, Section 2.)

2. Some Defined Notions. Let us now turn to several notions definable on the basis of 'Prfm', which seem not only interesting and important in themselves but useful as well.

It is assumed that '$=$' in contexts of the form '$f = g$' is admitted as a logical primitive, and hence that suitable axioms for it are available. Further, distinct constants for action kinds are to designate distinct action kinds. Thus '$\sim f = g$' always holds where in place of 'f' and 'g' distinct constants for action kinds are inserted.

Closely related to identity is what may be called '*performative equality*', more specifically, *absolute* performative equality. An action kind f is said to be *performatively equal* to an action kind g *in the absolute sense,* if and only if everyone who ever performs f on any x also performs g on x at the same time, and conversely. The word 'absolute' here is to suggest the universal quantifiers implicitly involved.

Clearly, identical action types are performatively equal, but not necessarily conversely. Hence it is important to distinguish performatively equal but not identical action types. It might well happen that whenever one action type is performed the other is also, and conversely. However, even if this should hold, the system should presumably be rich enough to distinguish these action types in other ways, that is, to ascribe to one some property not ascribed to the other. (See Section C below.) If the system is not rich in this way, identity and performative equality should be regarded as the same.

Various types of *relative* performative equality may be distinguished, relative, that is, to a given person, to a given object, or to a given kind of object, or to both a given person and a given object or kind of object, or so on. First f is said to be performatively equal to g *relative to person* X if and only if for all x and t, $X \operatorname{Prfm}_E f,x,t$, if and only if $X \operatorname{Prfm}_E g,x,t$. Similarly, f is said to be performatively equal to g relative to the *object* x if and only if for all X and t, $X \operatorname{Prfm}_E f,x,t$ if and only if $X \operatorname{Prfm}_E g,x,t$. Also f is performatively equal to g relative to *both* X and x where for all t, $X \operatorname{Prfm}_E f,x,t$, if and only if $X \operatorname{Prfm}_E g,x,t$. And so on for the other kinds.

Suppose, for example, that whenever a person X sits on a four-legged chair he touches the front legs of the chair with his heels, and conversely. These two action kinds are then performatively equal relative to X. Similarly, because whenever one stands on a floor $x,$ one is in an erect position and has one's feet on x and vice versa, the action types of *standing on* and *of being in an erect position and of having one's feet on* the floor are performatively equal in the absolute sense. Each of these types of performative equality might be useful for the phenomenological analysis or description of some situation.

One action kind f may be said to be a *part* of another g (in one sense) if and only if for all x, X, and t, if X performs g on x at t he also performs f on x at some temporal part of t, but not necessarily conversely. There are undoubtedly other part-whole relations to distinguish here, but this is the only one that is needed for the present.

To illustrate this notion, let 'g' stand for the action kind of lighting a cigarette in the usual way and let 'f' stand for the action kind of drawing in on the cigarette while it is between one's lips. Then clearly f is a part of g, because whenever X lights a cigarette x in this way he draws in upon it while it is between his lips. (It is assumed that the cigarette is between his lips for a part at least of the time during which he is lighting it.)

Several *relative* part-whole relations between action types may also be defined, relative to a given person, to a given object, or to both, analogous to the various notions of relative performative equality.

The various relations of performative equality and of part to whole clearly have the appropriate properties of identity and part-whole relations.

An action type is said to be performatively *null* if and only if it is never performed by anyone on any object. However, it need not be assumed that there are null action types. This is a matter to be decided by observation. It might so happen that some action types are null or it might not. Neither possibility should be excluded.

An action type would presumably be performatively *universal* if everyone is always performing it on everything. There seems no need to introduce action types of this kind, however, and in fact it is quite clear that there are none unless one stretches enormously the ordinary meanings of 'action'.

Let us consider now certain kinds of performative *sums* and *products* of action types.

Suppose that X performs an action of the kind h upon x at t if and only if he performs *both* f on x at t as well as g, for all X, x, and t. The action type h is then a kind of *simultaneous product* of f and g, more specifically, an *absolute* simultaneous product because of the reference here to all X, x, and t. The complex action type of writing (composing) while typing, for example, is presumably the absolute simultaneous product of composing and typing, because whenever X writes-while-typing a page x at time t, he both composes the page and goes through the mechanical motions of typing, and conversely, for all X and x.

However, there is also a notion of simultaneous product *relative* to given X, x, and t. Thus h is said to be the simultaneous product of f and g *relative to* X, x, and t where X performs h on x at t if and only if he performs both f and g on x at t. Suppose X holds a book x in his hands during t and reads it at the same time. The complex action type holding and reading *relative* to that X, x, and t is then the simultaneous product of the action type holding and of the action type reading, *relative* to X, x, and t.

It seems natural to assume the existence of the absolute simultaneous product of any two action types (as confined to the same objects). It might so happen that this product is null, but still it should be regarded as a suitable action type even if no one ever happened to perform it. It follows that for any X, x, and t, there is a relative simultaneous product for any two action types, even if null.

In a similar way *absolute* and relative simultaneous *sums* of two action types may be introduced. It is not clear that such notions would be very useful, however, and, given any two action types f and g, it need not be assumed that there is an action type h as their absolute simultaneous sum or as their relative absolute sum.

Other kinds of product are, moreover, the so-called *absolute* and *relative successive products* of two action types. Suppose that for all *t*, *X*, and *x*, *X* performs *h* on *x* during *t* if and if for some t_1 and t_2, *X* performs *f* on *x* at t_1 and *h* on *x* at t_2, where t_1 and t_2 are successive, exhaustive, temporal parts of *t*. Clearly *h* is then merely the product of *f* and *g* performed at successive times.

As in the case of simultaneous sums, it is not clear that absolute, and hence relative, successive products need be assumed always to exist. *f* and *g* might be quite separate action types performed on *x* at successive times. There seems to be little reason to allow action types always to be combined to form a successive product. Unless a strong reason is forthcoming, the realm of action types should not be overpopulated unnecessarily.

Some action kinds exhaust or fill the time in which they occur, so to speak, others do not. (Recall Chapter IX, Section 2.) The lighting of a cigarette during time *t*, for example, takes up the whole of the time *t*, and cannot take place within half of *t*, say, or within three quarters of *t*, or within a time containing *t* as a proper part. In other words, if *X* lights a cigarette *x* during *t*, he can light *x* at no proper temporal part of *t*. Nor can he light *x* during the whole of a time of which *t* is a proper part. However, other action kinds need *not* fill up the whole of the time in which they occur. If any person *X* sits on a chair *x* during time *t*, he is also sitting on *x* during every temporal part of *t*. (All times *t* are continuous, so to speak, and must contain all parts between any two separate parts.) Action kinds of the former sort are said to be *exhaustive* with respect to the time in which they occur; of the latter, *non*exhaustive. Thus in general *f* is said to *exhaust t*, or to be *exhaustive with respect to t*, if and only if for all *X*, *x*, and t_1, if *X* Prfm_E *f,x,t* and also t_1 is a proper temporal part of *t*, then it is not the case that *X* Prfm_E *f,x,t_1*. Also, *f* is said to be *nonexhaustive* with respect to *t* if and only if for all *X*, *x*, and t_1, if *X* Prfm_E *f,x,t* and t_1 is a temporal part of *t* (not necessarily proper part), then *X* Prfm_E *f,x,t_1* also.

Corresponding relative notions may be defined here also.

The question arises as to whether all action kinds are either exhaustive or nonexhaustive.

Consider the action kind *eating*, more particularly, eating a meal *x* during the time interval *t*. The ordinary use of the word 'eat' is presumably such that this action kind is neither exhaustive nor nonexhaustive. If one eats a meal *x* from 1 to 2 P.M. on such and such a day, it does not follow that he is eating the whole of *x* at every temporal part of that interval. Of course he might be eating a *part* of the meal *x* at every temporal part of that time interval.[1] This,

---

[1] A part-whole relation between individuals has not been explicitly admitted here, although it would no doubt be desirable to have it available.

however, is a very different matter. Nonetheless it would still be appropriate to say that he is eating x during the whole time interval. Thus there seem to be action kinds that are neither exhaustive nor nonexhaustive with respect to the times at which they occur. Such action types may be said to be *interrupted* with respect to the times at which they occur. The corresponding relative notions may also be defined.

Let us reflect now a little more closely upon the part-whole relation between action types and of how action types may be analyzed into parts. First, what are the minimal or atomic parts of an action type? It seems reasonable to require that action types be analyzable into parts and that this analysis must stop at some point with *minimal* parts. There seems to be no clear-cut or obvious way of carrying out such an analysis unless the time factor is brought in. Minimal action types are presumably performed during moments, that is, the shortest time intervals. More specifically, an action type might be said to be *absolutely atomic* if and only if it is nonnull and any time at which it is performed is momentary.

As a matter of fact, however, this definition would not be very useful if there are no action types satisfying it. One and the same person often performs the same action type at different speeds, as it were, and different persons most surely do. A more useful notion is therefore that of being an atomic action type *relative* to a person and a time. An action type f is atomic *relative to* X and t if and only if that action type is performed by X at t and t is momentary.

Suppose X moves a physical object from one place to another at time t and suppose t consists of three consecutive moments, t_1, t_2, and t_3. It seems reasonable to analyze this action type into three parts, f_1, f_2, and f_3, where f_1 is atomic relative to X and t_1, f_2 atomic relative to X and t_2, and f_3 atomic relative to X and t_3. The whole action type consists in moving an object from place A to place B. There are intermediary places A_1 and A_2 such that f_1 is the action type consisting of moving an object from A to A_1, f_2, A_1 to A_2, and f_3, A_2 to B. The velocity or acceleration or other such physical properties need not enter into our considerations here. Strictly, f_1 is the action type of moving an object from A to A_1 with such and such a velocity or acceleration or so on.

Observe that absolutely atomic action types performed at t, as as well as action types relative to X and t, are both exhaustive and nonexhaustive with respect to t. There are thus action types that are neither exhaustive nor nonexhaustive, as well as action types that are (trivially) both exhaustive and nonexhaustive, with respect to the times at which they are performed.

There are surely ways of determining minimal action types other than that suggested. If attention is confined solely to certain specified action types, which in the given context need not be subdivided, those very action types may themselves perhaps be regarded as minimal. For example, if the context is a legal one involving, say, action types concerned with the driving, parking, and so on, of motor vehicles, these very action types may be regarded as minimal. To determine the minimal action types other than by reference to temporal moments, would seem then to involve fundamental reference to some special set of action types germane to a given context.

Finally, a few virtual classes of particular interest are as follows.

Consider the virtual class of all monadic action types performed by a person X during his lifetime. This is obviously a very important class, completely characterizing the person X with respect to his monadic action types. Let this class, that is, the virtual class of all f's such that there exists at least one x and at least one t such that $X \, \mathrm{Prfm}_E \, f,x,t$, be called 'the *total monadic performative class* of X'. Such a class, together with the analogous dyadic one, and so on, should clearly be of interest for ethics, if moral responsibility is thought to attach primarily to actual behavior. Perhaps some restrictions on t here would be desirable, so as to relativize X's actions to given selected times.

Another closely related virtual class is that of all objects upon which X has performed some monadic action type or other during his life span. Such a class comprises the total environment of objects upon which X acts, the *total monadic performative environment* of X, as it were.

Consider also the virtual class of all monadic action types ever performed upon some given object x. Again, such a class completely characterizes x insofar as x is a component or factor in monadic actions. Such a class might be called 'the *total monadic actional class* of x'. In the behavioral sciences, physical objects are of interest not because they possess given physical properties or stand in given physical relations to other physical objects, but because they are termini, so to speak, of action, because people perform certain action types upon them. The total monadic actional class of x is thus presumably of greater interest to the behavioral scientist than is x itself.

Again, the virtual class of persons who ever perform some action or other on a given object may be an interesting class, in connection, for example, with the problem of giving a precise analysis of such notions as 'role', 'status', and so on. Also of interest is the class of all persons who perform some given action on a given object. The former class is the total *monadic human environment,* so to speak, whereas the latter is the total monadic human environment with respect to the one given action type.

3. Rules of Performance. Whenever new primitives are introduced, axioms or rules must be laid down to characterize them. As rules governing the primitive 'Prfm', the following are suggested somewhat tentatively.

First it may be assumed that there is *at least one nonnull* action type and that there is *no universal* action type, that is, there is no f such that for all X, x, and t, $X \operatorname{Prfm}_E f,x,t$. Also, the existence of *at least one absolute simultaneous product* of any two action types is assumed. In many cases, of course, this product may be null. Uniqueness with respect to absolute performative equality readily follows, in the sense that if h and h' are both absolute simultaneous products of f and g, then h and h' are performatively equal in the absolute sense. As a result of this law we have also uniqueness of the absolute simultaneous product with respect to the various kinds of relative performative equality introduced.

The next rule, which may be called the *Rule of Atomic Parts*, states that if $X \operatorname{Prfm}_E f,x,t$ and t_1 is any mometary part of t, then there is a g such that $X \operatorname{Prfm}_E g,x,t_1$. As a result of this rule, all action types actually performed by X at t may in effect be decomposed into action types performed by X at momentary parts of t. These various action types may or may not be distinct from each other, but they are atomic relative to X and t_1, and hence (trivially) exhaustive of the times at which they take place.

The pure theory of action kinds has been distinguished from the applied theory. The pure theory may be regarded as characterized by these general assumptions, together with further ones should they be needed. The pure theory is concerned with properties of all action kinds but without naming any specific one. For the pure theory no constants for action kinds are required, although they may be present. In the applied theory, specific action kinds are not only named but suitable properties of such kinds are laid down axiomatically. Among such axioms there are certain ones that we shall call *Rules of Kind*. Usually there will be of the form that if $X \operatorname{Prfm}_E f,x,t$, then x is a member of such and such a virtual class F of objects. To return to the example already given, if 'f' stands for the monadic action kind of lighting a cigarette, then 'F' here would stand for the virtual class of cigarettes. This Rule of Kind would then make explicit that if X performs f on x at t, then x is a cigarette.

In the applied theory there might of course be other types of axioms laying down properties of specific action kinds and showing how they are interrelated. The specification of such properties and relations is of course a part of the analysis of those action kinds, of their phenomenology, as it were. However, in the general theory under discussion here, no such axioms need be specified. Note that the theory is being set up in such a way that such rules can easily be added. The presence of constants for action kinds is optional, as has been noted.

As an example of such additional axioms needed in the applied theory, consider the following. Suppose 'A_1', . . . , 'A_k' are primitive predicate constants taking variables or constants for action types as arguments. Each of these predicate constants stands for a property of action types. 'A_1', for example, might be the set of all action types involving the human arm say, in one way or another, 'A_2', the human foot; 'A_3', on the other hand, might be a set of certain kinds of verbal actions requiring the use of the mouth, throat, and tongue. Presumably, 'A_1', and so on will be chosen so as to allow a suitable classification of the action types to be considered in the given application of the theory. Further axioms would stipulate other properties of, or inter-relations between, their properties, depending upon the phenomenology of the particular action types considered. Still further axioms might stipulate that such and such a person or persons have in fact per-formed such and such action types on certain objects at particular times.

4. Social Action. Closely related to the notions of performance introduced above are some notions that appear essential for certain contemporary sociological theories.

In *Toward a General Theory of Action*, edited by Parsons and Shils,[2] sociology is regarded primarily as the systematic study of *social action*. Social action, however, is not mere performance in this sense. Rather, it is performance oriented to the gaining of certain *ends* or *goals*. Further, any performance takes place in certain "situations" or contexts; it is "normatively regulated" and involves the expenditure of energy or effort on the part of the agent or performer. To borrow an example from Parsons and Shils, the behavior of *a man driving his automobile to a lake to go fishing* may be analyzed as involving these various factors. To be fishing is the goal or end of the action. The "situation" or context consists of the road and car and the present locale of the man. The man must actually expend energy to perform the given action of driving his car. Further, his behavior is normatively

---

[2] (Cambridge: Harvard University Press, 1951), especially pp. 55 ff.

regulated, that is, his present action is a reasonable or "intelligent" means for achieving the given goal.

Let us look at this a little more closely and consider a suitable new primitive for handling this type of goal-directed behavior. Driving an automobile to a given place we may regard as a dyadic action type. Of course a time factor also should be introduced, although Parsons and Shils do not do so explicitly. How now should the goal—fishing— be handled? Fishing might be handled as a monadic action type, fishing for a fish z. However, the goal remains the same even if there is no fish actually caught or to be caught. Thus, for the present purpose, it seems better to regard fishing as zero-adic.

Let

(1)   '$X \text{ Prfm}_E f,x,y,t,g$'

read 'X performs f on x to y at t *in order to perform g*'. This perhaps may be regarded as the fundamental kind of locution for the social theory of action. More extended forms must also be considered, allowing for action types of all degrees both as present actions and as anticipated goals.

Precisely what Parsons and Shils mean by 'a situation' is not too clear. Presumably the situation is wholly determined by the agent X, the objects x and y (y in the example given being a place), the time t, and the goal g. If so, "situations" are adequately handled by expressions of the form (1), and no new variables need be introduced to range over them.

Note that no provision is made in (1) for the "normative" factor regulating action. However, this normative factor is presumably a sentence of some language system that itself talks about or is relevant to action types. The given sentence is presumably accepted *as a basis for* the given action. In the example cited, one normative principle is perhaps to the effect that whenever one drives his car along such and such a road he in due time (*ceteris paribus*) reaches the given lake. This sentence is accepted by person X at the time to a high degree. He bases his present action upon it, as well as upon many other relevant sentences. Thus, no specific mention need be made in (1) of the normative principle or principles involved. It seems likely that they can be handled by reference to the notions of acceptance and acceptance as a basis for action. (See Chapter XII, Sections 7 and 8.)

Parsons and Shils point out that social actions are not "empirically discrete" but take place in clusters or "constellations." These clusters, they tell us, are of three kinds, "social systems," "personalities," and "cultural systems."

The agent X is always a human agent. The objects x, y, and so on, in (1), however, may themselves be in turn either human agents or not. The kind of locution needed for the discussion of social systems must allow for this. Social systems involve "interaction" between two or more human agents. Thus they consist of action types that human beings perform upon human beings. A locution of the form

(2)   '$X \, \mathrm{Prfm}_E \, f,Y,t,g$'

is then needed in place of, or in addition to, (1). A social system is then presumably a virtual class of action types f such that for some X, Y, t, and g, $X \, \mathrm{Prfm}_E \, f,Y,t,g$. Other conditions should perhaps be added, but at least this much is needed. Personality systems, on the other hand, are relativized to a given "actor." Thus a personality system relative to person X is presumably the virtual class of all f's such that for some Y, t, and g, $X \, \mathrm{Prfm}_E \, f,Y,t,g$. Here likewise some further conditions are no doubt needed, but this much at least is basic. Finally, cultural systems are constituted by the "organization of the value, norms, and symbols which guide the choices made by actors and which limit the types of interaction which may occur among actors." As suggested, the "norms" are presumably sentences relevant to actions accepted by members of the social group to a high degree. Perhaps therefore this notion may be handled as a suitable virtual class of sentences.

In these few comments it has merely been suggested that the preceding material may be suitably extended to provide a basis for some notions needed in contemporary social theory. These notions must then be extended to the behavior of social groups. However, difficult problems emerge here that are beyond present concern. Also, the choice of Parsons and Shils for discussion is merely illustrative and alternative theories could have been used equally well. Here we have been concerned merely with the linguistic form or forms needed, and these or similar ones should presumably be useful in other sociological theories as well.

5. Authorship and Purposiveness. Another approach to the problem of characterizing goal-directed behavior is that of Henry Leonard. In several papers Leonard has put forward an analysis of "productive" discourse in which meaning or signification is related to a purpose of the author.[3] More particularly, Leonard seeks to analyze the relations

---

[3] Henry S. Leonard, "Authorship and Purpose," *Philosophy of Science* 26 (1959), 277–294, and "Authorship of Signs," *Papers of the Michigan Academy of Science, Arts, and Letters* XLV (1960), 329–340.

between a person's actions and sentences or statements by means of two primitive relations that may be described approximately as follows.

Let 'B$^t(X,a)$' express that person X "brings it about at time t" that a holds, that is, that person X performs a certain action or actions in order to make a certain sentence a true. Leonard cites an example as follows: if at 11 P.M. I set my alarm clock for 7 A.M., then at 11 P.M. I bring it about that my alarm clock is set from 11 P.M. to 7 A.M. to ring at 7 A.M. Leonard's second primitive 'W' is significant in contexts of the form 'W$^t(X,a,b)$', which may be read 'X *works* at time t at bringing it about that a holds in order to bring it about that b holds'. 'W' will be reflected upon in a moment. First, let us consider the primitive 'B' a little more closely.

Rather than the sentences of some language system L, Leonard takes as the second argument of 'B' names of unanalyzed "propositions" or propositional variables standing for or ranging over "states of affairs." These are rather obscure, as noted above. More will be said in Section 8 below about any method that uses such entities unless suitably analyzed. Little change need be made in Leonard's formal material, however, if sentences are used in place of propositions.

Let a be some sentence about action types. Suppose it says in fact that the alarm clock is set for 7 A.M. To say then that B$^t(X,a)$ is to say that X performs at t on the alarm clock x the action type of setting for 7 A.M. It follows from this statement concerning X and t that in fact the alarm clock is set for 7 A.M. In general, then, Leonard's locution 'B$^t(X,a)$' should be definable in terms of 'Prfm' within the theory of action kinds suggested above. In general 'B$^t(X,a)$' seems to mean merely that the sentence a holds (more strictly, *is true*) and furthermore because X performs or performed at t such and such an action type upon some x.

Perhaps it should be required here also that X *accepts* the sentence a at t, or accepts it to such and such a degree. X performs f at t on x with the conscious intent of bringing about a and hence is presumably aware that he is doing so, this awareness being reflected in his acceptance of a.

The other primitive 'W' is designed to accommodate *purposive* behavior. Suppose a and b are two sentences of L about actions. If person X works at time t to bring about a *in order to* bring about b, he then performs an f on some x at t so that either at t or a later t, he may perform g also. One way of construing 'W' might therefore be in terms of (1) of the preceding section, the notion of 'Prfm' as needed in Parsons and Shils' theory of social action. To say that X Prfm$_E$ f,x,y,t,g, it will be recalled, is to say that X performs f on x to y at t *in order* to perform g either at t or at a later time. The sentence a here would say something to the effect that X does perform f on x (to y) at t, and b that X performs g at such and such a time. (Whether the action types are medadic, monadic, dyadic, and so on is immaterial here.)

6. Actions and Events *Sui Generis*. An alternative handling of actions and events has been suggested recently by Donald Davidson.[4] Of the three methods of treating events suggested in Chapter IX, Section 1, he apparently espouses the one in which both physical objects and events in some sense *sui generis* are taken as values for variables. Davidson is more interested in the logic of sentences describing actions than he is in those describing events in general.

Davidson's method can best be approached by considering his example,

(1)   'I flew my spaceship to the morning star'.

This becomes for him, where 'x' now is a variable ranging over events in general,

(2)   '$(Ex)(Flew(I,my\ spaceship,x) \cdot To(the\ evening\ star,x)$'.

Here 'Flew' is a three-place predicate, the third argument of which is an event, and 'To' is a two-place predicate, the second argument of which is an event. Now,

'Flew(I,my spaceship,x)'

presumably is to express that x is a flying event, as it were, involving me and my spaceship.

'To(the evening star,x)'

expresses that x is a To-event, as it were, involving the evening star.

It is not necessary, Davidson says, "to separate off the To-relation; instead we could have taken 'Flew' as a four-place predicate." (This latter is essentially the same as given above, in Chapter X, Section 2.) However, Davidson thinks it "a merit of [his] . . . proposal that it suggests a way of treating prepositions as contributing structure." Now

[4] See his "The Logical Form of Action Sentences" in *The Logic of Decision and Action*, ed. by N. Rescher (Pittsburgh: University of Pittsburgh Press, 1966) and "Facts and Events" in a University of Western Ontario volume (in preparation).

structure is what we want, and this much is surely to the good. "Not only is it nice to have the inference from (1) to . . .

(3)   '(Ex)Flew(I,my spaceship,x)';

it is also nice to be able to keep track of the common element in 'fly to' and 'fly away from' and this of course we cannot do if we treat these as unstructured predicates."

Again, surely no predicate should be treated as "unstructured." However, that the treating of prepositions in the way suggested contributes to structure, seems doubtful. For one thing, Davidsonian relations such as To, Away From, perhaps With, Of, and so on remain rather murky. At best we need to be told a good deal more about them. What is *their* structure? Also an inference to something like (3) from (1) can surely be arranged, taking 'Flew' as a four-place predicate. Thus surely,

(4)   'I flew my spaceship somewhere',

which is presumably inferable from (1) by a law of logic, is essentially like (3). In fact (3) might be thought to be mere ellipsis for (4). Also, 'away from' and 'to' ought somehow to be definable in terms of vectors, or coordinates, or something of the kind, so that the "common element" in 'fly to' and 'fly away from' need not be lost. Surely then acceptable reasons for introducing such mysterious relations for handling prepositions have not been given.

Nor does Davidson offer us any analysis of the internal structure of events. Events, it is to be feared, remain for him "unstructured." Surely structure is what we are trying to find almost always in logical analysis. Further the structure is there, and if we fail to locate it something is amiss.

Davidson notes that predicates other than action predicates have "event-places" or events as arguments. "Indeed," he writes, "the problems we have been mainly concerned with are not at all unique to talk of actions: they are common to talk of events of any kind." An eclipse of the morning star is an eclipse of the evening star. Do we handle this, by parity of method, as

(5)   '(Ex)(Eclipse(x) · Of(morning star,x) · Of(evening star,x))'?

It is not the concern over the identity of events that need worry us here, but rather the use of 'Of'. If we are not careful, we could make too much of 'Of'. Why not handle 'Cain is the brother of Abel' as

'(Ex) (Brother(Cain,x) · Of(Abel,x)'.

After all, 'of' occurs in 'Cain is the brother of Abel' and it would be good to bring out the common structure in the two uses of 'of' in this and in 'An eclipse of the morning star is an eclipse of the evening star'. It is not clear that Davidson would go quite so far as this. The brakes would perhaps have to be put on at some point, but just where? And just why there? Better not to need the brakes at all and to treat prepositions syncategorematically.

The 'Fido'-Fido principle, so-called and disparaged by Ryle, requires that to every word of a language there corresponds something or other that it designates. Perhaps no one now takes this principle seriously, unless suitably restricted. According to it, to prepositions there are some corresponding objects, perhaps the Davidsonian relations To, From, and so on. Davidson does not explicitly invoke the discredited 'Fido'-Fido principle, but his recognition of prepositional relations is uncomfortably in accord with it.

There is also an increase in ontology, and hence in ontic commitment, with the new sort of variables over events. The problem for Davidson remains of showing us precisely how this new ontology is related to the one of physical objects. In Chapter IX, Section 2, the attempt was made to construct an ontology of events in terms of the latter. In Chapter IX, Section 3, the alternative was considered of admitting events as values for variables, but with suitable types of predicates applicable to them. Thus, in that method, explicit indication is given as to how events and physical objects are interrelated. It is thus far from clear that Davidson's strange machinery enables him to do anything that cannot be done, perhaps more naturally, by the methods sketched above.

7. Performance and Deontic Logic. Von Wright, in his papers on deontic logic, has noted that in ordinary language 'act' is ambiguous.[5] Sometimes the word is used for properties of a certain kind, sometimes only for instances of such. Action types he regards as a certain kind of property, 'act properties' he calls them, and what he calls 'act individuals' are then instances of such properties. Act individuals are presumably the same as what we have called 'action events'. Von Wright notes that in order to describe an act individual there must be mention of both an agent (or performer) and an "occasion" on which the act is performed. The occasion is presumably uniquely determined by the time and the object or objects upon which the action is performed.

[5] See, for example, *An Essay in Modal Logic*. See also his "An Essay in Deontic Logic and the General Theory of Action," *Acta Philosophica Fennica* 21 (1968), which appeared too late for discussion here.

Von Wright's purpose in discussing act properties at all is as a basis for introducing the so-called *deontic modalities*. As the basic deontic modality he takes the notion of *permission* symbolized by '*P*'. Let 'f', as above, stand for some action type. '*Pf*' then reads 'the action type f is permitted'. On the basis of '*P*' other deontic concepts may be introduced, as we shall see in a moment.

Concerning action types, von Wright utilizes operations of *negation, conjunction, disjunction*, and so on. Given any two action types, their conjunction and their disjunction are assumed to be action types. Likewise, given any action type, its negation is assumed to be an action type also. It may well be questioned whether such a plethora of action types is really needed.

Note that in the preceding sections the notion of the negative of an action type has *not* been introduced. If *X* is *not* performing f on *x* at *t*, it need not be postulated that there is always a *g* that he *is* performing on *x* at the time. This is unnecessary and would involve what would seem to be rather strange suppositions. Think of the enormity of action types one would always be performing—all humans to date would every moment have been performing the action type of not looking at the other side of the moon, for example. *X* would be performing in fact at time *t* the negative of every action type he does not perform at *t*. On the other hand, *some* action types might well have negatives. Suppose that it is not the case that there is a cigarette *x* such that *X* is smoking *x* at *t*. *X* might then be said to be *abstaining* from cigarette smoking at the time. In general f may be said to be a *negative* of *g* if and only if for all *X*, *x*, and *t*, $X \mathrm{Prfm}_E f,x,t$ if and only if *X* does not perform *g* on *x* at *t*. Note that an action type may have several distinct negatives, all of them performatively equal in the absolute sense.

Von Wright also assumes that there are such things as "tautological" and "contradictory" act properties. A tautological act property is the logical disjunction of an act property with its negative. Presumably *all* action events are then instances of such an act property. Similarly, a contradictory act property is the logical conjunction of an act property with its negative, and presumably no action events are instances of such an act property. It is not clear, however, that such act properties, or action types, are needed. Nor is it very clear what it might mean to say that person *X* performs the "tautological" action type upon *x* at *t*. What test can the experimenter use in order to decide this? Similarly, what observations or experiments should be made in order to decide that no *X* ever performs the contradictory action type upon *x* at *t*? Also, if no one ever performs it, why introduce it at all?

Also, von Wright's treatment seems unable to handle action events. Permission, obligation, and so on, should surely, it would seem, be relativized to given persons, objects, and times. Some persons are permitted (in whatever sense this word is taken) to perform given actions, others not. Persons under a certain age, for example, are not legally permitted to drive a car, whereas older persons are. Some actions are permitted at some times and not at others, for example, parking a car at a given place. Likewise, it is permitted to perform given actions on certain objects, not on others. For example, in some countries it is legally permitted to ride a bicycle on streets, but not on sidewalks. Thus it is not sufficient to formulate a deontic logic merely for action types. Action events must be taken account of fundamentally. Also it is important, as already noted, to distinguish monadic, dyadic, and so on, action types, just as in the theory of relations dyadic, triadic, and so on, relations must be distinguished from one another. Von Wright in effect makes no such distinctions but groups all of these action types together.

Also, it seems that within von Wright's theory no comparison can be made between what is permitted and what is actually performed. Surely such comparison is vital for most if not all interesting applications. For this, the theory of performance developed above is needed, or at least something similar.

Let us attempt now in rough outline to reformulate deontic logic as a suitable extension of the theory of performance given above.

Von Wright introduces 'P' as a one-place primitive applying to action types. This may be reconstrued now to apply to (monadic) action events. We have noted above that action events are not needed as values for variables, the effect of having such being achieved in another way. Thus, 'P' may be reconstrued here as a four-place predicate. To suggest the word 'permitted' let us use 'Pmtd' in place of 'P', and let this be significant in contexts of the form

$$\text{'}X \text{ Pmtd } f,x,t\text{'},$$

read 'X is permitted to perform f on x at t'. The exact interpretation to be given to 'Pmtd' in given applications of the theory is left open, just as the exact interpretation of 'P' is left open in deontic logic.

On the basis of 'Pmtd', 'P' is readily definable. To say that the monadic action type f is permitted, in general, is to say that everyone is always permitted to perform it on every object. Of course there may be bounds here on the range of the variables, the X's concerned being just members of the relevant social group, the x's the appropriate kind of objects, and the t's the times under consideration.

According to von Wright, an action type is *forbidden* if and only if it is not permitted. Also, an action type is said to be *obligatory* if and only if its negation is not permitted. The notion of being obligatory is definable in this way because the negation of every action type is itself assumed to be an action type.

The question arises now as to how the notion of being obligatory can be introduced here. For an action type f that has a negative, f may be said to be obligatory provided it has a negative and all of its (performatively equal) negatives are forbidden. Another method is to introduce a predicate for being obligatory as a primitive. Let 'Oblg' be a four-place predicate significant in contexts of the form

$$\text{'}X \text{ Oblg } f,x,t\text{'}.$$

This may be read 'X' is obliged to perform f on x at t'. Here also the exact empirical interpretation is left open.

The notions of being permitted and of being obligatory are the two fundamental notions of deontic logic, so that in terms of 'Pmtd' and 'Oblg' the further notions should be definable, provided the underlying ontology of action types is sufficiently rich.

Even more important than the notions considered here, "absolute" deontic notions, as von Wright calls them, would be *relative* ones. Permission and obligation are perhaps best thought of as relative to a given moral code. For this the locution might be 'X is permitted to perform f on x at t according to a given code C'. What are moral codes and what kinds of statements comprise them? Precisely how are codes related to specific statements of obligation and permission? Careful answers to such questions would have to be given. Indeed, it would seem that the most interesting applications of the deontic notions would in fact be as relativized in this way.

Now, a few critical comments on von Wright's method in general.

8. An Alternative Method Rejected. In Chapter IX, Section 4, an *analysis* of propositions was suggested. The entities that result are of course *analyzed* propositions, constructed as nominal entities. The use of such entities in philosophical analysis is to be contrasted sharply with the use of unanalyzed propositions in the guise of values for a special kind of variable. Yet curiously, the use of unanalyzed propositions, together with variables thereon, is rampant in the literature, especially that concerned with the logical analysis of sentences concerning belief, action, and the like.

Perhaps the use of unanalyzed propositions is a reasonable first step in logical analysis. After all, Russell first put forward, in *PM*, a theory of unanalyzed propositions as a prelude to breaking them up, as it were, by exploring their inner structure and their connection with quantification. This is all now a rather murky chapter in the history of logic. After sentences (or statements) and propositions have been distinguished, and in general the use and mention of expressions, and after the syntactical and semantical components of language systems have been suitably characterized, there is no further need of un-analyzed propositions. To use them is, again, to return to the horse-and-buggy days.

Some logicians, as we have noted, condone such forms as

'*X* believes that *p*'.
'*p* is believed',

and similarly for knowing,

'*X* brings it about that *p*',
'*X* prefers *p* to *q*',
'*p* is preferred to *q*',
'*p* transforms into *q*' (von Wright's 'T'),

and so on with unanalyzed *p*'s and *q*'s. Von Wright in fact is perhaps the most influential writer who condones such forms, and others have followed in his footsteps. Let us therefore examine what appear to be his most extensive comments concerning what propositions are, for a doctrine of unanalyzed propositions underlies all of these forms.

"What is a proposition?—An attempt to answer this question in a satisfactory way would take us out on deep waters in philosophy."[6] Precisely, and without such a voyage we will not have a clear under-pinning for our subsequent analyses, as von Wright would no doubt agree. He assures us that there are such things as propositions, but tells us nothing of their structure. It is good to be assured of their existence, but not without a delineation of inner structure. Straight-away propositions are allowed to be true or false. The view here, and of modern semantics, however, is that only declarative *sentences* can significantly be said to be true or false in the most fundamental sense, and that analyzed propositions may then be said to be true or false only in a derivative sense. (Recall Chapter IX, Section 4.)

The semantic view has been fully worked out and constitutes what may be regarded as a completed science. The propositional view,

---

[6] G. H. von Wright, *Norm and Action* (London: Routledge and Kegan Paul, 1963), pp. 22 ff.

on the contrary, at best has not been satisfactorily worked out, as von Wright would surely admit. The semantic view takes us over deep waters safely. The propositional voyage has not even started. The attitude taken here is that in philosophic analysis we ought to avail ourselves of the best, and best worked-out, methods known at the time. Von Wright does not reject the semantic view explicitly, but only by innuendo or indirection, by not using it. This is especially to be lamented in view of the wide influence his writings have exerted.

Von Wright distinguishes between *generic* and *individual* propositions.

> The individual proposition has a uniquely determined truth-value; it is either true or false but not both. The generic proposition has, by itself, no truth-value. It has a truth-value only when coupled with an *occasion* for its truth or falsehood, that is, when it becomes 'instantiated' in an individual proposition.

An occasion may perhaps be construed as an ordered couple of a place with a time, somewhat in the manner of Chapter IX, Section 2. In any event, a generic proposition has a truth value only when coupled with an occasion, whereas an individual proposition has a uniquely determined truth value once and for all.

Let 'Tr p' express that the proposition p is true. We are not given an analysis of the predicate 'Tr' and no axioms are laid down for it. But suppose this were done. Let $\langle s,t \rangle$ be the couple (virtual?) of the place s with the time t. In addition to 'Tr p' we should need another form then, 'Tr $p,\langle s,t \rangle$' to express that p is true *on the occasion* $\langle s,t \rangle$. We should need, for von Wright's distinction between generic and individual propositions, *two* truth predicates, not just one. This duplication by itself seems rather needless. Also it is not clear without further ado that such duplication would be sound. There is no need for two truth predicates in Tarski's theory, for example, or in *Truth and Denotation*. Nor does Frege have two "objects," each of which are the True. (See Chapter XI, Section 4.) That they should be needed here surely requires independent justification.

If von Wright were to admit just one truth predicate, the distinction between the two types of propositions might be preserved if we were to regard the generic proposition p as the ordered couple of p with an occasion. A generic proposition would then be of an altogether different logical type, however, from an individual one, and this would surely be awkward.

If we were to be told something about the inner structure of propositions, we could perhaps see how places and times might be accommodated or referred to within them. It is interesting that von Wright puts quotes around 'instantiated' when he notes that a generic proposition becomes "instantiated" in an individual proposition. Strictly instantiation of course takes place only as between sentences or statements. To be clear as to what instantiation is is to be clear about the inner structure of whatever it is that is instantiated.

Also it is very doubtful that 'true at time *t*' or 'true on occasion $\langle s,t \rangle$' can be given a sound meaning independent of semantics. It is better to incorporate the time or the occasion into the sentence *in the object language*, and then keep the semantical predicate 'Tr' timeless and spaceless, as it were. Not to do so is to embroil the analysis of truth unnecessarily with the analysis of space and time.

"Occasions are not to be confused with (logical) *individuals*," von Wright tells us. "Individuals could be called 'thing-like' logical entities." The locution 'logical entity' is surely unhappy. It invites the question "What are *non*logical entities?" Clearly there are only entities. We can speak of a logical *constant*, such as 'V' for disjunction, or of a *non*logical *constant*, say, 'w' for *Waverley*. There is no entity for 'V' to designate, however, whereas there is for 'w'. There are no "logical" entities, only entities in space or time or wherever.

To get at the structure of a proposition, von Wright refers to the sentence that "expresses" the given proposition. This is then presumably to give the proposition structure by proxy. However, does not this really amount to mistaking the structure of the proposition for the structure of the sentence? Proponents of unanalyzed propositions would answer 'No'. If all they tell us about the structure of a proposition is in fact derivative from that of the sentence that expresses it, however, do not their words betray them? Is not this just one more instance of mistaking the thing for its expression, which Frege bewailed? (See Chapter I, Section 5.)

Russell too, in a timely but forgotten passage, wrote that

> unless you are fairly self-conscious about symbols, unless you are fairly aware of the relation of the symbol to what it symbolizes, you will find yourself attributing to the thing properties which only belong to the symbols [or conversely]. That, of course, is especially likely in very abstract studies such as philosophical logic, because the subject-matter that you are supposed to be thinking of is so exceedingly difficult and elusive. . . . That is why the theory of symbolism has a certain importance, because otherwise you are so certain to mistake the properties of the symbolism for the properties of the thing. . . .[7]

---

[7] In "The Philosophy of Logical Atomism," in *Logic and Knowledge*, p. 185.

Fortunately progress has been made on the theory of symbolism and its relation to the nonlinguistic world in the years since Russell wrote. Unfortunately, however, proponents of propositions *sui generis* take little account of it.

Further, almost all such proponents fail to use quotation marks with consistent correctness and hence to observe the distinction between the use and mention of expressions. This in itself is not perhaps especially significant. It is what this failure leads to that is philosophically so unfortunate. On the other hand, those philosophers who do meticulously distinguish use and mention, for example, Frege and Carnap, are rarely if ever referred to by von Wright. In a footnote, von Wright writes that "we shall, for the sake of typographical convenience, throughout avoid the use of quotes round symbolic expressions such as p, $\sim p$, $p \& q$, etc. . . ." This is of course not objectionable in itself. The difficulty is that what originates as a mere "typographical convenience" leads us astray, or at best does not help us when we move on to such fragile matters as "facts," "events," "states of affairs," and the like.

Von Wright moves on to "facts," stating that "when a (contingent) proposition is true there corresponds to it a *fact* in the world." There are three types of facts, "states of affairs," "processes," and "events." Again, however, we are not told what it is that a contingent proposition, when true, "corresponds to," so that we are scarcely better off than before. Are propositions somehow not "in the world" whereas "facts" are? If so, where are they? Are they spatio-temporally located? Von Wright thinks facts can be named, but this is doubtful, as we have learned from Russell and Ramsey. At any event, it is to be regretted that von Wright does not press his analysis more deeply, for much of his subsequent discussion depends rather intimately upon what he says about facts. In a genuine sense, a philosophical superstructure is no firmer than the foundations upon which it is built, however attractive the decorations, balustrades, cornices, and lintels may be.

Von Wright does not emphasize the different levels of language, object language, metalanguage, and so on. However, the sharp differentiation of levels is surely conducive to clarity and essential for consistency, as we now know. It is interesting that many philosophical logicians do not explicitly recognize these different levels, however, but commit what might be dubbed the *object language fallacy*. They seem to think that they need discuss only an object language and say *nothing whatsoever* about its metalanguage. Terms under philosophical analyses are almost always, they think, to be couched in an object language. Natural language, they say in effect, is one vast object language. They fail to realize that there are metalanguages even *for* natural languages, as well as *within* natural languages, and that these are now beginning to attract the attention of workers in structural linguistics. They also fail to note that many philosophical notions are most directly and efficiently to be handled as metalinguistic terms and hence to be given analysis only in a metalanguage.

9. On Hintikka's System. Nothing has been said thus far concerning Hintikka's *Knowledge and Belief*. Readers friendly to that book will think this a serious omission. The book has been widely praised and has been said to contain "the single most important contribution to philosophical technology since C. I. Lewis's invention of the systems of strict implication."[8] It has been urged in Chapter III above, however, that these latter have little if any philosophic interest (aside perhaps from their model-theoretic interpretations). Some think nonetheless that Hintikka has in effect answered the objections put forward above and that his book contributes to the analysis of knowing and believing. A dissenting opinion must be recorded here. An exhaustive discussion of minutiae will not be given, but merely a few rather fundamental critical comments.

The first sentence of Hintikka's book is: "The word 'logic' which occurs in the subtitle of this work is to be taken seriously." To do so is, however, in the first place, to consider a language system with articulated primitives. Strictly, there is no such thing as a logic aside from a language system, as has been urged above. Two of Hintikka's basic forms

$$`K_a p` \text{ and } `B_a p`$$

read respectively 'person a knows that p' and 'person a believes that p'. In place of 'p' here we are allowed (pp. 3–4) to put in an "independent clause." However, just where these independent clauses come from we are not told. For a serious logic of belief, these clauses should be built up in specified ways in terms of the primitives allowed, as Ramsey was perhaps the first to suggest. If the independent clauses are supposed to belong to a natural language such as English, then the logic of belief is apparently a part of the "logic" of natural language. Whatever this latter is, however, we surely know very little about it at the moment. Hintikka's view is dangerously reminiscent of the English view criticized by Peirce. (Recall Chapter III, Section 4, above and see Chapter XII, Section 10, below.)

To take logic seriously is, in the second place, to make use of

---

[8] See H.-C. Castañeda's review of *Knowledge and Belief* in *The Journal of Symbolic Logic* 29 (1964).

notions of syntax and semantics, and hence to bring in a metalanguage fundamentally. Hintikka, like von Wright, never quite does this explicitly enough. Of course some metalanguage is being used, but its character is not too clearly delineated. Also, Hintikka seems to commit what has just been dubbed 'the object language fallacy'. No attempt is made to differentiate between sentences that belong to an object language from those that belong to a metalanguage. Thus, knowing and knowing that one knows are handled within the same language, as are knowing and knowing that such and such is true.

In particular, Hintikka does not bring in explicitly the semantical notion of truth. That it is eminently desirable to do so has been urged throughout. It is thus not really clear how, for Hintikka, what is said to be known can be said to be true. It has been urged, he writes approvingly, that "it is a statement, and not a sentence, that strictly speaking ought to be said to be true, . . ." and, " a statement is an event of a certain kind while a sentence is not. More explicitly, a statement is the act of uttering, writing, or otherwise expressing a declarative sentence. . . . In order to specify a statement one has to specify the occasion on which it was uttered or written and to specify the speaker or writer. . . ." Truth for Hintikka is presumably a property of statements so conceived. However, he tells us little more than this, and nothing about "acts" and "occasions." A full theory of truth as a property of such "acts" (or end products) is needed before we have a suitable philosophic foundation for his "logic" of knowledge and belief. Obviously it is not the semantic notion of truth that he has in mind, but rather a pragmatic one, the character of which remains to be worked out.

If the sentences from which Hintikka's "statements" are formed are from a natural language, difficulties are bound to arise. For, on Hintikka's view, some of the properties truth must have should presumably be analogous to some of those of the semantical notion of truth. Unless we are careful here, we might have an inconsistent language form. Also, there are difficulties about truths of truths. Hintikka's worry about knowing that one knows does not, curiously, lead him to worry about the truth of truths.[9] It should (should it not?), if knowing that one knows is equivalent to knowing (as for him) and if what is known is regarded as true (as seems natural). Because, then, for any statement that is known to be known, it is also true that it is true.

Difficulties also arise over Hintikka's use of 'entails'. Perhaps, as has been suggested above, suitable relations of entailment may be introduced, and expressions for them defined, in terms of 'analytic

[9] *Knowledge and Belief,* pp. 103 ff.

truth'. In any event, 'entails' is surely on a par with 'truth', 'analytic truth', and the like, and a whole semantic theory must be presupposed to explicate them. Hintikka follows the usual practice of decision theorists, subjectivists in probability theory, and some statisticians in limiting himself to statements, all of which are made on one and the same occasion. However, much of interest in the logic of belief depends upon change of belief over time. Hintikka cannot handle this and similar phenomena. The simple way of doing this, as suggested above, is of course to append a simple topology of temporal flow and to add a time parameter at appropriate places.

Also, Hintikka is nowhere concerned with the experimental basis for establishing in a given case how or whether '$K_a p$' holds or not. Nor does he handle a locution of this kind as within the context of a pragmatical metalanguage. He handles it rather as a theoretical locution to be axiomatized *ex cathedra logicae*. In effect, arguments against such axiomatization have been urged above. Such axioms, like those of certain modal logics, may exhibit interesting mathematical structure—but this is beside the point. Axiom sets governing belief and knowledge are rather to be transformed into formulae definatory of certain *patterns* of belief or knowledge. Also, allowance is made for all manner of alternative patterns, some of them "rational," some not. For Hintikka there is only one pattern, axiomatized once and for all. Hintikka must thus face the very difficult, if not insoluble, problem of giving a full philosophical justification of that one pattern. Precisely why this one and no other?

Hintikka's critics have generally agreed that his requirement that one knows everything entailed by what is known is too strong. Perhaps he tends now even to agree with his critics on this matter. In any event this requirement is surely not needed. We might well wish to define a *pattern* based on it—and an interesting pattern it may well be—but we would not wish to require the pattern to hold in full generality. (Recall Chapter V, Section 9, above.)

We need not tarry further with minutiae of Hintikka's system. Enough has been said, however, to suggest that Hintikka's book cannot be regarded as having provided a viable approach to the problems it treats. There is too much neglect of necessary logico-semantical prologomena. Also, extraordinary as it may seem, it contains not one reference to such basic contributions to the subject as those of Adjukiewicz, Frege, Carnap, Church, Ramsey, or Tarski, and only nugatory or more or less irrelevant ones to Peirce, Quine, and Russell. It is difficult to discern what Hintikka thinks is to be gained by disregarding the work of these authors.

CHAPTER XII

Some Further Relations of
Pragmatics and Epistemics

General semiotics conveniently divides into logical syntax, semantics, and pragmatics, as has been noted. The three areas are not mutually exclusive, but rather are cumulative in the order given. Pragmatics thus includes semantics, which in turn, as we have seen, is a kind of extended syntax. Syntax and semantics are by now well-developed areas of logical theory. Pragmatics, however, is still largely in its infancy, a fertile field crying for workers.[1] Attention has been called in the preceding chapters to some useful pragmatical relations. In the present chapter several further such relations will be introduced. We shall not pretend to exhaust the list of the important ones, but merely pick out a few that seem to be fruitful and about which we can at the moment be reasonably clear.

We shall be concerned only with certain pragmatic *relations*, and not with such *entities* as experiences, beliefs, states of brain or mind, events, facts, states of affairs, and the like. Expressions for such "entities," as has been noted throughout, usually remain rather obscure and in need of analysis.

Certain relations of an *epistemic* type will be considered. Semantics and systematic pragmatics are no doubt of interest for epistemology, but precisely how seems not to have been shown too clearly. Let us distinguish between pragmatics and *epistemics* somewhat roughly as follows. In pragmatics there is concern with relations between the user, human or otherwise, of a language and words or phrases or

---

[1] See R. Carnap, "On Some Concepts of Pragmatics," in *Meaning and Necessity*, and the author's *Toward a Systematic Pragmatics*.

sentences of that language, as we have noted. In epistemics relations between the human being and the various "objects" and "conditions" of his belief and knowledge are considered. Such relations are the common stock of the epistemological analyst, although all too rarely explicitly recognized as relations. Pragmatics and epistemics thus overlap in important ways, and it would be idle to try to separate them too sharply.

Attention has been called in Chapter XI to certain relations needed for the theory of action, which (following Kotarbiński) might be called '*praxiology*'.[2] We could distinguish then a wider domain of pragmatics embracing pragmatics in the narrow sense just considered, epistemics, and praxiology. In any event, the theory of actions is surely a desirable adjunct to pragmatic and epistemic study, as we have already observed. In Chapter XI the theory of action was incorporated in an object language. Now let us incorporate it rather within the wider pragmatical metalanguage.

In this chapter, then, a rough inventory is given of what appear to be some of the most important relations of pragmatics in the broad sense. No attempt at completeness is aimed at, however, as has already been mentioned, and significant items will no doubt be left out. Nor can a full or really deep analysis be given of any one. Instead, we merely list them, hinting here or there at what may be needed by way of analysis or offering suggestions that seem not unworthy of further development.

1. Carnap on Pragmatics. Carnap thinks it best to regard relations of a pragmatic type as "theoretical constructs in the theoretical language" rather than as "behavioristically defined disposition concepts of the observation language."[3]

Let

[1]   '$B(X,t,p)$'

express that "the person at time t believes that p." This form presupposes the presence of variables over analyzed propositions. [1] is to be "understood in a weak sense," Carnap says, "as not implying either that X is aware of the belief or that he is able to verbalize it." The relation B is an epistemic one, not a pragmatic one in the narrow sense. Carnap also lets

[2]   '$T(X,t,S,L)$'

express that "X at t takes the sentence S of the language L to be true

[2] T. Kotarbiński, *Praxiology* (Oxford: Pergamon Press, 1965).
[3] *Op. cit.,* p. 248.

(consciously or not)." For [2] we must have variables over sentences as well as over language systems.

Both [1] and [2], Carnap thinks, should be useful. The two relations B and T, he thinks, are to be interrelated by a relation of *intension*. Let

[3]   'Int(p,S,L,X,t)'

express that "the proposition p is the intension of the sentence S in the language L for X at t." In addition Carnap lets

[4]   'A(X,t,S,L)'

express that "X at t wills deliberately to utter a token of S as a sentence of the language L in the sense of an *assertion*." Also, Carnap lets

[5]   'U(X,t,R)'

express that "X at t produces with his speaking organs a series of audible sounds R." Carnap needs also then

[6]   'U(X,t,S)'

to express that X *utters* the sentence S at t. However, we should note that if R is a token of type S and if U(X,t,R), then and only then presumably does U(X,t,S). (Recall 'Utt' of Chapter VIII, Section 6.)

Carnap's form (1) may be criticized on the ground that its introduction within the framework of theoretical pragmatics commits us to abstract, and indeed unanalyzed, propositions. Similarly, the use of [3] involves us at once in an intensional metalanguage. Carnap thinks, however, that "there is no compelling reason for avoiding the use of an intensional language for science, because such a language can be completely translated into an extensional one . . . ." However, if this is the case, why not avoid intensional languages for the same reason? The intensional notions are highly obscure, as Carnap admits, and are understood only in terms of their extensional translations.

In forms [2], [3], and [4], there is explicit reference to a language system as a value for a variable. This too is a bit murky, as (we recall) Quine has pointed out. It is doubtful that such reference is needed, and at any event we shall avoid it here. Form [5] uses a variable over series of audible sounds. It is doubtful that these need be introduced. Why not interpret [6] as expressing that X utters at t a token of type S? We can then drop [5] altogether. Thus, of Carnap's six forms, [6] as thus reinterpreted seems the most suitable for a system of theoretical pragmatics. Some of Carnap's other forms may be provided for in a slightly different way.

2. A Review. Let us recall briefly various pragmatic relations that have been introduced above, and then suggest a few new ones.

First, there is the notion of testing mentioned in Chapter V. We let, it will be recalled,

[7]   'X Tst$_E$ a,t'

express that an experimenter E is testing the sentence a of a fixed language system L at t with respect to the reactions of the subject X to it. And similarly with *acceptance*.

[8]   'X Acpt$_E$ a,t'

expresses that X accepts the sentence a of L at time t, according to the experimenter E. Of course [7] and [8] are mere linguistic forms. The real flesh and blood is to be found in the interpretation given to them in specific contexts of use.

Note that only *sentences* as wholes are significantly under test or accepted in accord with these forms. Single words, such as an individual constant or a predicate constant, cannot be accepted. They function only as parts of wider sentential contexts. Of course X may well react to single words and nonsentential phrases in specified ways, but these are not covered by 'Acpt'. Once we have a clear vocabulary for handling reactions to single words or phrases, these latter may then be studied along with their connections with acceptances. In any event, acceptance of whole sentences seems the more significant and useful notion, at least at the present stage of research, and has been used throughout. Acceptance here seems very close to Carnap's T of [2].

There are at least two kinds of *rejection*. X can reject a sentence a at t if and only if he accepts the *negative* of a. Or he can reject a in the sense of not accepting a at t, leaving it open as to whether he accepts the negative of a or not. The two are by no means the same. They may be symbolized respectively in the forms

[9]   'X Rjct$_E$^{1} a,t'

and

[10]   'X Rjct$_E$^{2} a,t'.

X can be said to be *indifferent* to a at t if he accepts neither a nor the negative of a at t. This of course is *cognitive* indifference, not evaluative. To say that X is indifferent to a states nothing about X's desires or valuations. We can let

[11]   'X Indiff$_E$ a,t'

be defined as suggested. Also we can say that X prefers a to b at t, again in a purely cognitive sense, merely by requiring that X Acpt$_E$ a,t but it is not the case that he accepts b at t. Thus, he cognitively prefers any sentence he accepts to any he rejects in the sense of 'Rjct$_E$²'. We let

[12]   'X Prfr$_E$ a,b,t'

symbolize this relation in context.⁴
    We also let (in Chapter XI)

[13]   'X Prfm$_E$ f,x,t'

express that X performs at t an action of the kind f *upon* the object x at t. However, action kinds vary as to degree, as observed there. Thus, we might wish to say that X performs an action of the kind g upon x *with* y at t. To express this, a form such as

[14]   'X Prfm$_E$ g,x,y,t'

is needed. By the use of different action kinds of differing degrees, different prepositional phrases may be accommodated.
    Further relations Prfm may be admitted to handle goal-directed behavior. Thus,

[15]   'X Prfm$_E$ f,x,t_1,g,y,t_2'

may express that X performs f on x at t_1 with the purpose (perhaps conscious) of doing g on y at some later t_2. However, such a notation conceals as much perhaps as it reveals. [15] entails not only that X actually performs f on x at t but also that X at time t_1 *intends* to perform g on y at a later time t_2. Yet, the notation does not enable us to single out what we wish to say here about *intending*.
    Let, then,

---

⁴ Neglect of my distinction between cognitive and evaluative preference and indifference is at the root of some of the criticisms of the foundations for the theory of subjective intensions in *Intension and Decision*, made in the review by Montague, *loc. cit.*, and its echo by John M. Vickers, *The Journal of Philosophy* LXIV (1967), 193–200.

[16]   'X Intd$_E$ t_1,f,x,t_2'

express that X *intends* at time t_1 to perform f on x at time t_2, according to E. Here again an interesting case is where X and E are the same. If they are, [16] expresses X's conscious intent. If not, it is E who, by studying X's behavior or by questioning him, assumes responsibility, as it were, for attributing intention to X. Using [16], the entailment mentioned in the preceding paragraph may easily be handled. It is no doubt good to have [16] and its cognates for action types of higher degree available anyhow.

[16] might be criticized on the grounds that intending should be handled intensionally. Of course the 'f' in [16] can in effect be nominalized by replacing it by some expression designating or L-designating f. Alternatively, in place of 'f' we could write '$\langle f,a\rangle$' where a is an expression designating f. These moves can of course be made only in an appropriate metalanguage. (See Section 5 below.)

Suitable forms for knowing and believing, as introduced in Chapters V, VI, and IX, are of course epistemic forms *par excellence*. These are forms akin to Carnap's [1] and are presumably "theoretical constructs" in a suitable sense.

3. Assertions and Questions. The study of *judgment* and *assertion* has been a significant part of traditional logic. The subject is as old as the hills, but very little new or enlightening seems to have been written on the subject in recent years. Strictly, it belongs to pragmatics, so we think, and an exact theory of assertion can be given presumably only within a systematic pragmatical metalanguage. The failure of logicians to turn to systematic pragmatics for the analysis of assertion has perhaps helped to keep the subject in limbo.

Carnap's form [6], suitably interpreted, may be used to handle utterance. How now can *assertion* be handled? Suppose X both utters a sentence a at t and accepts it also. Perhaps he may then be said to *assert* it. Thus, we may perhaps introduce

[17]   'X Asrt$_E$ a,t'

in this way, defining it in terms of the conjunction of [6] with [8]. [17] is comparable to the form in Chapter IX, Section 6, for the assertion of analyzed propositions.

It is a commonplace to note that language is primarily a *dialogue*, not a monologue, a social phenomenon rather than a merely private one. The forms [6] and [17] are essentially monologic, however, and perhaps therefore not suitable for a full theory of utterance and assertion. One utters sentences not solely for one's own pleasure or benefit. One usually directs them to others, who then should perhaps be explicitly referred to in our form for handling utterance. In a special case the other can of course be the utterer himself. Let

[18]   'X Utt$_E$ a,Y,t'

express that (according to E) X utters a to Y at t. In terms of [18] the dialogic and social character of language may be explicitly brought out. [6] may then readily be defined by existentially quantifying the 'Y' of [18], and hence may be dropped. Assertion, if regarded as simultaneous utterance (as in [18]) and acceptance, also now becomes essentially dialogic. For this we should need the form

[19]   'X Asrt$_E$ a,Y,t',

and then [17] could be defined.

A similar pragmatical handling of *questions* suggests *itself*. Various alternative approaches to the logic of questions and answers have been given.[5] It is not clear that any of these approaches views the subject as one squarely of pragmatics, however. The fundamental locution needed, we wish to suggest, may be of the form

[20]   'X Asks$_E$ a,Y,t',

expressing that X asks a of Y at t in the sense of uttering certain sounds in a certain way. Asking is other-person directed, just as utterance is. Here too, one may ask of oneself. If the form [20] is sound, no special domain of interrogative sentences need be recognized. There are only declarative sentences given interrogative status on the occasions of being asked.

Suppose X asks a of Y at t_1. How can Y's *answering* X at a later time t_2 be handled? Perhaps no new relation is needed here. We ought perhaps to be able to handle answering in terms of assertion. If a is asked and is the kind of question that admits of itself or its negative as an answer, then Y answers X if and only if Y Asrt$_E$ a,X,t_2. Or suppose a is a disjunction of a_1 and a_2 and that X Asks$_E$ a,Y,t_1. Then Y answers X at t_2 if and only if Y Asrt$_E$ a_1,X,t_2 or Y Asrt$_E$

---

[5] See *inter alia* D. Harrah, "A Logic of Questions and Answers," *Philosophy of Science* 28 (1961), 40–46, and *Communication: A Logical Model* (Cambridge, Mass.: The M.I.T. Press, 1963), and Nuel D. Belnap, Jr., *An Analysis of Questions,* Technical Memorandum of the System Development Corp. (Santa Monica, California).

a_2,Y,t_2. If this mode of treatment should prove *un*satisfactory in general, however,

[21]   'X Answr$_E$ a,Y,t'

may be taken as a new linguistic form.

Note that in terms of the theory of events given in Chapter IX, a theory of *linguistic events* or *acts* emerges. Thus

$$\langle X \text{ Utt}_E \, a,t \rangle^\text{e}$$

may be regarded as an utterance event,

$$\langle X \text{ Asks}_E \, a,t \rangle^\text{e}$$

an asking event, and so on.

4. Some Relations of Sense Awareness. There are many further relations of an epistemic type to be considered. We shall merely list a few of these in exploratory fashion without settling upon any final forms.

Especially interesting for our purposes is Woodger's discussion of the "proper objects" of sensation.[6] What are, namely, the objects or termini of seeing, hearing, tasting, feeling, and touching? Historically there are two general answers, *physical objects* or phenomenal *sense data* in some sense. Let us reflect first upon the latter.

Woodger introduces a relation of *getting,* the use of which may be illustrated by the following sentences:

'By carefully listening Tom is getting a sound of a nightingale in St. James' Park',

'By stroking his horse Tom is getting a feel of velvet',

'By looking eastward from Waterloo bridge, Tom is getting a view of St. Paul's',

and so on. In each case what is gotten is a sensation or sense datum of some sort correlated with a physical object. Let

[22]   'X Gts s,x,t'

express that X gets the sense datum s of x at t. We can distinguish then five different kinds or sorts of sense data, depending upon the

* See especially J. H. Woodger, "Proper Objects," *Mind* LXV (1956), 510–515.

sense involved. Or we could distinguish five different relations Gts, one for each sense, and let our new variables 's', 's_1', and so on, range over sense data indiscriminately. In either case a new domain of "proper objects" of sensation must be introduced. The question as to whether this is the wisest course to follow for the theory of perception[7] may be left aside. Surely, however, sensations are good data for science; they can be measured, there are certain psycho-physical laws about them, and so on. Hence, relations such as Gts seem fit subjects for epistemic study.

Epistemologists unwilling to introduce a separate realm of sensations will favor alternative relations with no variable for sensations as argument. Presumably forms such as

[23]   'X Sees x,t',
                                          'X Hears x,t',

and so on, would then be needed to handle seeing, hearing, and so on. Perhaps *both* types of forms are to be admitted, those of [23] as well as [22]. This kind of treatment seems advocated by, for example, Reichenbach.[8] He distinguishes a realm of subjective "fictitious" objects, very akin to sensations. We *perceive* subjective things but *observe* physical objects, put loosely, according to him. (Reichenbach is talking only about visual perception here.) To perceive for Reichenbach is thus very much like Woodger's getting a view of, whereas to observe (visually) is presumably to be handled in terms of some forms such as those of [23].

5. On Concepts and Conceiving. We are assuming that our object language is of the familiar physicalistic or reistic kind, and we have been considering how to introduce within such a language suitable epistemic relations to handle perception. Our language also contains predicates standing for virtual classes and relations. We should now ask, what epistemic relations, if any, stand between persons and "abstract" objects such as virtual classes and relations?

Traditionally we have here relations of *conception*. We may be said to conceive or to "have" a concept or conception of such and such an abstract object. To characterize this, let us go back to Frege's notion of an object in a given "mode of presentation." Consider a

---

[7] See, for example, W. V. Quine, *op. cit.*, J. L. Austin, *Sense and Sensibility* (Oxford: Clarendon Press, 1962), and R. Chisholm, *Perceiving* (Ithaca: Cornell University Press, 1957).

[8] H. Reichenbach, *Elements of Symbolic Logic* (New York: The Macmillan Co., 1947), Chapter VII.

virtual class $x\mathbf{\mathfrak{z}}(\text{—}x\text{—})$ and a given expression a that designates it. a may be thought of as representing a "mode of presentation" of $x\mathbf{\mathfrak{z}}(\text{—}x\text{—})$. Of course there are other modes also, as many as there are distinct PredConOne's designating it. We now wish to bring $x\mathbf{\mathfrak{z}}(\text{—}x\text{—})$ and the mode a to form a single entity. It is the notion of a virtual-class-in-the-given-mode-of-presentation-a that is of interest here. This notion is easily accommodated by the ordered couple

$$\langle x\mathbf{\mathfrak{z}}(\text{—}x\text{—}),a\rangle.$$

Roughly speaking, then, a virtual-class concept now consists of two components, the virtual class itself and an expression that denotes its members. For example, let M be the virtual class of men. The ordered couple $\langle M,a\rangle$ is then a class concept if a denotes just the members of M. a could be 'M' itself. Or a could be a suitable expression in the language translating the English 'featherless biped', or translating 'rational animal'. The concept of M in the mode of presentation 'featherless biped' is a very different concept from M in the mode of presentation 'rational animal', the second components being different expressions.

A virtual-class concept is what we may be said to "have" at certain times when we entertain the concept or conception of that class. Thus we now let

[24]   'X Has $\langle x\mathbf{\mathfrak{z}}(\text{—}x\text{—}),a\rangle,t$'

be significant in the metalanguage to express that person X has or entertains the given conception of the virtual class $x\mathbf{\mathfrak{z}}(\text{—}x\text{—})$ at time t. This form in the theory of conception will play the role of [22] for Gts in the theory of perception. Class concepts function here in place of sensations. Supplementing [24], additional forms for dyadic relation concepts, and so on, are needed.

Of course we must worry long and hard as to the precise interpretations for [24] and cognate forms. Perhaps they are definable in terms of the relations above, although this seems unlikely. Conceiving is perhaps in some sense *sui generis* and is not to be reduced to other kinds of relations. Better to regard the relations of conceiving as "theoretical constructs" of epistemology and then to worry about their exact logical and other connections with each other and with the relations of Section 4.

Having gone as far as this, we would naturally condone a form for *individual concepts* also. Let

[25]   'X Has $\langle x,a\rangle,t$'

express that X has the conception $\langle x,a \rangle$ of x at t, where $\langle x,a \rangle$ is the object x taken in the mode of presentation a.

Concepts have an internal structure. The class concept $\langle x\ni(\!-\!x\!-\!),a \rangle$, for example, consists of the virtual class $x\ni(\!-\!x\!-\!)$ as its object and the expression a as its mode of presentation. The individual concept $\langle x,a \rangle$ has x as its object and a as its mode of presentation. The mode of presentation provides, as it were, the intensional component of the concept. The intentional (with a 't') component enters by means of the relation Has. A concept as actually had by someone is presumably an intentional (with a 't') object of some kind or other. However, such objects are not to be confused with intentions-to-do as handled by [16].

Let us reflect now upon epistemic relations between persons and *events*. Consider

'Bertrand sees John kiss Mary'.

Here, the object of seeing is not just John, not just Mary, nor the relation of kissing, but rather the event of John's kissing Mary. Can this be handled in terms of the foregoing forms or must new ones be introduced? The event of John's kissing Mary at time t, we recall, may be regarded as the quadruple $\langle j,K,m,t \rangle^e$, where j is John, m is Mary, and K is the dyadic relation of kissing, and t is the time at which John actually kisses Mary. Then, where b is Bertrand,

[26]   'b Sees $\langle j,K,m,t \rangle^e,t$'

seems a reasonable locution to admit. This would presumably entail that Bertrand sees John, or at least has a sensation of him, at t. Also, that he sees Mary, or at least has a sensation of her, at t. However, does it not also entail some conceptual element, namely, that Bertrand has a conception of kissing at the time? If so [26] would entail also that

b Has $\langle K,a \rangle,t$,

for a suitable a describing some conception of K. More, however, is involved in [26] than merely these three entailments, for Bertrand sees the actual kissing, not just John and Mary with a conception of K thrown in. [26] should also entail that John does kiss Mary at t. In any case, the seeing of events is closely linked in some way with the seeing of objects, or at least of getting sensations of them, and with the having conceptions of virtual classes and relations.

If one prefers [22] to [23] as a form for handling the perception of objects, one would no doubt reject the form [26] in favor of some form such as

[27]   'X Gts $s,\langle j,K,m,t\rangle^e,t$'.

By use of [27] one would contend that one gets visual sensations of events but perhaps does not "see" them directly.

6. Sensations, Space, and Time. In his recent *A Deductive Theory of Space and Time*,[9] Saul Basri has put forward some interesting suggestions concerning the foundations of the theory of *general relativity*. The weakest part of Basri's construction, philosophically, is perhaps at the beginning, in which a theory of sensations is used fundamentally. Basri introduces in effect some relations closely akin to the Gts relations above. Let us examine these very briefly in passing.

Of course no temporal factor can now be an argument of any primitive relation, for time, the theory of time order, and so on, as well as space and hence geometry, are to be constructed or formulated as the theory develops. We shall not consider this technical development. Instead we shall be concerned only with the foundations of Basri's formulations, parting considerably from his actual work.

Basri's ontology consists roughly of observers, sensations, physical particles (without extension in space), and events (more particularly, the *point events* of relativity theory). We have available from above expressions for all of these, which can now be used with only small changes. The variables 'X', and so on will suffice for observers, and 's', and so on, for sensations. Events—or at least kinds of events— may be handled essentially as above but with of course the time parameter dropped. Our physical objects x, and so on, are now to be regarded as extensionless particles and kinds of point events as virtual ordered couples of these particles and suitable properties.

Let

[28]   'X Gts s_1,s_2,x'

express that the observer X has, according to himself, simultaneous sensations s_1 and s_2 with the particle x regarded as their source. We can then get at three of Basri's primitives as follows, where 'S_1' and 'S_2' are taken as expressions for virtual classes now of sensations. Let

[9] (*Studies in Logic and the Foundations of Mathematics*, Amsterdam: North-Holland Publishing Co., 1966).

[29]   'S_1 SimSen X'

express that S_1 is then a virtual class of X's *simultaneous sensations* provided X gets at least one sensation s (of some particle), every member of S_1 is a sensation that X gets simultaneously with s (of the same object actually), and S_1 is nonnull. Basri does not introduce the source x here, but its presence does no harm, and is essential if [28] is taken as a primitive form.

Attribution to a source is handled by the next notion. Let

[30]   'X IdSrc S_1,S_2'

express that X attributes the sensations of the nonnull virtual classes S_1 and S_2 to the same particle as source. Perhaps [30] may be defined by saying that S_1 and S_2 are nonnull, and that there is an object x and a sensation s such that X Gts s,s,x, every sensation s_1 in S_1 is such that s_1,x, Y Gts s_2,s_2x, every sensation s_3 of S_1 is such that X Gts s_1,s_3,x, Similarly, let

[31]   '$\mathrm{Crsp}(X,S_1,Y,S_2)$'

express that observers X and Y establish a *correspondence* between their respective classes of sensations S_1 and S_2, attributing them to the same source. This is perhaps definable by saying that S_1 and S_2 are nonnull and that there exists an x, and s_1, and an s_2 such that X Gts s_1, s_1,x, Y Gts s_2,s_2x, every sensation s_3 of S_1 is such that X Gts s_1,s_3,x, and every sensation s_3 of S_2 is such that Y Gts s_2,s_3,x.

Point events, or rather *kinds* of them, in accord with the analysis suggested, are to be handled as virtual ordered couples of particles with suitable properties. Now apparently, the properties that are of interest here are those of *suddenly appearing* or *suddenly disappearing* in a given visual field.

> Since the only events of interest in physics are *point-events,* the changes must be *sudden* (no extension in time) [Basri explains (p. 28)], and the objects affected must be *particles* (no extension in space). In order for a change in sensations to be sudden and distinct, it is necessary that it starts or ends at a level above the threshold of both intensity and quality. For instance, the light from a particle must be bright enough to be clearly seen, and its color must be well within the visible range of red to violet.

Let 'A' stand for 'appears suddenly in the visual field of' in the sense of this explanation. Consider then the point-event-kind $\langle x,A,X \rangle^{\mathrm{e}}$. Basri

takes as a primitive an expression by means of which we can ac-
comodate the locution 'the observer X perceives the event e of the
sudden appearance of particle x within the field of perception of X.'
This we may perhaps handle here as

[32]   'X Sees $\langle x,A,X \rangle^e$',

an adaptation of [26] above. Similarly, where 'D' expresses 'disappears
from the visual field of', we would have

[33]   'X Sees $\langle x,D,X \rangle^e$'.

It is perhaps curious that, having made so much of sensations,
Basri speaks of perceiving here rather than of having a sensation of.
The following locutions could be introduced and would perhaps be
more in accord with the spirit of his inquiry, namely,

[34]   'X Gts $s,\langle x,A,X \rangle^e$'

and

[35]   'X Gts $s,\langle x,D,X \rangle^e$'.

These are adaptations of [27], and presumably would enable us to ac-
complish whatever could be done with the two preceding ones. Or
perhaps we need here rather adaptations of [28].

Basri's final primitive concerns the *perceived coincidence* of
point events. We wish to be able to say that the observer X perceives
(or has a sensation of?) the coincidence of events e_1 and e_2 of specified
kinds. Let 'CoIncd' be the new primitive here, in contexts such as

[36]   '$\langle x,A,X \rangle^e$ CoIncd$_X$ $\langle y,D,X \rangle^e$',

with all possible combination of 'D' and 'A.'

Events of the kind $\langle x,A,X \rangle^e$ and $\langle x,D,X \rangle^e$ might be called '*percipient
events*'. Other types of percipient events would involve relations other
than D and A. However, it is not clear that all of our events need to be
percipient ones, although this might actually be the case in parts of
relativity theory.

With suitable axioms we can no doubt go a long way now in
building up the theories of space and time. Basri makes fundamental
use of set theory. With the use of so powerful a substructure it is not
surprising that one can do almost anything one wishes. In the fore-

going brief sketch such powerful procedures have been avoided. It seems very likely, however, that our use of merely virtual classes would not suffice here for all we wish. This, however, is a bridge we can cross when we get to it.

Of course no axioms have been suggested for the epistemic 'Gts'. Also, the difficult problem as to how sensations are individuated must be faced. Here some relation of *felt similarity* will no doubt play a crucial role.[10] Perhaps

[37]   '$s_1 \, \mathrm{Sm}_X \, s_2$',

read 's_1 is taken by X to be similar to s_2, s_1 and s_2 both being sensations in X's visual field'. Perhaps a comparative notion of similarity, and even a quantitative one, can be introduced. In any event a much deeper analysis of sensations is needed before we can recognize in 'Gts' a suitable primitive for a part of relativity theory.

The various definitions and forms [28]–[37] are not to be taken too seriously and are merely exploratory. They are put forward more as a *jeu d'esprit*, intending to suggest that, with suitable adaptation, the preceding material can perhaps be extended to deal with sophisticated matters in the foundations of the sciences. On the other hand, from the point of view of the physicist, more particularly the epistemologically oriented theorist of relativity, the forms [28]–[37] (with perhaps some omissions) may be the fundamental ones, in terms of which some at least of the preceding, [1]–[26], should be definable. There are two points of view here, that of the pragmatic analyst and that of the theorist of relativity. It would be idle to make a quarrel, however, for both points of view need looking at *from close to* and have much to contribute to each other.

7. On Acting on a Belief. Let us now turn very briefly to another kind of pragmatic relation, that of *acting upon a belief*, a notion at the very heart of pragmatics. Yet the notion remains somewhat obscure and seems never to have been given a very thorough analysis.

In his interesting discussion of this subject, Chisholm is surely quite right, in stressing that the notion of *acting upon* is "one of the points at which we find the link between thought and action."[11] His analysis is illuminating in helping to bring to light important features

---

[10] See R. Carnap, *The Logical Structure of the World* and *Pseudo-Problems in Philosophy,* tr. by R. George (Berkeley and Los Angeles: University of California Press, 1967), and N. Goodman, *The Structure of Appearance* (Cambridge: Harvard University Press, 1951).

[11] R. Chisholm, "What Is It to Act upon a Proposition?" *Analysis* 22 (1960), 1–6.

that must surely be taken into account. He is quite right also, it would seem, in stressing that there are several notions of *acting upon*, to be distinguished carefully from one another but no doubt with family resemblances. What are needed now are analyses that not only illuminate but reduce the notions involved in the analyses to others that in some sense are clearer or more acceptable or more amenable to exact logical characterization. Although one finds much to agree with in Chisholm's account, some of the notions used by him seem themselves to have resisted precise logical analysis and insofar remain suspect.

It is often said that to believe a "proposition" is to be prepared to act upon it. No doubt this statement contains the core of something sound and our task is to make sense of it. "Yet," Chisholm notes, "a rational man may act upon propositions" which he does not believe, just as he may believe propositions upon which he does not act. Indeed such a man may act upon a proposition while he is also acting upon its contradictory; in setting out to walk he acts upon the proposition that it will not rain, and in carrying his umbrella he acts upon the proposition that it will rain." Now Chisholm is not saying here that a rational man can perform *one and the same action at the same time* on the basis of both a "proposition" and its contradictory. Thus, 'acting upon' is not the notion we wish to get at, but 'acting *so and so* on' or 'performing *such and such an action* upon'. A man may perform the action of setting out to walk at a time *t* on the basis of his belief that it will not rain, whereas he performs the action of carrying his umbrella on the basis of his belief that it will. The air of paradox here vanishes when the different relevant actions or action kinds are explicitly brought in. Of course, the whole matter is more complicated, for probability considerations, or the man's *estimates* of such, must no doubt be brought in also. If so, it is doubtful that a *rational* man ever acts or performs such and such on "propositions" in which he does not believe. Chisholm does not tell us how 'rational' is to be understood here. Of course a man may take chances or may be committed to a course of action in which he no longer believes, but he is then acting with considerable risk upon a quite complicated set of beliefs, or half beliefs, or hunches.

Chisholm suggests that there are four different senses of 'acting upon'. He points out several spurious senses that, he thinks, fail to take account of the fact that "to act upon a proposition is to act in a way that is relevant or appropriate to the proposition." "It would be easy enough," he says "to define 'acting upon' in terms of relevance or appropriateness—'to act upon a proposition is to act in a way that is relevant to the proposition's being true'—but it is just this concept of *relevance* which we originally set out to find."

To act upon is presumably to act, and hence we cannot be very clear about *acting upon* unless we are a great deal clearer about *acting*. What is needed here is a theory of actions or performance—perhaps the one of the preceding chapter—as a prelude to the theory of acting upon. In addition, a theory of acceptance, or something like it, is surely needed in order to take account of the "propositional" factor. Chisholm does not press his analysis so deeply as this, but he is quite right, it would seem, in having located a notion of relevance here as a key notion.

Chisholm's first sense of '*S* acts upon *h*' is: *S* acts in order that if *h* should be true, a certain end would then be realized. However, the notions involved in 'acts in order that' and in the "realization" of ends, to say nothing of the use of the subjunctive conditional, are themselves rather obscure, as Chisholm would no doubt admit. Surely, a person may act on a true *h* with a view to "realizing" a certain end, even though something transpires to prevent its realization. *S* may take along his umbrella on the "proposition" that it will rain in order to keep himself dry by using the umbrella. However, the moment he steps out of the door it may cease to rain, or a friend by chance may be driving by and give him a lift. Or a frightful wind comes up and blows his umbrella inside out beyond repair, or blows it away altogether. He has still acted upon the proposition that it will rain, but the end-in-view of keeping himself dry by means of the umbrella is not realized.

Chisholm's second sense of 'acting on' fares no better: *S* acts in order that, if *h* should be true, a certain end would then be realized; and *h* is true. (Semanticists have done rather well, as we have noted, with 'true', but it is not clear that it is their sense that Chisholm is using here.) A third sense involves the notion of 'relying on': *S* acts upon *h* if and only if *S* relies on *h*'s being true. However, the definition of 'relying on' must presumably hark back to the notions already noted, as does the fourth sense.

Also, there are surely senses of 'acting on' in which the ends are not explicitly taken into account. Chisholm is concerned rather with 'acting on . . . in order that —' or 'acting on . . . for the purpose of —'. *S* may go for a stroll with no special end in view worth the mentioning. Or he may act out of sheer habit or caprice. Must we always ascribe to our actions a given purpose? The fact is that very often we do not.

For the analysis of 'acting upon' and allied notions, a suitable vocabulary is needed, and we are indebted to Chisholm for calling attention to some of the notions that, no doubt, will be useful. There are difficulties here, however, it seems, and to overcome them a deeper probing is needed, using only secure logical tools.

8. On Hempel's Analysis. An important special case of the notion of *acting upon* is the notion of *acting rationally upon*. In his presidential address, Hempel has put forward many illuminating comments concerning the latter, which we will do well to examine.[12]

Hempel's remarks concern the following schema for "explaining" why person X did so and so.

(1) X was in a situation of type C.
(2) X was a rational agent.
(3) In a situation of type C, any rational agent will do f.
(4) Therefore X did f.

This schema—let us call it *Schema R*—in turn is a modification of one due to Dray.[13]

Note that in (1) there is explicit mention of the "situation" in which X finds himself at the time. Of the situation, Hempel says that its "description would presumably include a specification of [X's] . . . objectives and relevant beliefs." Objectives and beliefs relevant for doing just f, or more generally? Hempel does not say, but note that the specific action kind f is explicitly brought in.

The key notions of being a "rational agent' is crucial in Schema R. This notion, Hempel says, must

> be conceived as a descriptive-psychological concept governed by objective criteria of application. [It is a] broadly dispositional trait: to say of someone that he is a rational agent is to attribute to him, by implication, a complex bundle of dispositions, each of them a tendency to behave in characteristic ways in certain kinds of situations (whose full specification would have to include information *about the agent's objectives and beliefs* [italics added], about other aspects of his psychological and biological state, about his environment, *et cetera*).

Dispositions have been the object of intensive study for many years, but to date they have resisted clear characterization. Let us

[12] C. G. Hempel, "Rational Action," *Proceedings and Addresses of the American Philosophical Association* 35 (1961–62), 5–23. See also the relevant pages in *Aspects of Scientific Explanation*.

[13] W. Dray, *Laws and Explanation in History* (Oxford: Oxford University Press, 1957), pp. 123 ff.

avoid them here altogether, or at any event as much as possible. The notion of *rational agent* should presumably be definable in terms solely of *actual* acceptances or beliefs and *actual* performances. If we define it in terms of dispositions, the notion is left hanging in midair. In any event we should hope that adequate characterizations would be forthcoming without them.

Note that Hempel's description of the notion of *rational agent* includes information about the agent's objectives and beliefs. However, such information is also included, it will be recalled, in the description of the relevant "situation" C. Presumably, the objectives and beliefs are the same in both descriptions, and it is not clear why they should be repeated. In fact it might be better to construe the "situation" more narrowly as involving only the relevant physical and perhaps biological properties and relations. The "situations" clearly may vary with time, so that it would no doubt be good to bring in a time parameter explicitly. Also, the "situation" is to be regarded presumably as for the doing of f only, not for the doing of some other g or in any more general sense. In place of 'C' we should more properly write '$C_{X,f,t}$', indicating the relativization of the "situation" to X, f, and t.

Statements (2) and (3) of Hempel's schema seem to presuppose that there is one and only one notion of "rational agent," the same for all kinds of actions. This seems doubtful. There seem to be many alternative—some of them competing—notions of rationality to be taken into account. A person may well be a rational agent with respect to one class of action types but not with respect to another. Also, what notion of rational agent is common to the businessman selling his odious goods, the lonely poet writing with no thought of commodity, and the saint in solitary meditation? It would very likely be advisable therefore to speak more specifically of a "rational agent of type R_f," that is, of the type relevant for the doing of f, in (2) and (3).

Hempel calls statement (3) a "descriptive generalization." Note that it gives in effect a necessary condition for being a rational agent. It says, in a logically equivalent formulation and with the refinements suggested,

(5)   For any X, f, and t, if X is a rational agent of type R_f, then in a situation of the type $C_{X,f,t}$, X does f at t.

We may well ask whether the converse of (5) also holds. In behavioral terms, is not X a rational agent of type R_f (of the type, that is, relevant to the doing of f), if for all t, if he is in a situation of type $C_{X,f,t}$ then he performs f at t? The possibility that this might hold is worth exploring. If it were to hold, we should then have both a necessary and sufficient condition for being a rational agent of type

R_f and there would be no need to enter the devious and dubious path of dispositions.

Of course we are speaking here not of a rational agent in general, but only of a rational agent of the type relevant to the doing of the specific action kind f. However, is not this a desirable restriction anyhow? Once clear concerning this restricted notion, we can then generalize to other action kinds, and then to all action kinds of a given class. Perhaps even generalization beyond such a class is possible. In the face of so difficult a notion as that of *rational agent* in general, however, sound methodology surely advises a cautious stepwise procedure.

Whether this notion of *rational agent* is defined dispositionally or introduced in some fashion as a theoretical construct, (5), and its converse if it holds, would obviously be useful in interrelating this notion with actual behavior. And of course similarly for more general forms of (5), and for the converse of these if they hold.

Rational agents are those who act in certain "situations" upon the basis of rational beliefs. What are rational beliefs and what does it mean to act upon the basis of them? We are led back to the original problem of trying to be clear concerning 'acting upon'. Situations we can presumably characterize without too much difficulty, and rational beliefs we can no doubt get at by means of rational and normal acceptance patterns of various kinds.

9. Some Steps Forward. Let us glance now at a few notions that are of interest in themselves and that help to illustrate the theoretical interweaving of some of the notions just suggested.

Suppose we are given a sentence a of L. Consider now the virtual class of all monadic action types f such that for all X and for all t, if X accepts a at t he performs f (on some x) at some t' later than or simultaneous with t. Let this virtual class be F_a. Quite clearly F_a is a significant class determined by a. We might call it 'the *total* (*monadic*) *actional content* of a'; it is the class of all (monadic) action types actually performed upon the acceptance of a. The quantifiers over time and over all persons gives the class F_a the needed universality.

A related class is that of all sentences a such that for all X and t, if X accepts a at t he performs f (on some x) at some t' later than or simultaneous with t. This class, F_f, we might call 'the *total acceptance basis* for performing f'. Of course some members of F_f might be "irrelevant" for doing f. Some members might be undesirable for other reasons. However, among the members of F_f some are surely relevant *sufficient* conditions for performing f.

Narrower classes may be introduced by putting further conditions on a or f. Such classes give the partial actional content for a or partial acceptance bases for f. For example, we might wish to rule out all analytic or logically true sentences. Or we might wish to restrict the actions under consideration to just those of a certain type or to those concerned with behavior of such and such a kind. Also, the sentences involved might be required to contain a name for the action f, or be sentences in some sense "about" f.

We might also consider relevant *necessary* conditions for performance. Let the virtual class be that of all sentences a such that for all X and for all t, if X performs f on some x at t he accepts a at t. This class constitutes the sentences, acceptance of which is necessary for the performance of f. Presumably no one ever (under normal circumstances) sits on a chair without accepting at the time that it will not break. The acceptance at t of a sentence expressing that the chair x will not break during t is a necessary condition for one to sit on x at t. The set of all such conditions constitutes the *total necessary acceptance basis* for f.

Consider also the set (or virtual class) of all monadic action types f such that for all X and t, if X performs f on some x at t then X accepts a at t. This class we might call 'the *total monadic actional basis* for the acceptance of a'. It consists of just those actions, the performance of which always leads to the acceptance of a.

Consider now the *relation* between an action f and a sentence a (relative to a person X, as it were, parametrically) where for all t if X performs f on some x at t he accepts a at t. Here we can say that X's acceptance of a is a necessary condition for his performance of f, or that X performs f on his acceptance of a. In the interesting cases a will be "relevant" for f and will be of general form, a principle of some sort about all actions of the appropriate kind.

Rather than mere performance, let us consider for a moment performance of f for the purpose of doing g. Suppose that whenever X performs f on some x in order to do g he accepts a. Whenever X carries along his umbrella in order to keep himself dry he accepts a sentence expressing that umbrellas help to keep one dry. X is surely then performing f in order to do g upon his acceptance of a. If a is a general principle "about" f and g in some immediate sense, then we seem to have here a relation not too remote from *acting upon*.

Can one act on a *single* belief? Presumably not. Beliefs come in clusters. One acts at a given time on a cluster of beliefs held at the time. We may consider then the following form:

[38]   'X performs an action of type f at time t upon the basis of a virtual class F of sentences accepted by X at t'.

This form would appear to provide the minimal kind of locution required for a logic of *acting upon*. No factor may be omitted. Clearly there must be reference to the person X and the time t. Likewise, relativization to a specific action kind f is required, as we have noted above. Also, because beliefs come in clusters, virtual classes of them must be brought in explicitly.

A cognate locution brings in the purpose, or end-in-view, with which Chisholm is concerned. For this we need

[39]   'X performs an action of type f at time t upon the basis of the virtual class F, of sentences accepted by X at t, in order to perform an action of type g'.

Here, however, the virtual class F should presumably contain not only sentences about the action type f but statements concerning means and ends as well, for example, that f is a suitable means for doing g.

In place of Hempel's "conditions" C, or more specifically $C_{X,f,t}$, let us now use

[40]   '$C(X,t,f,Y,t')$'

to express that X is at time t in a situation, for the doing of an action of the type f, similar to that of Y at t'. Using [40] we shall have no need to speak of "situations" in any sense in which we should have to recognize such entities as values for a new kind of variable. Phrases of the form [40] are in effect a kind of *ceteris paribus* clause. In some specific context or application of the theory, in which all the action types considered are enumerated primitively and the circumstances under which they are performed suitably characterized, [40] may perhaps be forthcoming by definition and 'similar' would take on a very specific meaning. Meanwhile, we use [40] without definition, following Hempel anent "situations."

However, enough of this *Überblick* of some of the terrain of pragmatics. Let no one complain now that he does not grasp the significance of the foregoing forms, or that he fails to grasp the point of the whole enterprise of systematic pragmatics. Like any scientific theory, pragmatics contains a logic as a part plus suitable extra-logical notions with attendant principles. These later notions are meaningful only as they occur in certain atomic sentential forms. [1]–[40] have been suggested as a few such forms. If not these, then other suitable ones should be forthcoming. It will not do to confine logic and the search for logical forms to mathematical and scientific contexts only, as some pragmatists and philosophers of science apparently wish to do. Nor will it do to confine logic itself to the state of its development at the time of Stuart Mill, as though Frege, Russell, Carnap, Leśniewski, Quine, and others had never written.

10. On Natural Language. It is usual, in studies such as the present one, to be concerned, at least indirectly, with natural language. Thus, the theory of intensions here, the theory of belief, the considerations concerning ontology, and so on, should presumably have some interest for the study of natural language. The theory is couched in a semantical metalanguage, however, with a suitable L as an object language embodying a first-order logic. Natural language does not apparently contain a first-order logic, or at least not *prima facie*, nor is the notion of a semantical metalanguage of a natural language altogether clear or unambiguous. Thus, the *exact* connections between a theory such as the present one and natural language, the bridges, as it were, are not too clear and remain to be characterized.

Church notes that it is often the purpose of studies such as the present one

> to provide an abstract theory of the actual use of language for human communication—not a factual or historical report of what has been observed to take place, but a norm to which we may regard every-day linguistic behavior as an imprecise approximation, in the same way that e.g. elementary (applied) geometry is a norm to which we may regard as imprecise approximations the practical activity of the land-surveyor in laying out a plot of ground, or of the construction foreman in seeing that the building plans are followed. . . .[14]

Church is concerned only with semantics, not with a pragmatics. This latter *par excellence*, however, is concerned with "the actual *use* of language for human communication" whereas in semantics we are more concerned with norms. However, whether everyday linguistic behavior *should* be regarded as an "imprecise approximation" to these norms may be doubted. The gap is too wide and perhaps unfathomable. The norms, as laid down in suitable semantical metalanguages for appropriate object languages, seem very different *in principle* from whatever it is that the student of natural language is seeking. Also, there is the suggestion in Church's statement that the norms are somehow *better* than the everyday linguistic behavior, the latter being, prejoratively perhaps, mere "imprecise approximations." However, natural language, it may be urged, is *precisely what it is* and is not an imprecise approxi-

[14] In "The Need for Abstract Entities in Semantic Analysis."

mation to anything at all. Nor does it strive, as it were, to be anything different from what it is. Our task is to study it *precisely as it is*, not to try to improve it or "regiment" it or anything of the kind.

How then are we to think of constructed language systems as related to actual language? Surely there is or ought to be some useful interconnection. The exact study of this interconnection, however, remains to be undertaken. In closing, let us offer a very tentative suggestion concerning such study.

We assume before us two *prima facie* quite diverse phenomena, a natural language such as English and an artificial or constructed language system, each with its separate dignity and function. The language system we may, for present purposes, presume to be a pragmatical metalanguage developed along the lines suggested above. How now are we to go about bringing these two quite separate phenomena together?

We should consider first English words as *coordinated* with the special symbols of the constructed system and then proceed to phrases and whole sentences and thence to classes of sentences. Let us consider first *coordinating rules* for logical constants. Consider the English word 'and'. We usually assume, without much thought about it, that this word can be coordinated somehow with the symbol for logical conjunction, '·'. This, however, is premature. Only *some* uses of 'and' in English are handled, directly at least, by '·'. 'And' as between interrogatives or imperatives or exclamations, for example, is not. Compound noun phrases ('a cigarette and a match'), compound adjectival phrases ('large and expensive'), and compound adverbial phrases ('slowly and carefully') can sometimes be coordinated with '·' by defining the whole context containing them as a conjunction. But not always. The 'and' in "All philosophers and mathematicians are invited' seems best correlated with 'V'. We need an exhaustive account of the English 'and' with a full classfication of its various uses. Then and only then could we legitimately contend that some of these uses can be suitably coordinated with '·', either directly or indirectly; others not.

The very meaning of 'coordination' here is not too clear. The word is purposely chosen to avoid "correspondence' or 'correlation', which have preempted mathematical overtones. The relation of coordination would presumably be a primitive in the comparative metalanguage being envisaged. The aim of our inquiry would be to sharpen this notion and to lay down specific rules to govern it. Coordination is not just translation, although the latter, in the special case here as a relation between words of natural English and symbols of our language systems, should be somehow definable in terms of it. Nor is it paraphrase, in, for example, Hiz's[15] sense, for paraphrase is intralinguistic, co-ordination being interlinguistic. Although neither one nor the other, it has of course family resemblances to both.

We should go on to coordinate rules for other truth-functional constants, for quantifiers, for identity, for nonlogical individual, class, and relational constants, for the notions of syntax, semantics, and pragmatics. At every step our path is strewn with difficulties. There is also much here to learn from empirical and structural linguistics. Roughly and hopefully, we would end up with a kind of "logistic grammar" as envisaged by Reichenbach (*loc. cit.*).

To conclude. Much ground has been covered in this book, some of it rather too cursorily. Much of the material is tentative and much more remains to be said. The various constructive suggestions are perhaps far from adequate. Concerning some of them we have been much too brief, and some of them have perhaps been belabored. However, even brief, inadequate, tentative analyses of the topics covered are not without value should they lead to something better. Even so, they must be labeled 'fragile' and 'handle with care'. In sending them through the philosophic mails, we can only hope that they will not arrive at their destination in tatters. At the very least, however, it must be admitted that the first-order, extensional point of view has been pressed here further than ever before and than has usually been thought possible. Moreover, the extreme simplicity and elementariness of the methods used throughout carry with them their own recommendation.

---

[15] See H. Hiz, "The Role of Paraphrase in Grammar," reprinted from *Monograph Series on Language and Linguistics, Report of the 15th Annual R.T.M. on Linguistics and Language Studies* (April, 1964), pp. 97–104, and other works.

INDEX OF SUBJECTS

281

INDEX OF NAMES

INDEX OF
SPECIAL ABBREVIATIONS